The Balkans Divided: Nationalism, Minorities, and Security

EURO-ATLANTIC SECURITY STUDIES

Edited by the NATO Defense College

Band 1

PETER LANG

Frankfurt am Main · Berlin · Bern · New York · Paris · Wien

Andrey Ivanov

The Balkans divided: Nationalism, Minorities, and Security

PETER LANG
Europäischer Verlag der Wissenschaften

Die Deutsche Bibliothek - CIP-Einheitsaufnahme

Ivanov, Andrey:

The Balkans divided : nationalism, minorities and security /
Andrey Ivanov. - Frankfurt am Main ; Berlin ; Bern ; New
York ; Paris ; Wien : Lang, 1996
   (Euro-Atlantic security studies ; Vol. 1)
   ISBN 3-631-50006-8

NE: GT

ISBN 3-631-50006-8
US ISBN 0-8204-2999-6
© Peter Lang GmbH
Europäischer Verlag der Wissenschaften
Frankfurt am Main 1996
All rights reserved.

Printed in Germany 1   3 4 5 6 7

TABLE OF CONTENTS

6

FOREWORD

AVANT-PROPOS

This book inaugurates the new Euro-Atlantic Security Studies series which replaces the NDC Monograph Series of publications on the international research seminars which are conducted at the College on issues of immediate concern to the North Atlantic Alliance's security policy.

In 1992, at a time when the process of armed forces restructuring had begun to gain momentum, the College conducted a Research Seminar on "The Role of Military Education in the Restructuring of Armed Forces." Similarly, the topic chosen for the 1993 Seminar, "Peacekeeping Challenges to Euro-Atlantic Security," reflected the high political interest this issue had assumed. The 1994 Seminar focused on "Democratic and Civil Control over Military Forces—Case Studies and Perspectives," which is a major objective of NATO's Partnership for Peace (PfP) programme.

These International Research Seminars on Euro-Atlantic Security, and their corresponding monographs,

Cet ouvrage inaugure la nouvelle série d'études consacrée à la sécurité euro-atlantique qui remplace celle des monographies liées aux séminaires internationaux de recherche organisés par le Collège sur des thèmes touchant directement la politique de sécurité de l'Alliance de l'Atlantique Nord.

En 1992, alors que s'affirmait le processus de restructuration des forces armées, le Collège avait choisi pour thème de son séminaire de recherche: "Le rôle de la formation militaire dans la restructuration des forces armées". Dans le même esprit, le sujet du séminaire de 1993: "Les défis du maintien de la paix pour la sécurité euro-atlantique" reflétait l'intérêt politique aigu que revêtait alors cette question. Le séminaire de 1994 était, lui, axé sur: "Le contrôle démocratique et civil des forces armées— Etudes de cas et perspectives", illustrant ainsi l'un des principaux objectifs du Partenariat pour la Paix (PpP).

Ces séminaires internationaux de recherche sur la

were only part of the new ground the College was breaking in its response to historic changes in the security environment. A further innovation was the introduction of fellowships for visiting researchers to study topics of particular relevance to both the North Atlantic Cooperation Council (NACC) and the Partnership for Peace programmes. We are now sponsoring two four-month research fellowships per year, and the fifth fellow has recently been welcomed to the College. Indeed, no other NATO institution offers Partnership countries the opportunity for such intensive scholarly cooperation.

The results of these studies have usually been published as NDC Occasional Papers. Two Fellows have, however, taken advantage of the opportunity to expand their papers into monographs. Dr. Andrey Ivanov, the author of this book, was the first Fellow to do so. Dr. Daniel Daianu from Bucharest was the second, and his monograph on "Economic Viability and Vitality—A Dual Challenge for European Security" will probably be the next book in this new series.

In addition to opening our series of publications to visiting researchers, the College's

sécurité euro-atlantique et les monographies correspondantes ne représentaient qu'une partie du terrain défriché par le Collège en réponse aux bouleversements historiques touchant la sécurité. Autre innovation, celle des bourses permettant à des chercheurs invités d'approfondir des thèmes liés aux programmes du Conseil de coopération nord-atlantique (CCNA) et du Partenariat pour la Paix. Nous parrainons chaque année deux bourses de recherche, d'une durée de quatre mois chacune, et nous venons d'accueillir notre cinquième boursier. Aucun autre établissement de l'OTAN n'offre aux pays du PpP une telle occasion de coopération intensive dans le domaine académique.

Jusqu'ici, les résultats de ces travaux ont généralement été publiés sous forme d'études spéciales. Cependant, deux de nos boursiers ont saisi l'occasion d'en faire de véritables monographies. C'est M. Andrey Ivanov, auteur de cet ouvrage, qui a ouvert la voie. Il sera probablement suivi de M. Daniel Daianu, de Bucarest, avec sa monographie intitulée "Viabilité et vitalité économiques: un double défi pour la sécurité européenne".

Une fois la série ouverte aux chercheurs invités, notre objectif a été d'attirer sur elle

next goal was to bring its publications to the attention of the wider international strategic community. This goal is, of course, far easier to achieve through a respected publisher rather than through in-house publications. I would, therefore, very much like to thank Peter Lang Publishing, Inc. for agreeing to publish this series.

Thus, the two main components of the NDC's long-term research project on Euro-Atlantic security, the research seminar and the fellowship programme, which I have briefly outlined above, are now firmly anchored in the College's standard task catalogue and will be further strengthened by this new series. It should be stressed that all the College's educational tasks continue to serve NATO's Military Cooperation Programme and the NDC's Senior Course which is the cornerstone and the core of all College activities.

Dr. Andrey Ivanov is to be congratulated for completing a solid piece of academic work on a topic of interest to the transatlantic community. Although the study underwent considerable change during the course of its research and preparation, his high level of commitment and analytical powers enabled him to keep pace with events as

l'attention des milieux de la stratégie internationale. Entreprise grandement facilitée si l'on s'appuie sur un éditeur respecté plutôt que de s'en remettre à ses propres moyens. C'est pourquoi je tiens à remercier la maison Peter Lang Publishing, Inc. d'avoir accepté de publier cette série.

Les deux piliers du projet de recherche à long terme du Collège de Défense de l'OTAN sur la sécurité euro-atlantique, à savoir le Séminaire de recherche et le programme de bourses, brièvement décrits ici, sont désormais fermement ancrés dans les activités du Collège, et cette série viendra encore les renforcer. Il va de soi que toutes les activités pédagogiques du Collège concourent au Programme de coopération militaire de l'OTAN comme à notre session principale, pierre angulaire de nos activités.

M. Andrey Ivanov mérite des éloges pour avoir mené à bien un travail académique de qualité sur un sujet qui intéresse la communauté transatlantique. Contraint de réaménager en cours de route le plan de son étude, il a su, grâce à sa persévérance et à sa clairvoyance, suivre les événements et faire des propositions utiles aux praticiens et aux responsables de la sécurité. Adressons aussi un re-

10

well as to formulate useful conclusions for practitioners and policy makers in the security field. A special word of thanks is due to Dr. Detlef Herold for being instrumental in launching this new series, and to Mrs. Mary Burke for reading and improving the final text and all earlier drafts of this monograph since work began on its preparation. Miss Michèle Mangani's editorial assistance and preparation of the final manuscript for publication were also much appreciated. This monograph provides a promising start to the new series.

merciement particulier à M. Detlef Herold pour le rôle joué dans le lancement de cette série, et à Mme Mary Burke, dont le travail de relecture et d'amélioration du manuscrit a accompagné cette monographie depuis son ébauche jusqu'à sa version achevée. Nous sommes également reconnaissants à Mlle Michèle Mangani du soin apporté à la présentation du texte en vue de sa publication. Cette monographie constitue un début prometteur pour la nouvelle série.

Richard J. EVRAIRE
Lieutenant General Lieutenant-général
Canadian Army Armée canadienne
NATO Defense College Collège de Défense de l'OTAN
Commandant

INTRODUCTION

European security and stability is not a new issue, but since the end of the Cold War and bipolarity it has acquired new dimensions whereas the significance of some traditional pillars of European security has somewhat diminished. While the old security system based on the global opposition between the two super-powers did provide a sense of stability, there was still the constant threat of a large-scale conflict with the potential to evolve into a nuclear one. In fact, the unpredictability of the Cold War era was limited to the technical dimensions of security issues since the actively involved political actors and their interests and rationales were clearly defined and provided the basis for strategic political decision making.

After the collapse of the communist system, the great adversary—ideological and military—vanished and so did the basic security threat. However, new challenges—let us call them security risks—have now emerged as a result of the democratization process that began in Eastern Europe in 1989 and one of the consequences of this process has been the proliferation of political actors capable of upsetting regional security balances. At the same time, the decline of the military threat has increased the relative significance of other dimensions of security—economic, ecological, demographic, migrational.

One of these challenges is the minorities' issue which had previously been confined to a secondary level by the global politico-military threat. In fact, under communist regimes ethnic or other minorities had only two options—refraining from defending their rights or facing direct or indirect repression—and in many cases it was not even safe to declare and insist on belonging to a minority. The situation changed dramatically in 1989 when groups and individuals became free to defend their particular affiliation and Eastern Europe's ethnic and national mosaic, which had rarely been mentioned before, was suddenly uncovered. It was for that reason that minority issues appeared to explode virtually simultaneously with the process of democratization.

In some areas of Eastern Europe—mainly the former Yugoslavia and some of the former Soviet republics—these issues have turned into long-lasting bloody conflicts and civil wars. In other areas they are still at the crossroads, with two basic, equally probable, possibilities for their future evolution—violent or peaceful. The common denominator in minority conflicts in Eastern Europe, and especially in the Balkans, is usually their nationalistic component. In fact, most of these conflicts are not ethnic or religious, although they are usually **presented** and **perceived** as such, and in most cases the underlying causes are mainly political or economic. In addition, nationalism and nationally-motivated mobilization provide the emerging political elites in this region with an effective instrument for obtaining public support and legitimacy, and nationalist appeals, to which the Balkan peoples are extremely susceptible, are also widely exploited at the political level.

Although the Yugoslav crisis is still the most tragic example of a minority conflict in the former Eastern Europe (excluding the former USSR), there are other potential sources of tension in the region. Indeed the various aspects of the minorities' issue represent a common European problem. This means that European security is indivisible as local conflicts have a direct or indirect impact on the whole continent—as refugee flows, as threats of spill-over into bordering countries, thereby enlarging the circle of countries involved, or simply as demoralizing examples of how policy should not, but nevertheless can be, conducted. And this is one of the reasons why the issue of ethnic and minority conflicts is not locally but globally significant. Bearing this in mind, it is important to analyse the roots of some of the most significant ethnically-based (or ethnically-worded) conflicts in Europe, to define their participants' **rationales**, and to answer the question of how they relate to the issue of European security. These are the objectives of the present monograph.

The analysis concentrates on the Balkans, because this region provides the most blatant examples of violent ethnically-worded nationalism. It is based on two case studies, former Yugoslavia and Bulgaria. One of the reasons why these two countries were chosen for case studies is that, from the very beginning of their statehood, they were competing and rival sides, with their common Slav origins representing a dividing rather than a uniting element. Faced by a powerful Austro-Hungarian rival in the north, the Serbian state looked to the south as the natural and the only possible direction for its expansion. The same was true of the Bulgarian state and the powerful Ottoman Empire and Greece in the nineteenth century—the only feasible direction for its expansion lay in the north-west. And Macedonia was the region where these two, and later three, competing sets of interests collided. While historical analogies are always risky, it is worth bearing in mind this constant Serbo-Bulgarian rivalry which has shaped much of the Balkan context up to the 1990s.

However, the main reason for which these two countries have been chosen as case studies is their different approach to minority issues. In fact, we can speak of two models in the Balkans: one is the Yugoslav approach, secessionist-oriented self-determination, and the other is the Bulgarian approach, non-secessionist self-determination with limits to minority rights.

Of course, the scale of the problems and that of the competing minorities are not always comparable. This is partly due to the fact that Bulgaria has one dominating—state—majority whereas all the constituting nations of the former Yugoslav federation were minorities in absolute terms. In addition, account must be taken of the unique historical background of these two countries which represent two distinct groups of states in the Balkans: satisfied and dissatisfied in terms of territory. Throughout the twentieth century, Yugoslavia has been a typical example of a satisfied state and Bulgaria of a dissatisfied one, and there has always been a direct link between the degree of territorial satisfaction and the intensity of minority conflicts. Hence, increasingly aggravated minority problems were, and still are, the inevitable price which has been paid at various times by all Balkan states for territorial satisfaction. That is why the Yugoslav period is treated as an introduction to today's status quo, whereas after the collapse of the federation most of the post-Yugoslav states moved closer to the Bulgarian model, i.e. one dominating national minority, which makes the comparisons more relevant.

Mutual relations between seemingly separate issues have also governed the content and structure of this monograph. Since current Balkan politics is always deeply rooted in the historical context, any research on this region calls for some broad historical introduction in order to formulate the distinct (but vivid) current points of concern and sources of arguments used in discussing the minorities' issue. This is the aim of Chapter 1 which should be considered as a broad, but mandatory, introduction to the issue and not just as a survey of the region's ancient and medieval history.

The unique historical experience of the Balkan peoples predetermines both the importance of history and the significance of the concept of nations together with the Balkan peoples' susceptibility to nationalist appeals—both in the past and now. Hence Chapter 2 attempts not only to present nationalism as it was conceived and developed in the Balkans, but also to explain the effectiveness of nationalist-based mobilization in the region in the twentieth century—both between the two World Wars and since 1989.

Chapter 3 addresses the direct historical, as opposed to the distinct historical, i.e. often mythological, roots of minority problems in the region. It traces the evolution of the state's approach to the issue in satisfied Yugoslavia and frustrated Bulgaria. This period was crucial for building different attitudes to what a state or a group is entitled to in terms of territory and minorities. Both attitudes were in some respects biased, and in the Serbian case this was the period which produced the unique tradition of historical egoism, of interpreting extraordinary historical circumstances as natural events. This formed part of the intellectual background to Serbian policy after 1991 (the Serbo-Croatian war), especially in Bosnia-Herzegovina in 1992 when ethnic cleansing was considered justifiable in terms of the Serbs' natural right to be the majority in certain territories. In the Bulgarian case, the interwar period was the one when revanchist attitudes gained broader ground in society.

The basic factual material for the monograph is provided in Chapter 4, which approaches the minorities in Bulgaria and former Yugoslavia from the perspective of their impact on regional security, i.e. minorities which can raise claims for secession and threaten the territorial integrity of states. Since the question of secession and self-determination is not that clear-cut, this ambiguity is analysed in Chapter 5 and the two basic options—secessionist and non-secessionist self-determination—are examined, again using the Yugoslav and Bulgarian examples.

Chapter 6 discusses the impact of the Balkan crisis on international relations. The newly-emerged political parties to local conflicts and their interests are defined as well as the Western response to the crisis in the former Yugoslavia. On that basis an attempt is made in Chapter 7 to go beyond regional security issues and to put the problem of Balkan security into a broader European perspective. This includes an examination of the possible ways of dealing with the security vacuum which has emerged since the dissolution of the Warsaw Pact, in particular addressing the question as to whether NATO membership is the only solution to Eastern Europe's security concerns or whether there exist other—regional—options. In the last part of the chapter the idea of a regional defence structure is analysed.

In view of the very different dimensions—historical, political, sociological—of the minorities' issue in the Balkans, the proportion of data and theory varies from chapter to chapter. For this reason each chapter begins with a short description of the terminological framework and ends with current conclusions which provide the starting point for the next chapter in the monograph.

CHAPTER 1
MINORITIES IN THE BALKANS:
THE HISTORICAL ROOTS

Almost everything about the Balkans is disputable as, to a certain extent, is the geographical definition of the region. However, there are three irrefutable geographical facts about the Balkans: first, it is a peninsula in south-eastern Europe; second, it is surrounded by the Black, Aegean, Ionian, and Adriatic Seas; and, third, it is a mainly mountainous region whose very name is derived from its mountain relief.[1] The northern and north-western borders are not so easy to define. Although some specialists point to the Rivers Danube and Sava in the north and to the Kupa in the north-west as natural borders, this is rather a narrow approach and a certain extension of the region's geographical borders up to the Transylvanian Alps in the north and to the Julian Alps in the north-west is justified if only to include countries which are perceived, and perceive themselves, as Balkan countries.[2]

One of the region's major features is probably the predominance of politics and its overrepresentation in all aspects of Balkan life. In a much more tangible way than elsewhere, politics determines economics, geography, and even history which is often rewritten in a purely Orwellian way, according to the last directives.

In political terms, the Balkans refers to both a strategically more or less important region[3] and a group of countries situated in this region. Until 1991 the list of countries traditionally regarded as Balkan states comprised, in alphabetical order, Albania, Bulgaria, Greece, Romania, Turkey, and Yugoslavia. With the collapse of the communist

---

[1]In Turkish, mountain sounds like balkan, which is also the common name for the biggest mountain range in the peninsula—Stara Planina in Bulgaria. See Map 1.

[2]For more details on the geographical aspects of the Balkans and the influence of its geography on history and politics, see Robert Lee Wolff, The Balkans in Our Time (Cambridge: Harvard University Press, 1956), pp.10-24.

[3]More for some politicians, such as Winston Churchill, less for others, such as Otto von Bismarck.

system and the democratization process, four other countries have emerged and joined the Balkan list: Bosnia-Herzegovina, Croatia, Former Yugoslav Republic of Macedonia, and Slovenia. It is possible, however, that the list is not yet closed.

In addition to the emergence of new states on the Balkan map, the political changes which have occurred since 1989 have also created a certain amount of terminological confusion. To avoid any such confusion and for the sake of contextual clarity, the following set of definitions has been developed for the terminology which will be used throughout this monograph:

-   "Former Yugoslavia" refers to the former "Social Federal Republic of Yugoslavia";
-   "Yugoslavia" refers to the present-day federation between Serbia and Montenegro as a successor state to the former Yugoslav federation;
-   "Macedonia" refers to the territory of Macedonia as a geographical area and historical region;
-   "Macedonian" refers to the issues connected with the Macedonian question until 1991;
-   "Republic of Macedonia" refers to the "Socialist Republic of Macedonia" in the former "Socialist Federal Republic of Yugoslavia";
-   "Former Yugoslav Republic of Macedonia" (FYROM) refers to the political entity created following the declaration of independence by the former "Republic of Macedonia" in the former "Socialist Federal Republic of Yugoslavia."

This complicated set of definitions is in itself an indication of the complexity and high degree of politicization of Balkan issues. In the case of Bosnia-Herzegovina and Croatia, there should be no confusion as it will be clear from the context whether they are referred to in geographical terms, as republics in the former Yugoslav federation, or as state entities.

For more than forty-five years the region was divided into two-and-a-half hemispheres as part of the front line between NATO and the Warsaw Pact, with former Yugoslavia attempting to escape from bipolarity and actively promoting the non-aligned movement. This meant that different approaches were applied to the region as a whole, on the one hand, and to its individual countries, on the other. Regional stability was a residual value of global and European stability and any attempt to put the problem into regional dimensions was doomed to failure.[4] Nevertheless, concern about regional stability is the factor which unites the various Balkan countries, whereas the factor which divides them is different approaches to defining existing threats and possibilities of neutralizing them.

The aim of the present monograph is to answer some of the questions directly connected with regional stability in the Balkans. What are the existing minorities or, rather, the basic ones from the point of view of their strategic impact? How did they emerge and why did they become minorities? What are the basic conflict spots and the main conflictual issues? Is nationalism in the Balkans something exclusive or, rather, the materialization of some general civilizational trends? Is today's situation unique or have there been analogous ones in the past? Are the international community's responses to the present challenges adequate to the nature of the issue and, if not, why? If they are adequate, why are the responses not having the desired effect? Are there any resources available (both material and intellectual) for anticipating the appropriate responses to events, or are we doomed to just watch the events as they unfold? Who has the capability—and who is willing—to become actively involved in the Balkans? What role can NATO play in the region, and could the Balkan issue be one element in a broader security framework? Could the Partnership for Peace (PfP) programme provide such a framework?

These are some of the questions that inevitably arise when one hears the key words, "Balkans," "nationalism," "ethnic conflicts," and "European security." In fact all of them relate—directly or indirectly—to the minorities' issue. For historical reasons all the existing states in the region, as well as some non-Balkan ones which have traditionally close ties with the area, have bigger or smaller minorities living outside their borders. That is why we find Albanians in Greece, in the Former Yugoslav Republic of Macedonia (FYROM), in Serbia proper, in Montenegro, and mainly in Kosovo; Bulgarians in Serbia, FYROM, and Turkey; Croats in Bosnia-Herzegovina; Greeks in Albania; Czechs in Croatia and Serbia; Hungarians in Croatia, Serbia, and Slovenia; Italians

---

[4]As, for example, the unsuccessful efforts to create nuclear-free zones between 1957 and the late 1980s. For further details, see Athanassios G. Platias and R.J. Rydell, "International Security Regimes: the Case of a Balkan Nuclear-Free Zone," in South-Eastern Europe After Tito. A Powder-Keg for the 1980s? David Carlton and Carlo Schaerf (eds.) (London: Macmillan Press, 1983), pp.115-123.

in Croatia and Slovenia; Macedonians in Serbia and, with serious doubts about their Macedonian national affiliation, in Bulgaria and Greece;[5] Romanians in Serbia; Serbs in Bosnia-Herzegovina, Croatia, FYROM, Montenegro, and Kosovo;[6] and Turks mainly in Bulgaria, but also in FYROM and Serbia.

Until the war in Bosnia-Herzegovina, the Bosnian Muslims[7] and the Macedonians were the only national groups which did not have significant minorities living outside their republics—later independent states, Bosnia-Herzegovina and FYROM.[8] With the former, this was because religious affiliation (in this case to Islam) in the other neighbouring countries was not elevated to the status of national affiliation. Like the Pomaks in Bulgaria (Bulgarian Muslims), these communities are minorities which are distinguished according to religious criteria although they remain ethnic Bulgarians. In the case of the Macedonians, they do not have any minorities outside FYROM because the intensive nation-building process which created the Macedonian nation and its separate identity after 1945 was confined to the Republic of Macedonia of the Former Yugoslav Federation. The Gipsies constitute a significant minority without their own state, and a small number of Jews and Armenians also inhabit the region.

The commom denominator of all these completely different groups is the important role they play in Balkan politics, and this role is the general topic of this monograph.

---

[5]The problem with the Macedonians in Greece and Bulgaria will also be analysed within the framework of the Macedonian question. The general idea is that although Macedonian minorities do not exist in Bulgaria and Greece, the FYROM's quests for their recognition have a serious impact on security in the Balkans.

[6]For the purposes of analysis the Serbs in Kosovo will be treated as a minority although Kosovo is still part of Serbia.

[7]Serious terminological confusion has arisen since 1971, when the Yugoslav authorities officially recognized the descendants of Slavs converted to Islam as a separate nation and gave them the name Muslims. In order to distinguish Muslim as a religional affiliation from Muslim as the national affiliation of 43.7% of the population of Bosnia-Herzegovina, the latter will be defined throughout the analysis as Bosnian Muslims.

[8]On the refugee problem, see F.W. Carter, "Ethnicity As a Cause of Migration in Eastern Europe," Geo-Journal, Vol.3, No.3, 1994, pp.241-248.

Overview of Ancient and Medieval History

It is somewhat superficial to say that different ethnicities are intermixed in the Balkans. The minority map of the Balkans is really a mosaic and, therefore, the tendency to view the region's ethnic heterogeneity as one of the reasons for its conflicts is almost commonplace.

Some studies stress the irrationality of the processes taking place in the Balkans and describe ethnic conflicts as "violent, ruthless, and, most important to Western understanding, irrational. Ethnic violence is a release of long-suppressed hatreds awaiting the right spark to set them off."[9] Others attribute the blame for these conflicts to the "barbarian nature" of the Slav nationalities, which "are tribal societies, governed more by their emotions than by their intellects. Moreover, these emotions are primitive, atavistic, and not those shaped by late twentieth-century liberal values: concepts such as death before dishonour and the sacred duty to wreak personal revenge on those who have wronged oneself, one's family or one's country are still powerful motivators."[10] One interpretation stresses the strong traditionalist structures and the communal elements which go to make up the organization of these societies.

There is much truth in all these explanations, but "to assert temporal distance, such as by calling something 'ancient,' is a classic means of establishing the thing so called as inferior; this and the imagery of 'tribalism' and 'irrationality' make the explanation immediately suspect as ideology, not analysis."[11] And, unfortunately, there is a rational explanation for such an ideology because interpreting ethnic conflicts in the Balkans as irrational tribalism in many cases puts the broadly defined West in the extremely comfortable position of innocent superiority. The logical development of this interpretation not only presupposes non-intervention in conflicts and, whenever possible,

---

[9]Timothy L. Thomas, "Ethnic Conflict: Scourge of the 1990s?" Military Review, December 1992, p.15.

[10]C.J. Dick, "Serbian Responses to Intervention in Bosnia-Herzegovina," British Army Review, No.102, December 1992, p.18.

[11]Katherine Verdery, "Nationalism and National Sentiment in Post-Socialist Romania," Slavic Review, Vol.52, No.2, Summer 1993, p.181.

assigning them to the internal affairs of the countries in the region but, more importantly, it relieves the West of its share of responsibility for the present crisis in the Balkans.

Indeed, much of what is happening today in the Balkans is a far cry from even the most broadly-defined civilized rules. What is more, the events in the region often defy understanding in terms of West European democratic paradigms. However, this does not mean that the Balkan reality is irrelevant or surrealistic, but that it simply needs to be approached in a different way in order to be understood since its hierarchy of rational arguments is biased from the traditional West European point of view. Within this hierarchy, historical arguments constitute an important layer in the social consciousness—much too important according to Western standards. And for that reason any study of the causes of the Balkans' ethnically-based or ethnically-tinged crises must include an historical overview of how the problems emerged bearing in mind that history in the Balkans is a never ending story.

The region's current territorial and ethnic composition is the result of a long and complicated process of population migrations and invasions from both Europe and Asia Minor. For centuries the region was a terrain of rivalry between several civilizations and empires—Illyrians and Dacians, Ancient Greece, Macedonian and Roman Empires, Byzantium, Ottoman, Austro-Hungarian and Russian Empires. Since the Balkans has an extremely rich history, every nation in the region can trace back its roots to some glorious periods, events, or peoples in antiquity.

The oldest peoples in the peninsula are the Greeks and the Albanians, the latter claiming descendance from the ancient Illyrians. Towards the end of the fifth century, the Slavs, who probably originated from the lands of present-day Poland or, according to some theories, even from territories further to the east, gradually began to move southwards. This peaceful invasion took a century to complete and by the sixth century the Slavs occupied most of the Northern Balkans and had even moved into Greece.[12] As a result of this gradual moving apart by the various Slav tribes within the peninsula and its natural mountainous barriers, the Slav language split and the various dialects became separated from each other, giving rise to the four basic

---

[12]For more details, see E. Garrison Walters, The Other Europe (Syracuse: Syracuse University Press, 1988), pp.19-21.

South Slav peoples—Bulgarians, Croats, Serbs, and Slovenes—and to the three basic Slavic languages—Bulgarian, Serbo-Croat, and Slovene.[13]

By the seventh century the Slavs had been conquered by the Bulgar tribes, a non-Slav ethnicity which originated from the territories between the Azov Sea and the Kuban and Volga Rivers, and the first Bulgarian state was founded in A.D. 681. In A.D. 864 Bulgarian Czar Boris converted the Proto-Bulgarians to Christianity. This helped them to integrate with the Slavs, who had in the meantime assimilated their conquerors. The first Bulgarian Empire reached its peak during the reign of Simeon (A.D. 893-927), extending to the territories of today's Bulgaria and Macedonia as well as to parts of Albania, Greece, and Serbia (see Map 2). Byzantium was the main rival in the region and by the end of the eighth century it occupied the eastern and south-eastern parts of the Bulgarian Empire and in A.D. 971 its capital, Preslav, was captured. Attempts to resist the Byzantine invasion were organized by the district governor of Sredetz (today's Sofia), who was later to become the Bulgarian Czar.[14]

After a series of clashes, the Bulgarian Empire was confined to its western part, the territories of present-day Macedonia, and the capital was moved from Sredetz to Ohrid. Samuil died in 1014 when he

---

[13]The exact number of Slavic languages is also disputable. For decades two problems—whether Macedonian is a language separate from Bulgarian and whether Serbian and Croat are two different languages—focused on political rather than linguistic discussions. Language was reasonably perceived as an important instrument for nation building and for that reason the recognition of a distinct language was necessary in dealing with the Macedonian issue and dangerous in the Croatian one. For these internal political reasons, whereas, in the former Yugoslavia, Macedonian was granted the status of a distinct language immediately after the Federation's creation in 1945, Croat was not granted similar status until after the federation had fallen apart and an intense nation-building process had been launched in Croatia.

[14]A brilliant example of the political manipulation of history is the contemporary Serbian and Macedonian interpretation of Samuil's period of the First Bulgarian Empire. According to this interpretation and without even mentioning any Bulgarian state, "in the south-eastern Balkans, the Slavic tribes in Macedonia also began building their feudal states after having wrested themselves free from Byzantine and Bulgarian control. They reached the peak of their power during the reign of Emperor Samuel. After his death, the Macedonian state weakened, and its lands came again under Byzantine sovereignty." Branimir M. Jankovic, The Balkans in International Relations (London: Macmillan Press, 1988), p.25.

saw his soldiers blinded after being captured by Byzantine Emperor Basil II, known also (not only in Bulgarian, but also in English- and French-language monographs) by his Greek name Vassilios II Voulgaroktonos or "The Slayer of Bulgarians."[15] In 1018 the Byzantine army took Ohrid and the region passed into Byzantine possession for a century and a half. The second Bulgarian Empire was established after a revolt led by two nobles, Peter and Ivan Assen, in 1186. It reached its peak under Ivan Assen II and again became a major Balkan power. But soon internal rivalries began to weaken the empire and a century and a half later the leading role shifted to the Serbian state.

The first attempt to settle an independent Serbian state was made in 1166 by Stefan Nemanja, who expanded Serbian territory to the Adriatic (see Map 3). His son Stephen II assumed the title of king. The Bulgarian and Byzantine Empires were natural rivals and Bulgarian expansion after 1186 was to the detriment of the Serbian state. The subsequent decline of both rivals created the opportunity for Serbian expansion. In 1282 Serbian King Milutin took Skopje from the Byzantine empire and started to penetrate Macedonia. After defeating the Bulgarian army in 1330 the medieval Serbian state reached its peak under Stefan Dusan. Under his rule the political centre of the state was moved south to Skopje, and the territory of the empire was extended from the Adriatic to the Aegean. But, as in the case of Bulgaria, the Serbian Empire lacked internal cohesion and declined after Stefan Dusan's death in 1355.

There was a similar development in the western part of the peninsula, where, by the end of the tenth century, Croatia, Bosnia, and Albania were competing for supremacy. By the end of the tenth century the Croats had established an independent state with Biograd on the Dalmatian coast as its capital. However, it only lasted until 1102 when it was incorporated into the Kingdom of Hungary and later into the Habsburg Empire.[16] A Bosnian kingdom with a Bosnian Christian

---

[15]"It is well known that Byzantine Emperor Vassilios II has been called the Slayer of Bulgars (Voulgaroktonos) and not the Slayer of Macedonians. This is an historical fact and cannot be disputed." Macedonia and the Macedonian Question (Thessaloniki: Society for Macedonian Studies, 1983), p.41.

[16]What is interesting in the case of the Croatian state is the nature of its relationship with the Hungarian state, disputed for centuries. The Croats always insisted that the union rested on an agreement between two equal partners. Although the Hungarian

Church (which was not part of either the Orthodox or the Catholic hierarchy) also existed for a short period in the fourteenth century. Its most outstanding leader was Stephen Tvrtko who was crowned king of the Serbs, Bosnians, and Croats in 1377. His very title is symptomatic of the mingling into one ethnic and territorial affiliation—a phenomenon which is also familiar from contemporary Balkan history. The Bosnian kingdom, similar to other Balkan states, soon fell apart under the pressure of internal conflicts. As for Albania, it was a difficult area to conquer and above all to control. The native Illyrian population was not assimilated by the Slavs; it was organized into tribal associations and the local notables fought each other, united under the sceptre of Skanderberg in the middle of the 15th century.[17]

Thus by the end of the fourteenth century the foundations of modern national disputes had already been laid. The various ethnic groups were already separated and had two important distinctive instruments: separate languages and the factual basis of a glorious historical myth. Unlike France and England, these differences between ethnic groups were preserved but the different ethnicities were not assimilated and amalgamated into modern nations for various reasons. In the case of the Ottoman Empire it was probably the serious religious, cultural, and linguistic distinctions between the dominating majority and the subdued minorities, whereas in the case of the Habsburg Empire it was probably the latter's relative tolerance in the field of interethnic relations.

Under Imperial Rule

In the fourteenth century, the Ottoman[18] Turks started invading from Asia Minor through Macedonia and the Maritza Valley.

---

government did not accept this interpretation, Croatia enjoyed wide autonomy within the Hungarian kingdom.

[17]Skanderberg's original name was Gjergi Kastrioti. When the Ottoman invasions began in the fourteenth century, he was converted to Islam and given the name Skanderberg. In 1443 he re-embraced Christianity and successfully resisted Ottoman rule. After his death the country lost its independence until 1912.

[18]The name Ottoman derives from one of their prominent leaders, Osman or Othoman (1290-1326).

The most important Turkish victory was on the Maritza River in 1371 which gave the Turks control of the Bulgarian, Macedonian, and South Serbian lands. Step by step, significant areas fell under Ottoman control—Sofia in 1385, Nis in 1386, and Thessaloniki in 1387. In 1389, the army of Serbs, Bosnians, and Albanians was defeated at Kosovo Polje and this battle marked the end of the independent Serbian medieval state and opened the way for the complete conquest of the Balkans. The fall of Constantinople—the centre of Orthodox Christianity—in 1453 was of crucial importance for the further evolution of the Orthodox Church, its relations with the Ottoman state, and its role in the preservation of the local nations' consciousness.[19]

Few attempts to stop the Ottoman invasion were made by Western Christendom and all efforts failed. Bosnia was taken in 1463 and Herzegovina in 1482. The fall of Belgrade in 1526 opened the way to further expansion and the Ottoman Empire gained control over the greater part of Hungarian lands and Transylvania. After the failure of the Serbian uprising against the Ottomans in 1630, thousands of Serbs—as many as 100,000 according to some estimates—were expelled, mainly from Kosovo. This population was replaced by Muslim settlers from Albania, thereby launching the process of the Albanianization of today's province. After the second siege of Vienna in 1683, the Ottomans were driven out of Hungary and a military frontier was established by the Habsburg dynasty against the Ottomans. Serbian refugees were later settled there and given land in return for military service to defend the Habsburgs from the Ottomans. And this is where the present-day Serbian minority in Croatia comes from.

Thus, by the beginning of the sixteenth century some kind of status quo had been established in the Balkans which was to last for almost three hundred years: the two empires were rivals but they did not allow any drastic changes to be made which might have upset the existing balance. In fact, this concept of security was to last until World

---

[19]Of course, the contents of the term 'nation' as applied to entities from the end of the fifteenth century is completely different from that applied to such entities in the nineteenth century. It indicates the existence of single elements of the future nation-building process as separate languages, distinct cultures, and common myths. One of the most important elements of nationhood—the sense of a common belonging—was missing and this did in fact lead to the collapse of these old states in their rivalry with the Ottoman and Habsburg Empires.

War I. However, in no way did this solve the question of the conquered nationalities, and the reason why it remained unsolved was because it was not formulated in terms of a national issue. The explanation for this was simple: both the Ottoman and the Austro-Hungarian Empires were not national in the modern sense of the term. "Though dominated by one nationality, they were in essence military empires serving dynasties. Their major purpose was to collect taxes to support the armies that served the sovereign."[20] This fact had important consequences for the subordinate and, in many respects, oppressed minorities: their assimilation was not an imperial priority because the empires were designed as non-assimilative and multinational entities.

The Ottoman Empire was a theocratic one up to the end of the nineteenth century and its population was not divided along linguistic lines but along religious ones. Religious affiliation was the main factor in differentiating the various groups. This was the essence of the Millet system in which other, non-Muslim, religious communities were granted recognition and their religious leaders were leaders of the communities as a whole. The reason for this was often pragmatic: in the newly-conquered territories any form of civil administration was usually missing. The representatives of the old ruling elite had either been killed in battle or had fled so that the only hierarchy which remained was that of the church and the Ottomans used these well-designed structures which did in fact cover most of the peninsula. In fact, they were willing to cooperate with people of any monotheistic religion whose leaders recognized their authority. The fact that Orthodox communities were centralized under the authority of the Patriarch of Constantinople and that all appointments within the religious communities were under his exclusive jurisdiction was an additional advantage.

As far as the Orthodox hierarchy was concerned, cooperating with the existing state was already an established tradition. Of course, in this case the state was not Christian but, on the other hand, it was the Orthodox Church's main supporter in its rivalry with Catholic Rome. Even at the beginning of the Greek national and Serb liberation movements at the end of the eighteenth century the Orthodox establishment sometimes had difficulties in overcoming its devotion to the state. The patriarch of Jerusalem even declared in 1798 that God

---

[20]Thomas W. Simons, Jr., Eastern Europe in the Postwar World (London: The Macmillan Press, 1993), p.4.

had created the Muslim Ottoman Empire to protect the Orthodox Church against Roman Western culture.[21]

Of course, the non-Muslim Millets (in addition to the most numerous—the Orthodox—there were also Gregorian, Armenian, Catholic and Jewish ones) were subordinated to the Muslim authorities as Islam was the official and privileged religion. Muslim farmers, for example, who had settled in the Balkans after the Ottoman conquest, paid lower taxes and held their land on terms of virtual ownership.[22] Freedom of religious belief was also a one-way street since Christians were welcome to convert to Islam but "there was little chance of conversions from the Muslim community to Christianity, since this action was punishable by death."[23]

But the crucial element of the system was not even the possibility of exercising flexible political control over the non-Muslim population but the system's tax collecting mechanism. One main priority, as mentioned above, was not power per se but the stability of the tax flow. That is why "the patriarch was committed to support the government's demands for taxes from the Orthodox. He had no responsibility for collecting them, but it was his duty to put pressure on those who failed to pay taxes, if necessary to excommunicate them."[24] This duty was the price which had to be paid for the relevant ethnic or religious rights and freedoms and for a particular type of State-Church cooperation.

The situation of the Balkan peoples under Habsburg rule was more tolerable than under the Ottomans. For a certain period, the Habsburgs discriminated against some of its minorities, for example, the Protestants in Bohemia and the Orthodox in Transylvania. But it was tolerant towards the Orthodox Serbs who inhabited the military frontier. Discrimination finally came to an end in 1780 after Joseph II's Edict of

---

[21]Christopher M. Woodhouse, Modern Greece (London: Faber and Faber, 1984), p.127.

[22]Barbara Jelavich, History of the Balkans. Eighteenth and Nineteenth Centuries, Vol.1 (Cambridge: Cambridge University Press, 1983), pp.97-98.

[23]Ibid, p.53.

[24]Hugh Seton-Watson, Nations and States. An Enquiry Into the Origins of Nations and Politics of Nationalism (London: Methuen, 1977), p.144.

Toleration, although this did not weaken aspirations towards national liberation and self-determination which increased in the nineteenth century.

Neither of the empires was so liberal as to guarantee equal rights and freedoms to the subordinated national groups and minorities. What is more important is that the main social cleavage lines ran parallel to the ethnic ones, interlacing two types of conflict—the class or socio-economic conflict with the ethnic or nationalistic one—thereby fostering nationalistic prejudices and overexposing the nationalist component of conflicts.

This was one of the reasons why the quest for liberation and the setting up of independent states was constantly present at higher or lower levels of intensity during these centuries of oppression. There were serious grounds for such quests based on the various ethno-national cultures, languages, and traditions which had been preserved. At a certain point their further differentiation became simultaneously a reason for and a result of attempts to obtain national liberation. Thus, in the late eighteenth and the early nineteenth centuries, the ground had been prepared for a sharp rise in national consciousness.

Of course, at that time most of these glorious events were pages from history. Nevertheless, the memory of former glory helped to preserve national language and national cultural heritage throughout centuries of foreign rule. These memories and myths were strengthened as the decline of the various empires became more and more imminent. At the same time, the process of national awakening was making headway as the ideas behind the French and American Revolutions spread and as the number of educated local elites grew. Freedom was becoming a keyword, and in the Balkans and in Eastern Europe the distinction between individual and national freedom was often blurred. That is why the issue of nations, nationalisms, and nation-states became particularly important there.

The minorities' issue is an important one because minorities seem to be, or at least are commonly **perceived to be**, the basis for the conflicts in the region today. But in order to understand present-day events, one has to go back to the very beginning so as to have at least some general historical background to the events which already point towards some intermediate conclusions.

Although the Balkans is a commonly used definition, its contents in political and geographical terms are not immediately obvious. Certainly, for centuries it was a sphere of rivalry between two great powers, the Ottoman and Austro-Hungarian Empires, whose multinational character led to the emergence of an extremely mixed distribution of ethnic groups in the region.

All countries in the Balkans have had their own states and empires at some stage in their history but their existence was always cut short by conquest. The myth of a glorious past did, however, remain and foreign rule did not succeed in assimilating the various ethno-national groups because the empires which dominated the region (Ottoman and Habsburg) were not designed as nation-states. In fact, foreign rule provided a strong impulse for preserving and developing subordinated peoples' separate identities based on separate languages, religions, cultures, and historical myths. These were to form the basis of the intensive process of nation building which was launched at the end of the eighteenth century.

CHAPTER 2
NATION-STATES IN THE BALKANS

Before returning to the muddled issue of nation building in the Balkans, it is necessary to clarify a number of basic definitions which are also often disputable. What are nations, and when and how do they emerge? What is the difference between nation, ethnicity, and race? What is nationalism? What are nation-states and how do nations relate to them? How does a nation-state come into being, and which comes first—the nation or the nation-state? Answering these fundamental questions is a necessary precondition for understanding the specific historical and contemporary features of the Balkans.

From Ethnicities to Nations

There are two basic approaches to the concept of nationality—objective and subjective—depending on how one defines national affiliation. In view of the particular nature of the situation in the Balkans, giving preference to one of these approaches usually goes beyond a purely scientific choice and often also implies a political attitude. In very general terms, according to the objective approach, national affiliation is determined by objective criteria—kinship, territorial belonging (place of birth), inherited cultural distinctness and, above all, language.[25] In other words, nationality is **innate**. The individual is born with a particular national affiliation which is irreversible and in this respect the concept of the nation closely resembles that of race.

According to the subjective approach, it is just the opposite so that national affiliation is a result of a **conscious** act by the individual—be it a conscious choice of national belonging connected with territorial affiliation, as with American nationality in the case of former immigrants with distinct native languages, customs, religions,

---

[25]A contemporary example of an objective approach to national affiliation is the German one in which ethnicity, a blood tie, even a distant one, is of primary importance for naturalization. For that reason, the procedure for descendants of German immigrants in the former USSR, unlike that for German guest workers, is almost automatic, regardless of how long they have been residents in the country.

and traditions[26]—or an act of conscious individual or group self-determination in the national sense of the term. In this case, it is the individual, not fate or nature, who is responsible for his or her national affiliation. Though the two approaches overlap in many respects (for example, those who adhere to the subjective approach do not deny the importance of a common language), the role of free choice draws a clear distinction between them.

Both approaches concur that the nation is a **community** bound by some kind of ties. According to these various ties, different types of communities can be labelled as nations, and this gives rise to different definitions. For the purposes of analysis, it would seem reasonable to use a broader definition. Therefore, this monograph will consider the nation as "a community of people who feel that they belong together in the double sense that they share deeply significant elements of a common heritage and that they have a common destiny for the future... community with which men most intensely and most unconditionally identify themselves."[27] This common type of entity overlaps to include many other existing cleavages in human communities. Although people can be identified in different ways—e.g. as taxpayers, employees, employers, football-fans, members of a family, etc.—identifying people according to national affiliation is one of the few universal unifying criteria which overarches all other subcleavages, even religious and ideological ones. What is extremely important in this definition is the priority of self-assertion as a primarily subjective notion of common belonging.

The notion of common belonging and destiny is probably the basic indicator that a given community has reached the state of a nation. According to the degree and intensity of that notion, it is possible to construct a terminological hierarchy. At the first level of this hierarchy, we would have the ethnic group—a community with a

---

[26]"Americans have considered themselves exceptional because their nation is not based as others are on common history, culture, blood or religion, but on common allegiance to a system designed to accommodate wide differences. It is a system based, in principle, on the liberal idea of individual freedom." Michael Walzer, Edward T. Kantorowicz, John Higham, and Mona Harrington, Politics of Ethnicity (Cambridge: The Belknap Press of Harvard University Press, 1982), p.102.

[27]Rupert Emerson, From Empire to Nation (Cambridge: Harvard University Press, 1960), p.95.

common name, bound mainly by shared descent or common origin, which makes blood ties an important unifying element.[28] The next level would be the ethno-national group in which blood ties are of secondary importance to cultural and linguistic ones. Although ethnic components are still important at this level, they are no longer the basic binding element. The feeling of common belonging is now based on a broader cultural heritage but a common destiny is lacking (an example of ethno-national groups are the Gipsies or Romas).[29] Usually such groups are not bound to a certain territory, they are often of different religions, and their various segments exist separately from each other. At this stage of development, it is still possible for ethno-national groups to change their national affiliation so that the group is still open to assimilation. The other possibility is for ethno-national groups to evolve towards a completely separate national identity.

Here we have two important substeps. The first one is the so-called cultural nation which already has its own distinct consciousness, although it is not necessarily based on one single ethnicity. The cultural nation as a community is a necessary precondition for the next level of the pyramid, the nation-state. It is important to note that the cultural nation is usually multiethnic. A good example is the Indian nation: we can surely speak of a distinct Indian culture and nation although it is based on many ethnicities. For that reason we cannot treat the ethno-national group and the cultural nation as synonyms. The next substep would be the political nation, i.e. a community which is not only aware of its destiny but also of the need for political and legal structures to represent and defend the nation's destiny. In this respect the Jews have been a cultural nation for centuries, and, after developing Zionist doctrine, part of this nation moved closer to acquiring the characteristics of a political nation. The top of the pyramid is the legal and political embodiment of the nation—the nation-state.

---

[28]Timothy M. Frye, "Ethnicity, Sovereignty and Transitions from Non-Democratic Rule," Journal of International Affairs, Vol.45, No.2, Winter 1992, p.602.

[29]Anthony D. Smith points to six basic characteristics of the ethnic community: a common name, a myth of common ancestry, shared memories, a common culture, a link with historic territory, and a measure of common solidarity. Anthony D. Smith, Ethnic Origins of Nations (Oxford: Basil Blackwell, 1986), p.22-28. However, a community possessing all these characteristics is closer to the definition of a nation.

34

The nation-state is a kind of state, presumably dominated by one nation. Since nation-states are the legal expression of nations, they are the main actors in international politics. In fact, the term international means interstate because it defines relations between states, presumably embodying nations. The vast majority of states act as the legal expression of, presumably, one collective entity—the nation. However, this entity is imaginary. It consists generally of several distinct subentities in complex mutual relations. Usually one of the subentities, the nation, prevails, dominates over all others, and acts on behalf of them. It is not the absence of other nationalities that makes the state a nation-state but the acknowledged dominating status of one of the national groups. The other national or ethnic groups have a minority status and their rights are regulated by generally recognized procedures for minority rights.[30] Even if these rights are fully guaranteed, this does not change their minority status. And the main problem with nation-states lies in the possible and probable contradiction between the dominant nation and the minorities (national or ethnic).

Of course, real non-imaginary entity exists in every multiethnic nation-state in the form of its population or citizenry. Citizenship is the administrative aspect of relations between the individual and the state. It is belonging to the state as a subject of international law, unlike nationality which is belonging to a nation as a more or less informal community.[31] It is important to distinguish between these two affiliations not least because of the different types of ensuing loyalties. Nationality and citizenship may coincide but they do not have to, especially in multinational states; they are synonyms either in ethnically pure nation-states or in states which attempt to blur ethnically-based

---

[30]An exception are states built on the federal or confederal principle. However, first, they are also often dominated by one of the members of the supra-national community, and, second, the experience of recent years suggests that the first result of democratization of former closed societies is nation building which can make the federation principle extinct in the less developed parts of the world.

[31]A clear distinction between ethnic affiliation, which in some respects corresponded to national affiliation, and citizenship, as belonging to a concrete state entity, was made as early as A.D. 212 when Roman Emperor Caracalla granted Roman citizenship to all freemen of the empire. Roman was no longer an ethnic, linguistic, or territorial designation. The citizens of Byzantium also called themselves Romans although the principal language was Greek and most of them belonged to the Greek or other ethnicity.

distinctions and to move towards ethno-national unilaterality.[32]

The American approach is similar, though for completely different historical reasons, and nationality and citizenship are synonyms and treated as such in American English.[33] By being or, more precisely, **choosing** to be a citizen of the United States, one was automatically **choosing** American nationality and, at the same time, preserving one's ethnic affiliation. The whole concept of the American nation is concentrated in the words "E Pluribus Unum," "From Many One," and is in fact based on the assumption that nationality and citizenship define an identical voluntary affiliation to the American nation-state.

Closely related to the category of nation and nationality is that of nationalism, which is usually defined as "asserting the primacy of a group affinity based on a common language, culture, and descent—and sometimes on a common religion and territory as well—over all other claims on personal loyalty."[34] Today nationalism appears both as an ideology and as a political movement. Nationalism as an ideology is a system of beliefs which justifies the idea of the supremacy of one (the chosen) nation over the others, whereas nationalism as a political programme and movement does in fact aim at creating a nation-state for the chosen nation, which is often far removed from democratic traditions.

The second aspect of nationalism—understood also as "the readiness of people to identify themselves emotionally with 'their' nation and to be **politically** mobilised as Czechs, Germans, Italians or

---

[32]For a certain period the national policy in Bulgaria was based on the assumption that all Bulgarian citizens were of Bulgarian nationality, thereby abolishing the differences between the various nationalities and ethno-national groups. In Turkey and Greece citizenship and nationality are also treated as synonyms. These problems are discussed in detail in Chapter 4.

[33]"Nationality... indicates the status of belonging to a particular state... may also be acquired by marriage, adoption, legitimization, naturalization or as a result of transfer of territory from one state to another... As well as acquired, nationality can also be lost or denied." Graham Evans and Jeffrey Newman, The Dictionary of World Politics (New York: Harvester Wheatsheaf, 1990), p.262.

[34]M.A Riff (ed.), Dictionary of Modern Political Ideologies (Manchester: Manchester University Press, 1990), p.154.

whatever"[35]—is of crucial importance for any research on the Balkans because nationalism has become one of the most efficient instruments there for political mobilization even at the end of the twentieth century. However, this was not the case in the eighteenth century when the doctrine of nationalism emerged.

The Age of Nationalism

It is an open question as to when exactly nations emerged. Undoubtedly, before the French Revolution, people did not operate within the categories of nations and nationalities. Another term, people—or pueblo, peuple, narod, Volk—was used to define the broad community with a sense of common belonging. It was not until the end of the eighteenth and the beginning of the nineteenth century, when the cultural and political context changed, that today's synonym, nation—or nacion, naciya, nationalitat—came into general usage.

But what is more important is not **when** but **how** nations emerged. Unlike the Balkans, in Western Europe, mainly France and England, it was a gradual process of building a sense of belonging to a community. Up until the seventeenth century, both these states were monarchies whose subjects were mostly serfs (the concept of free citizens was just emerging in the cities and their relative weight in these societies was rather symbolic). The vast majority of the population did not participate in any way in public life and even spoke different languages. Gradually, as internal markets began to develop and to involve broader communities, the sense of belonging grew beyond the traditional nuclei to the state level.[36] However, the existing frontiers

---

[35]Eric J. Hobsbawm, The Age of Empire, 1875-1914 (New York: Pantheon Books, 1987), p.143.

[36]Although the logic of industry has a tremendous impact on a nation's evolution, Ernest Gellner seems to overestimate the purely economic and technological side of the process. See Ernest Gellner, Nations and Nationalism (Oxford: Basil Blackwell, 1983). Indeed, it is hard not to agreee with John A. Hall that "Gellner's trinitarian view of human history is too simple: he is too much of an economic materialist, almost a Marxist in reverse, in imagining that history is structured simply by evolution from foraging-hunting to agrarian production and then to modern industry." John A. Hall, "Nationalisms: Classified and Explained," Daedalus, Vol.122, No.3, Summer 1993, p.16. See also John A. Hall and Ian Jarvie (eds.), Transition to Modernity (Cambridge: Cambridge University Press, 1992).

and the constant wars between states limited this development within state borders so that, by the beginning of the eighteenth century, the inhabitants of each of these two monarchies could be distinguished not only according to local or regional criteria but as people of certain countries too, i.e. as Frenchmen and Englishmen.

This was the Western way to nationhood, a process which was preceded by the existence of a state (which was by no means yet a nation-state) and limited within state borders. As a result, "the shared experiences and myths producing British and French nationalism took their shape primarily from the shape of the state, rather than from the myths of primordial ethnic groups... nationalism became more tied to the notion of citizenship within a territory than to the notion of ethnic identity."[37] The other way to nationhood was the one which emerged in Eastern Europe or Germany and Italy where the emergence of national aspirations and general mobilization on a national basis, and, in the German case, the sense of belonging, preceded the creation of modern states.[38] This was also the case in the Balkans where nationalism was in many respects a liberation ideology.

Nationalism, both as an ideology and as a political programme, has its roots in the universal ideas of the Enlightenment. Coherent expression was first given to the notion of cultural patriotism by Johann Gottfried Herder in 1767. However, his fascination with the ethnic uniqueness of each and every people was a source of patriotic rather than nationalistic exaltation.[39] The real basis for future nationalism was the concept of the sovereignty of the people. The problem here is that the sovereign people as a group of individuals cannot act as a collective body unless it has its own—collective—will. As Rousseau formulates it, "Each of us puts his person and all his power under the

---

[37]Jack Snyder, "Nationalism and Instability in the Former Soviet Empire," Arms Control (C.S.P), Vol.12, No.3, December 1991, p.8.

[38]The time-lag between the emergence of a nation and its nation-state is the basis for another distinction between old nations which emerged before the constituting of nation-states and new ones which emerged after nation-states.

[39]Patriotism is the individual expression of attitude towards one's people. It existed long before nations and nationalism and it is directed from the individual to the community. With nationalism it is usually the opposite—since it is an ideology (although it often utilizes patriotism), it is directed from the community to the individual with high mobilizing purposes and effects.

supreme direction of the general will, and, in our corporate capacity, we receive each member as an indivisible part of the whole... This public person... is called by its members State when passive, Sovereign when active, and Power when compared with others like itself. Those who are associated in it take collectively the name of people, and severally are called citizens, as sharing in the sovereign power, and subjects, as being under the laws of the State."[40]

But this popular will lacked entity, and the solution to this problem was found by Emmanuel Joseph Sieyes, an influential personality of the French Revolution. In his seminal 1789 manifesto What is the Third Estate? he developed the potential totalitarianism of the general will which is inherent to the concept of popular sovereignty. He not only gave political dimensions to the term nation but did in fact also lay the ideological foundations for the future doctrine of nationalist absolutism: "The nation exists before all, it is the origin of everything. Its will is always legal, it is the law itself."[41] And this did not represent a betrayal of the humanitarian ideas of the Enlightenment, but was one of the logical developments of its concept. For that reason "nationalism is not an antithesis to the Enlightenment and its universal principles, but in fact is one of the modern ideologies springing directly from the Enlightenment principle of the sovereignty of the people. At its core, nationalism refers to the rights of the nation as a collective entity... There is one core idea of nationalism, which is based on an oscillating emphasis on the idea of sovereignty and on the ideal of ethnic continuity."[42]

This is where the persistent association of nations and nationalism with the French Revolution comes from. The French Revolution really drastically changed the nature of the process, secularized it, and, to a certain extent, directed it towards the elevated

---

[40]Jean-Jacques Rousseau, "The Social Contract or Principles of the Political Right," in Great Books of the Western World Vol.38, Robert Maynard Hutchins (ed.) (Chicago: William Benton, Encyclopedia Britannica, Inc., 1952), p.392.

[41]Cited in Conor Cruise O'Brien, "The Wrath of Ages. Nationalism's Primordial Roots," Foreign Affairs, Vol.72, No.73, November/December 1993, p.143. See also Philippe Braud and François Burdeau, Histoire des Idées Politiques depuis la Révolution (Paris: Editions Montchrestien, 1983), pp.52-56.

[42]Hedva Ben-Israel, "Nationalism in Historical Perspective," Journal of International Affairs, Vol.45, No.2, Winter 1992, p.368.

role of the institution. In this respect, its effect was completely different from that of the American Revolution—"the American Declaration of Independence of 1776 favoured popular sovereignty. The French constitution of 1791 declared that sovereignty belonged to the nation."[43] Translated into the language of nation building, this means that the collective body of the nation (Rousseau's general will), not the individual, is sovereign and its sovereignty is obtained by enforcement of the national identity: "By placing the rights of the nation before all, the French Revolution gave a mighty push to the sense of nationality that was beginning to emerge in Europe. Increasingly the state and the nation became identified with one another... it was that idea, and not democracy, that was the central contribution of the French Revolution."[44] This makes nationalism an extremely exclusive ideology based on the assumption that what divides people (nations!) is more important than what unites them. And this identification has nothing in common with what was mentioned above in connection with the American nation because the latter derived from the individual will whereas the former derived from the collective will.

The collectivist nature of the ideology of nationalism made it extremely explosive. It became the basis for the future rebirth of nations because it carried an extremely simple and attractive message: the freedom and self-determination of nations. And in many cases, especially in the nineteenth century, and particularly in Eastern Europe, it worked according to this ideal. The Balkans just developed this approach to its logical extremes.

The Rebirth of the Balkan Nations and the Advent of Nation-States

Nationalism had an extremely wide appeal in the Balkans for several reasons. The most important one was probably the absence of independent states. For centuries, the Balkans has had ethnicities and ethno-national groups whose sense of common destiny was strengthened even further by oppressive empires. But, as already mentioned, there were no state borders, as in the English and French case, to guarantee the gradual process of the formation of national

---

[43]Ruth Lapidoth, "Sovereignty in Transition," Journal of International Affairs, Vol.45, No.2, Winter 1992, p.332.

[44]Stanley Kober, "Revolutions Gone Bad," Foreign Policy, No.91, Summer 1993, p.71.

consciousness. That is why, in accordance with the terminology outlined above, the Balkan nations are definitely new nations with strong primordial roots.

National affiliation was not synonymous with a sense of belonging to a state. Thus, from the very beginning of the Balkan states' modern history, subjective national affiliation was replaced by an objectively defined one: "In view of the absence of a state with which the nation could identify, this objectively defined national affiliation was determined by pre-statal attributes such as language, ethnicity, tradition and culture."[45] The other consequence of long-lasting foreign rule, and hence of the liberation aspects of Balkan nationalism, was the shaping of national identification in the Balkans as a **political** affiliation. Nationality, no matter in what sense, was the basis for a **political project** such as constructing a state. Giving priority to subjective aspirations, and not the available resources, was a major step towards the assumption that "national self-determination up to and including the formation of independent sovereign states applied not just to some nations which could demonstrate economic, political and cultural viability, but to any and all groups which claimed to be a 'nation,' opening the way to the growing tendency to assume that 'national self-determination' could not be satisfied by any form of autonomy less than full state independence."[46] Or, according to Anthony D. Smith, the Balkan nations followed the "ethnic" pattern of nation formation with its typical "drive for autonomy and statehood, as a means for creating the nation and giving it a protective shell."[47] For that reason, the Balkan nations not only emerged before the corresponding nation-states (or, rather, re-emerged because the histories of the individual Balkan peoples were interrupted by conquests), but the ethnic, cultural, and traditional diversities also served there as a basis for a number of national aspirations which far exceeded the region's capacity for viable states.

---

[45]Gerhard Wettig, "Shifts Concerning the National Problems in Europe," Aussenpolitik, Vol.44, January 1993, p.72.

[46]Hobsbawm, The Age, p.144

[47]Anthony D. Smith, "State-Making and Nation-Building," in States in History, John A. Hall (ed.) (Oxford: Basil Blackwell, 1986), p.242.

Foreign rule had a questionable effect. On the one hand, the absence of state protection hampered the nation-building process, but, on the other, the conquests stimulated the preservation of ethnic attachments and identity, insulating ethno-national groups from the threats of assimilation and providing the basis for a burst of nation building in the eighteenth century. The multiethnic environment of the empires was not chosen, it was enforced, and thus remained alien. For that reason, it was a backdrop against which the basic elements of nationhood—the national language and a common religion—stood out. Since it is a relational ideology, i.e definable only vis-à-vis a reference point, nationalism needs a backdrop to throw it into relief—and this was provided by the oppressors. And, last but not least, a discontinuous national history is the ideal breeding ground for national historical myths. This national identity was, of course, far removed from the nation in the modern sense of the term—it would probably be reasonable to define this stage as "proto-nation," to use a term coined by Eric Hobsbawm[48]—because it lacked the necessary mobilizing element provided by the educated nations' elites.

These are the positive elements. The negative elements resulted from the overlaying of two processes—nation building and state building. First, this overlaying made the new nationalisms more suspicious and aggressive. Second, as in the case of Bulgaria, the rebirth of independent states often preceded the accumulation of administrative experience by a significant part of the nation's elite so that those engaged in policy making were often incompetent and state bureaucracies were extremely corrupt, a familiar phenomenon in the post-colonial countries' experiences.

The Pashalik of Belgrade became the centre of the first successful national revolution in the Balkans. In 1804 a revolt broke out, led by Karadjorje Petrovic. This revolt was not directed against the Sultan but against four local Janissary leaders, whose power had become increasingly predominant and who were terrorizing the local population. However, it soon developed into a broader movement with liberating ambitions. In 1805 the first major clash occurred between Serbian rebel troops and the Sultan's army and the Sultan's troops were defeated. This victory marked the beginning of the Serbian

---

[48]Eric J. Hobsbawm, Nations and Nationalisms since 1870. Programme, Myth, Reality (Cambridge: Cambridge University Press, 1990), pp.46-55.

revolution in the real sense of the word, and in 1806 Belgrade fell under Serbian control. As usually happens in the Balkans, the Great Powers soon became involved in intensive negotiations to save the fragile status quo. Eventually, the Ottoman army reoccupied Belgrade in 1813 bringing the first Serbian revolution to an end. The second Serbian revolt broke out in 1814 and in 1816 Serbia gained the right to internal self-government. The Ottoman empire partially recognized Serbian autonomy in 1826 and the Russo-Turkish war led to full autonomy in 1830.

The drive for independence in Slovenia was considerably weaker, probably on account of its relatively smaller size and population although French, German, and Italian influence did foster the development of an educated national elite. Another reason was the fact that the cultural and linguistic lag between the nation-state and the subjected ethno-national group was smaller under the Habsburg rule than it was under the Ottomans. That is why the situation in Croatia was in many respects analogous: the Croat-populated territories were under Hungarian domination and there was a significant national elite. Moreover, as already mentioned, the Habsburg Empire was rather tolerant towards its minorities so that they had less reason to revolt than in the Ottoman Empire. From that point of view, it is no surprise that Croat troops were used to suppress the Hungarian revolution of 1848 and to stabilize the Habsbury Empire for a certain time.

During this period Greece was also undergoing serious cataclysms which, as it turned out, opened the way for other significant events in the region. In 1814 a conspiracy, the Society of Friends, was organized in Odessa by Greek merchants with the aim of liberating the peninsula from Turkey with the aid of Russia. After a series of uprisings between 1821 and 1827 Greece was finally recognized as an independent state by the London Protocol of 3 February 1830. These liberation trends also had a considerable impact on the development of other Balkan nations, in particular Bulgaria. Up until the beginning of the nineteenth century the Greeks had a privileged position in the Ottoman Empire because of the official domination of the Greek Orthodox Church. The Greek revolts discredited the Greek positions vis-à-vis the Ottoman authorities and opened the way for the strengthening of the new merchant class in Romania and Bulgaria and, above all, the emancipation of the Bulgarian Orthodox church from Greek influence. This long and persistent process included the setting up of a new Bulgarian education system and the distribution of Bulgarian-language literature.

In all cases, national revivals were launched by the intellectual and enlightening activities of educated, patriotic elites. But the case of Bulgaria was probably most typical. The Bulgarian monk, Paisi, from the Hulendar monastery at Mt. Aton (or Atos), who is considered to have launched the revival of Bulgarian national consciousness in 1762 when he completed the Slavico-Bulgarian History, begins his book with the words "Oh, imprudent, why are you ashamed to call yourself Bulgarian?" This did in fact constitute the first step towards overcoming the national inferiority complex which is a necessary condition for building national consciousness. According to Liah Greenfeld's approach to nationalism, one essential element of nationhood is the feeling of dignity: "The remarkable quality of national identity which distinguishes it from other identities—and also its essential quality—is that it guarantees status with dignity to every member of whatever is defined as a polity or society... To be a Russian at the end of the nineteenth century was an embarrassment. One way of dealing with this embarrassment was... to transcend the nation for a class or to present it as a class."[49] In the Balkans the logic was identical, although in practice it worked in reverse: being Bulgarian or, in broader terms, Orthodox Christian under the Ottoman Empire was also an embarrassment. This affiliation was synonymous with the definition "raja," a scornful term referring to the lowest level of the socio-economic hierarchy.

One way of dealing with this embarrassment was to change at least one's religious affiliation and to convert to Islam. The other way was to ignore the socio-economic dimension, to reinvent ethnicity, and to find new sources of dignity in the nationalist-type affiliation. In fact, we can say that the new Balkan nationalisms began at the very time that the old embarrassments were being replaced by new—historical and national—sources of dignity. In the case of Bulgaria this process culminated in 1870 when a separate Bulgarian Orthodox Church was established with its own exarch at its head. During these four decades, literacy grew at an astounding rate and in fact a sine qua non educated elite was formed for a national revival.[50]

---

[49]Liah Greenfeld, "Transcending the Nation's Worth," Daedalus, Vol.122, No.3, Summer 1993, pp.49 and 57.

[50]For further details see Diana Mishkova, "Literacy and Nation Building in Bulgaria 1878-1912," East European Quarterly, Vol.29, No.1, Spring 1994, pp.66-75 and 85-89.

The next important change on the Balkan political scene occurred after the Russo-Turkish war of 1877-1878. The war was triggered by the uprisings in Bosnia-Herzegovina in 1875 and in Bulgaria in 1876. After they had been crushed in an extremely bloody and ruthless way, a real Slav holocaust became probable in the Balkans so that Russia had no option but to intervene. The result was the defeat of Turkey and the establishing of an independent Bulgarian state at San Stefano in March 1878.

This state included territories north and south of Stara Planina, Macedonia, and large sections of Thrace. Its borders corresponded in general to the distribution of the main ethnic groups in the region and included territories in which the Bulgarian population constituted the majority. However, since the idea of San Stefano Bulgaria had no support outside Russia and Bulgaria, the newly established state was truncated into three parts by the Berlin Congress of the same year: Bulgaria as an autonomous tributary principality (the territory north of Stara Planina); the semi-autonomous region of Eastern Rumelia with an Ottoman-appointed Christian governor; and Macedonia and Thrace which were returned to the Ottoman Empire. After a revolt, Eastern Rumelia voted to join Bulgaria in 1885.

The Great Powers' reactions to unification were equivocal: although unification was the manifestation of popular will, it violated the decisions of the Berlin Congress and was by no means welcomed, not even by Russia. But unification was just one element in a more complicated chain of events which led to the shift of Russian support from Bulgaria to Serbia.

Initially, after 1878, Russia supported Bulgarian unification as it expected Bulgaria to be a future loyal and powerful ally. However, the Russian authorities' interpretation of loyalty gradually shifted towards expectations of pure obedience and the newly established Bulgarian authorities were treated correspondingly. The first manifestation of disobedience was the constitution, adopted by the Grand National Assembly in Tirnovo in 1879, which radically changed the Russian draft, making it more liberal and putting real power into the hands of an assembly elected by universal manhood suffrage.

Gradually three centres of power emerged in the country: the

Russian agents, especially in the Bulgarian army[51] which was being formed, the prince, and the political parties. By 1883, the prince had become tired of constant Russian interference and he merged the political parties into a common front against Russian officers which made Russia reluctant and even hostile towards unification. When the revolt broke out in Eastern Rumelia, the prince had no option but to support the national movement and hence to preserve his throne. The crisis finally resulted in relations being broken off between the two Slav and Orthodox countries. In practical terms, it meant the withdrawal of all Russian officers from Bulgaria in an attempt to blackmail the disobedient former ally.

Having been practically independent for less then seven years,[52] the country lacked an experienced national administrative and bureaucratic elite and it was presumed that the army would in particular be defenceless. Expecting to face disorganized and demoralized troops, the Serbs immediately tried to take advantage of this opportunity and in November 1885 they launched a surprise attack in order to gain some territorial compensation—as E. Garrison Walters aptly puts it, "compensation for what was never clear."[53] Unexpectedly, however, the Bulgarian officer corps showed an extremely high level of military competence and the Serbian army was overwhelmingly defeated. The Bulgarian offensive could have led to the occupation of Belgrade had Austro-Hungary not intervened to protect its Balkan ally. In the end, it was decided to restore the pre-war Serbo-Bulgarian borders which did in fact legitimize unification, making Bulgaria an autonomous state within the Ottoman Empire.

A period of relative stability in the region followed until the first Balkan War in 1912, as a result of complicated and intensive negotiations between the Christian countries in the Balkans on the division of the Ottoman-occupied territories in the peninsula. Several agreements were reached in 1912 (between Serbia and Bulgaria,

---

[51]The Minister of War, General P.D. Parensov, was Russian as were all the officers above the rank of captain.

[52]Practically because only in 1908, after a revolt and internal disturbances in the Ottoman Empire, did Prince Ferdinand proclaim Bulgaria an independent state and himself Czar.

[53]Walters, Other, p.93.

between Bulgaria and Greece, and between Serbia and Montenegro) which also contained secret clauses, and the Serbo-Bulgarian agreement dealt with the division of a large part of Macedonia between the two countries.[54] When Montenegro attacked the Ottoman Empire on 8 October the other allies followed suit.

The Serbian and Greek forces had no difficulty in advancing in Macedonia and Albanian territories whereas Bulgaria had to face major Ottoman forces in Thrace. Both the Bulgarian and the Greek army raced for Thessalonika but the Greeks arrived there first. In May 1913 the fighting was over and the Ottoman possessions in Europe were limited to the Enos-Media line. Unexpectedly for Serbia and Greece, the Great Powers also insisted on the establishment of an independent Albanian state as a check against the neighbouring Slavic states. This deprived Greece and Serbia of territories they had expected to annex so that they turned to Macedonia for compensation, which they had occupied while the main fighting was going on around Odrin.[55] "In fact, the issue was not the national character of the lands in question, but the balance of power among the Balkan allies. Once again fearing Bulgaria as a chief competitor, Serbia and Greece came to a secret agreement on the division of the area in question and on mutual aid in case of war. The two governments were also in touch with Romania, Montenegro, and even the Ottoman Empire."[56]

The Bulgarian government did not have a sufficiently clear picture of the international diplomatic context and felt that it had been deceived by the allies. As a result, it miscalculated the situation in terms of the country's resources as well as the Great Powers' reaction

---

[54]According to Paragraph 2 of the annex to the Treaty, "Serbia obliges to have no claims over the territory beyond the line... starting at the first Turkish-Bulgarian border near the village Golem (north of Kriva Palanka) and runs southwest to Ohrid lake." Thus, only the territory north of that line was disputable, and an agreement on its possession had to be reached under the arbitration of the Russian Czar. Krasimir Uzunov and Evelina Csaneva, Hristos na Balkanite (English title: "The Christ of the Balkans"), Sofia 1993, p.12. See also Map 4.

[55]It is worth mentioning that, although Serbia remained dissatisfied, it obtained Kosovo solely on the basis of historical arguments notwithstanding the fact that the Albanian population already constituted the majority of the population.

[56]Barbara Jelavich, History of the Balkans. Twentieth Century, Vol.2 (Cambridge: Cambridge University Press, 1983), p.99.

and declared war on Greece and Serbia.[57] Romanian, Montenegrin, and Ottoman troops immediately joined the battle against Bulgaria which was naturally defeated. Macedonia was divided mainly between Serbia and Greece, with a small part for Bulgaria, leaving the Macedonian question not only unsolved but, from the Bulgarian point of view, wrapped in the mists of a new-born notion of historical injustice.[58] The main result of the war however was not a territorial readjustment but the emergence of a new actor on the Balkan scene—the state of Albania.

Of course, it would be naive for a state to operate in politics using moral categories unless it had the status of a super-power. From that point of view, the Macedonian question is both extremely complicated and extremely simple: even assuming that the Bulgarian claims that the inhabitants of the region were of Bulgarian ethnicity and, in broader terms, had every right to become part of the Bulgarian nation,[59] these claims were impossible to satisfy for political and strategic reasons. As already mentioned, throughout the eighteenth and nineteenth centuries the Balkans was a terrain of rivalry between the Habsburg, the Ottoman, and the Russian Empires. According to the requirements of the traditional European state system, there was no once-and-for-all distribution of power and status.[60]

Up to 1914, the supreme characteristic of the European state system was the search for a flexible equilibrium and the maintaining of the status quo in general: "If any state seemed to be getting overly

---

[57]In Bulgarian historiography, the Second Balkan War is defined as the interallied war which seems to be more appropriate.

[58]See Macedonia. Documents and Material (Sofia: Bulgarian Academy of Sciences, 1978).

[59]The self-affiliation of the inhabitants of Macedonia is the subject of numerous politico-linguistic and politico-historical disputes, but most of the objective evidence proves that, at the beginning of the twentieth century, Macedonian was defined as a metaphoric or a geographic but not a national affiliation. The problem is discussed in detail in Chapter 4.

[60]On the diplomatic activity of the Great Powers in Macedonia, see Nina Djulgerova, "The Macedonian Bulgarians through the Eyes of Austrian and Russian Diplomats in the 1890s and the Beginning of the 20th Century," Etudes Balkaniques, No. 4, 1993, pp.12-17.

powerful and ambitious in proportion to the others, the others sooner or later leagued together to set limits to the threat (though often creating a new one, which then set the process in motion again)... the balance of power remained the keystone of the European state system up to World War I, mechanically effective, accepted as such and buttressed by psychological and even ethical acceptance of its legitimacy."[61] This philosophy was also applied in full to the new Balkan states on a regional scale. It determined the existence of non-durable alliances which were dissolved just as easily as they had been formed. Traditional enemies often plotted together against potential long-term allies in order to gain short-term advantages, to prevent certain states from rising above the others, and to upset the equilibrium. The second Balkan War provides the best evidence of this.

This quest for a status quo was the basis of the Balkan countries' foreign policies and is the real reason why Macedonia was never allowed to unite with Bulgaria. If it had annexed Macedonia, the Bulgarian state would have become a major Balkan power. The frequent anti-Bulgarian alliances after the first Balkan War and between the two World Wars were not the result of any anti-Bulgarian feelings but of the fear of resolving the Macedonian question to the advantage of Bulgaria.

The last phase in the nation-building process in the region was completed after World War I, with the sole exception of the Macedonian nation. From the regional point of view, the main result of the war was the collapse of the Austro-Hungarian Empire and the subsequent creation of the next independent Balkan state in 1918, the Kingdom of the Serbs, Slovenes, and Croats, which was renamed Yugoslavia in 1929.

At the beginning of the twentieth century, the main actors, the new nation-states, had emerged on the Balkan political scene, usually as a result of the gradual collapse of the former empires. Simultaneously, the future points of conflict became increasingly obvious. One of the crucial ones was the historical heritage of the new nation-states. All their sources of national identity (typically for the new nations) were rooted far back in history and history in the Balkans was always divided and overlapping. But different visions of history have led to different concepts of what is just and what is not, and these formed

---

[61]Anton W. DePorte, Europe Between the Superpowers. The Enduring Balance (New Haven: Yale University Press, 1979), p.2.

the bases of incompatible sets of motivations on the part of the various parties to the conflicts.

In terms of current politics, this meant that the nationalist ambitions of all the ruling elites in the region were inevitably conflicting so that opposing historical arguments could be, and indeed were, easily converted into political ones and the latter into military ones. In addition, Balkan nationalisms were militant and aggressive, typical of new re-emerged nations. All this predetermined a constant desire to reshape the existing borders—invariably based on the assumption of historical injustice—and inevitably divided the Balkan states into two groups: satisfied and dissatisfied states.

Thus, by the beginning of the 1920s, the basic conflicts for the future decades were clear: the disputable interstate borders dividing the existing ethnic and national communities; the Macedonian question; and the division of states into satisfied and dissatisifed ones. In all cases the issue of ethnic and national identity and minorities was of crucial importance.

CHAPTER 3
YUGOSLAVIA AND BULGARIA AND THEIR MINORITIES
BETWEEN THE TWO WORLD WARS

After World War I the Balkan countries could be divided into two groups: satisfied and dissatisfied states. The first group was a replica of the secret alliance which had existed before the second Balkan War between Greece, Romania, Turkey, and Yugoslavia, whose nationalist territorial claims had all been satisfied but at the price of aggravated minority problems as a result of the newly obtained territories. Albania and Bulgaria were in the second group with their minorities living mainly outside their borders, and Bulgaria had an important but politically passive minority.

The Perceived Threat of Minorities

From the very beginning of the twentieth century, the minority issue had a strategic impact on regional stability for the simple reason that minorities and minority problems were traditionally viewed as a destabilizing element and were, therefore, perceived as a source of the strategic insecurity which was always present in the region.

This strategic insecurity, which was compounded by the fact that the independent Balkan nation-states had only been in existence for a short time, was further aggravated by the Great Powers' constant intervention in the internal affairs of these states, be it in the form of a Berlin congress or a Yalta agreement: "Caught between West and East, prevented by the three empires (Austro-Hungarian, Ottoman, and Russian) from an evolution towards a nation-state on the model of the West, they have suffered from permanent insecurity about their identity and their borders. This had led... to a kind of 'hysteria' (already present in the German case) expressed in the vital importance given to any territorial or minority dispute, since at any moment nationhood had to be tested against the competing claims of neighbours whose own national legitimacy also relied on mythical or at least debatable historical or linguistic claims."[62] To a great extent this hysteria was exaggerated by the minorities' intermingled distribution which provided the legitimate basis for territorial claims.

In this Chapter, pre-World War II relations between the new nation-states and their minorities will be analysed. Although decisive steps were taken towards national uniformity during this period, the sources of some of the region's current minority problems stem directly back to this time.

According to widespread opinion, ethnic rivalries and conflicts in Eastern Europe and the Balkans are a post-communist invention.[63] However, this is far from correct. The view that different ethnicities and nations in the Balkans and, more concretely, in former Yugoslavia have lived side by side in peace for centuries only to turn into enemies after the collapse of communism is somewhat ahistorical. First, this view does not take into account the fact that, for centuries, the various ethnicities and nationalities in the Balkans did not have the opportunity to compete on a national basis since they did not have their own nation-states. And, second, it overemphasizes the current political aspects of the issue—the role of non-ethnic factors and the manipulation of ethnic conflicts—which are discussed in detail in Chapters 4 and 5. The facts tend to show the opposite, and that is that periods of ethno-national harmony in the Balkans were brief and, as a rule, harmony was illusory, the temporary result of previous violent solutions to national issues. All the local wars in the Balkans in the twentieth century were fought in the name of reuniting nations and territories or, at least, contained an extremely strong nationalistic component. The same emotions also motivated the Balkan countries' choice of sides in both World Wars.

All this has shaped one of the special features of the Balkans—the unusually high sensitivity to the national issue on the part

---

[62]Pierre Hassner, "Culture and Society," The International Spectator, Vol.26, No.1, January-March 1991, p.145.

[63]For example, according to Jack Snyder, "Contrary to what some would have us believe, Serbs and Croats fought each other very little before this century: 29% of Serbs living in Croatia who married in the 1980s took Croatian spouses... the widely invoked schema of ancient unchangeable, irrational hatred is an inadequate basis for public discourse on nationalism." Jack Snyder, "Nationalism and the Crisis of the Post-Soviet State," Survival, Vol.35, No.1, Spring 1993, p.5.

of the people in the region and their extraordinary susceptibility to nationalistic appeals from both their own and alien leaders. As a rule, people in the Balkans succumb easily to the temptation of historical retaliation. Or, vice versa, if there is the slightest possibility of an historical retaliation vis-à-vis themselves, they immediately feel threatened. In other words, peoples in the Balkans are potentially much more open to manipulation on a nationalistic basis than are, say, peoples in Western Europe, whose nation-building processes were completed centuries ago and whose societies are divided along many more cleavage lines than purely ethnic ones. That is why ethnic and nationalist mobilization played a more important role in Eastern Europe and was widely used by the local elites.[64]

Nationalism, both in terms of doctrine and political movements, starts at the top. It is always elitist, and even "risorgimento" nationalism which, at first glance, appears to be an exception, was in fact initiated by an educated elite. For that reason, the main role of nationalism is an instrumental one. The ideology of nationalism is simply a technology, a means of mass mobilization, for utilizing individual attitudes, such as patriotism. These attitudes are utilized by an elite and as a result of an initiative taken by an elite and it is always an elite or an elitist group that launches a massive nationalist campaign.[65] In the

---

[64]Or, as Thomas W. Simons puts it, "the existence of national minorities provided an obvious focus for majority nationalism. Ruling elites, having just emerged from a national struggle for independence, understood conflicts between majority and minority populations in the same binary terms they had learned in the struggle against foreign empires... They tended to see the discontented minorities as agents of outside enemies, and, ironically, they used the old strategies of denationalization... in regarding the consolidation of the state as synonymous with the well-being of their ethnic group, and by treating ethnic minorities as 'objectively different,' East European elites strengthened ethnic divisions and guaranteed that minority nationalism would be passionate and exclusionary." Simons, Jr., Eastern, p.22.

[65]"Just as nations and states are necessary to nationalism, so too are national elites, who utilize the nation as a vehicle for advancing their political, material or cultural interests and launch struggles for independence, self-government or enhanced well-being. Such a view of nationalism necessarily assumes that elites, not masses, are the key actors in history, that elites invariably pursue power and influence precisely because they are capable of doing so and that they can successfully mobilize masses by means of various strategies, some focused on rational calculations of means and ends, others centered on perceptions of status, still others appealing to constitutive myths, or mythomoteurs." Alexander J. Motyl, "The Modernity of Nationalism. Nations, States and

Balkans, this has meant that, for decades, the ruling elite always succeeded in gaining support whenever it requested such support on nationalistic grounds.

The constant redrawing of borders and the mixed distribution of minorities gave a specific form to ethnically-based territorial claims which were made on the grounds of the right to self-determination or irredentism. The former was fashionable after World War I and was the essence of the Wilsonian-Leninist approach[66] but it had weaker resonance in the Balkans, probably because the local population had less opportunity to express its will and also because the region did not have a long tradition of democratic culture. However, the second type of policy orientation, irredentism, was a constant latent element in interstate relations in the Balkans since the countries in this region had alien minorities on their territories and minorities of their own outside the borders of their nation-states.

Irredentism, as it is used in this monograph, refers to a policy of territorial claims, which were mainly made on the grounds of historical arguments, by one sovereign state to territory outside its internationally recognized borders.[67] The final aim of irredentism is a territorial change, similar to that of secession except that, in the case of irredentism, the object and the subject of the conflict do not coincide. The claim comes from outside the disputed territory, which itself is only an object of rivalry and, in theory, may remain neutral. This makes the irredentist claim extremely vulnerable in terms of a possible act of aggression and, for this reason, cases of the direct raising of irredentist claims are relatively rare in international affairs. If such claims are laid, they are usually preceded by an unambiguous

---

Nation-States in the Contemporary World," <u>Journal of International Affairs</u>, Vol.45, No.2, Winter 1992, p.321.

[66]The problem of self-determination and its application after World War I is discussed in detail in Chapter 5.

[67]The definition itself derives from the Italian unification movement at the end of the nineteenth century—Italia Irredenta, campaigning in fact for the creation of a nation-state and a modern Italian nation.

declaration in favour of reunion[68] made by the population of the territory in question which makes the irredentist claim at least formally a reply. In most cases, these claims are connected with the ethnic affiliation of the population inhabiting the territory concerned, usually an ethnic minority living among the population of a neighbouring state.

Bearing in mind the motley ethnic, cultural, and religious map of the Balkans, it is easy to see that minorities were perceived as alien and as a potential source of threat to state integrity. Hence, policies towards minorities were based on the assumption of possible treason, which was only one step short of actually attempting to get rid of them. In fact, this was usually the policy adopted by govenments in the Balkans and, for reasons which have already been mentioned, there was always some minority to get rid of.

Yugoslav Attempts to Create a Nation-State

The Kingdom of the Serbs, Slovenes, and Croats is probably the most obvious example of a state which emerged after, and thanks to, the collapse of the Austro-Hungarian Empire. The new multinational entity—the future Yugoslavia—was in that respect a residual value of the global process of disintegration of the old European state system after World War I.

At the beginning of the war, neither the Serbs nor the other Yugoslav nationalities had ambitions for building a multiethnic state.[69]

---

[68]One example of irredentist policy is the Armenian claim to Nagorno-Karabakh, although in this case the claim is also underlaid by the enclave's attempts to achieve self-determination.

[69]"For the Yugoslavs, drafted into armies on both sides, World War I was a fratricidal and religious war... The Serbian Orthodox church, traditionally linked to the state, was fighting more for the Serbian kingdom than for the kingdom of God. The Roman Catholic church ardently supported the Apostolic Majesty in Vienna... After joining the Central Powers, the Sultan in Istanbul proclaimed a Jihad (holy war) against the infidels, including Serbia and Montenegro. Muslims in Bosnia and Albania were incited to fight for the Austrian imperial eagle, together with pan-Islamic Turks in Macedonia. Supporters of Yugoslav unification, fighting on the side of the Entente, all emphasized the wish of 'our people' to unite. It is almost impossible to gauge how much the population at large supported the idea of unification during the war...The mood was turning in favour of unification as the war approached its end." Dimitrije Djordjevic, "The Yugoslav Phenomenon," in The Columbia History of Eastern Europe in the Twentieth Century, Joseph Held (ed.) (New York: Columbia University Press, 1992), p.310.

Furthermore, during the first phase of the war, Serbia's military aims were unclear. Having been attacked, it had to organize its defence and it was only later that seeking an outlet to the Adriatic and expanding towards Bosnia-Herzegovina became an attractive option. Later, after military defeat had been followed by the Serbian Army's disastrous Albanian march, the Serbian government retreated to Corfu and found itself in an even less favourable position. Therefore, the idea of a large Slav state, comprised of Serbs, Slovenes, and Croats from the Austro-Hungarian Empire, which was beginning to take shape at the end of the war, was not a Serbian one. From the very beginning, this idea was pushed forward by Croatian emigres from the Habsburg Empire, members of the former Croatian-Serbian coalition in the Austrian Parliament. In 1917 they founded a Yugoslav Committee, and although this was an unofficial body, it actively campaigned for Southern Slav unification. Later, the idea was supported by Croatian and Slovene leaders in the country.

The Croats and the Slovenes had a clear interest in creating a united Slav state in view of the impending collapse of the empire as well as the growing trend towards nation building as a result of the revival of national sentiments at the beginning of the war. In this situation, the Slav minorities in the Austro-Hungarian Empire had two options: one was to remain divided between the nation-states—the existing ones or the ones which would probably emerge after the collapse of the empire (Serbia, Romania, and Hungary)—and the other was to unite in a Southern Slav state. They were obviously in favour of a united state, although the technology of unification which would determine its future shape was an open question.

With the fall of the Czarist regime in March 1917, the Serbs lost one of their strongest supporters and they became interested in unification although they saw this project as an extension of Serbian administration over the former Habsburg territories and Serbia as a liberator rather than a partner in liberation. As far as the members of the Yugoslav Committee were concerned, they did not have any clear and coherent idea about the structure of the future state, while the Croatian and Slovenian politicians in the country, who were quite active in the Austrian Parliament, preferred a two-stage form of unification: during the first stage, the Slavs of the Empire would be united in one political unit, and only after that, during the second stage, would negotiations begin with the Serbian government. This was the reason why the coalition of the 33 Southern Slav members of the Austrian

Parliament issued a declaration in May 1917, in which they demanded "the unification of all the lands of the Monarchy which are inhabited by Slovenes, Croats and Serbs, into a single, autonomous political body... under the sceptre of the Habsburg-Lotharingian Dynasty."[70]

The Serbian government, which was becoming more and more involved, invited the Yugoslav Committee to Corfu to negotiate on the future united state. The result was the declaration of June 1917 on the establishment of a Yugoslav state under the Karadjordjevic dynasty. The declaration was not binding but did indicate a clear commitment to the undertaking. Three Slav peoples were mentioned in the declaration—the Croats, the Serbs, and the Slovenes.[71] The Montenegrins had their own state, the Albanians were not Slavs, and the Macedonians and the Bosnian Muslims were not taken into account since at that time they were not treated as separate national entities. Bosnia-Herzegovina and Macedonia were treated as territorial, geographic entities and the latter was regarded by the Serbs as South Serbia until the end of World War II.

In October 1918, the Czech national organizations declared independence and the national leaders of Hungary and Austria followed suit in November. The empire was dissolved and there was no longer any possibility of achieving a solution within its framework. In October 1918, a National Council of Slovenes, Croats, and Serbs was formed in Zagreb, and by 3 November, when the armistice between the Habsburg representatives and the allies was signed, a political body already existed with effective control over Slav-inhabited territory. Opinions within this body were also split between those who supported the idea of first establishing a closer union of the former Habsburg lands, and those who advocated immediate unification with Serbia. The second approach, which was supported by the Serbian Independent Party and opposed by the Croats, prevailed and on 1 December 1918 the common state was established. National revolutionary organizations in Montenegro and Vojvodina also declared their decision to join the newly established state.

Although it was initially reluctant to support the idea of Slav unification, the Serbian government quickly realized that after the

---

[70]Michael B. Petrovich, A History of Modern Serbia, 1804-1918, Vol.2 (New York: Harcourt Brace Jovanovich, 1976), p.642.

[71]Ibid, p.644.

collapse of the empire the idea of a united Slav state offered them the opportunity for future dominance. By 1920, when the elections for the new state's constituent assembly were held, it was pushing even harder for a centralized, Serb-dominated state. The psychological side of the issue was the widespread notion amongst the Serbs that Serbia had liberated their Slav kin from imperial oppression. This was incorporated into the constitution and into the law governing the administration of the country, which was divided into 33 departments, eliminating the four historical provinces.

Consequently, for the Serbs, "Yugoslavia was not a new state, but the final product of Serbia's wars (1912-1918) for the unification of all Serbs within a single state. It was therefore only natural that Serbia's state institutions (monarchy, army, administrative apparatus) should be extended to the 'newly-liberated territories' of former Austria-Hungary, enabling Serbia to dominate in the political affairs of the Yugoslav state, just as she had dominated in military affairs. Moreover, the new state should be administered from a single centre, without recourse to any federal arrangements. Federalism would be permitted only after a redrawing of internal frontiers, meaning that the Serbs would then incorporate practically all areas of Yugoslavia, with the exception of Slovenia and Northwest Croatia."[72]

None of the Croatian parties accepted this approach and with good reason since the situation of the Croats in the newly established state—after its liberation from the Serbs' point of view—was worse than it had been under Austro-Hungarian rule when they had had an autonomous administration with their own assembly and their own leaders. The opposite was true in the case of the Slovenes and the Bosnian Muslims who gained some political advantages under the new system; for example, the Slovenes saw unification, even under Serbian domination, as a form of protection against Austrian ambitions. For that reason, the mainstream political conflict between 1921 and 1928 was Serbo-Croatian rivalry in which the main issue was the Croats' quest for a federate state and the Serbs' opposition to it.

In January 1929 King Alexander dealt with the problem by suspending the constitution and establishing a personal dictatorship. Political parties and trade unions were abolished and the country was

---

[72]Ivo Banac, "Nationalism in Serbia," in Balkans: A Mirror of the New International Order, Gunay Goksu Ozdagan and Kemali Saybasili (eds.) (Istanbul: Even, 1955), p.141.

divided into nine provinces with the aim of weakening and destroying traditional loyalties. The broader intention was to create a new identity—a Yugoslav one—to replace the inherited national cleavages and serve as the basis for a uniform, centralized state which by 1929 already had its new name—Yugoslavia. But, in fact, "once in practice, these measures served to enhance Serbian domination"[73] since the new provinces were designed in such a way that the Serbs represented the majority in six of these provinces, the Croats in two, and the Slovenes in one.

In response to these developments, a Croatian emigre, Ante Pavelic, formed in Italy, with the support of Mussolini, the Ustashi (Insurrection) Movement with the goal of achieving Croatia's independence, even by violent means. An analogous Serbian nationalistic organization, the Yugoslav National Movement, was established in the early 1930s. The final ingredients of the future Serbo-Croatian conflict were added by the Orthodox Catholics' hostility. After the government had concluded a concordat with the Vatican recognizing the equal rights of the Roman Catholic and the Orthodox Church, the latter's opposition was so violent that the government had to withdraw from the concordat, thereby providing the Catholic Croats with further evidence of the existing national and religious inequality.

The Serbo-Croatian conflict dominated interwar Yugoslav history and the approach to national minorities' problems was in line with the general concept of the national question. This was solved, typically, by majority nationalism, by trying to impose Serbian dominance—in the form of an extension of the Serbian-dominated administration, in the form of direct suppression of the Albanian population in Kosovo, or in the form of creating a new collective identity, the Yugoslav nation. The latter was regarded with considerable suspicion by the other nationalities as a possible instrument for suppressing their individual national identities.

From today's perspective it is clear that the non-recognition of Yugoslavia's multinational character undermined it from the very beginning: "Confident that they could control or assimilate the 16.67 percent of non-Slavic minorities, the authorities in Belgrade refused to exchange reciprocal neighbouring populations, as stipulated in the peace treaties of other Balkan states. Deprived of their national rights,

---

[73] Jelavich, History, Vol.2, p.200.

the dissatisfied minorities turned into destabilising factors, feeding both the extreme political right and left, encouraged and supported by revisionist European powers."[74]

Prior to the outbreak of World War II, the Croats were granted limited autonomy, but it was too little and too late. Although it was not a massive phenomenon, the militant minority nationalism embodied in the Ustashi movement not only precursed the Croats' puppet state supported by Hitler but also embittered Serbo-Croatian relations. The fact that it was the Ustashis, and not the Germans, who committed most of the atrocities against the Serbs during World War II is in itself evidence of the failure of the Yugoslav approach towards the national minorities' problem during the interwar period.

The Frustrated Bulgarian State

Military defeat in the second Balkan War and the unfortunate choice of allies in World War I had a tremendous impact on Bulgarian society. The country was absolutely exhausted by the wars in which it had suffered enormous casualties. The lost territories produced more than 200,000 refugees, whom the new Greek and Serbian authorities forced to leave.[75] This immigrant community created a strong and influential Macedonian lobby in Sofia, and its military wing had an extremely disturbing influence on Bulgarian internal affairs.[76]

The partition of Macedonia aggravated both the country's economic problems and the dominant feeling of historical injustice. It should be remembered that, at that time, the majority of the population in the Macedonian territories identified themselves as Bulgarians and were indeed closely related to them in the linguistic, cultural, and ethnic sense. Perhaps the best evidence of this is the fact that these people

---

[74]Djordjevic, "The Yugoslav," p.316.

[75]"All Balkan countries (Turkey inclusive) have resorted to similar solutions in trying to solve their minority problems in the new context: emigration and assimilation. The culminations of the first solution were surely the major population shifts following World War I, both interstate and internal ones..." Maria Todorova, "The Ottoman Legacy in the Balkans," in Balkans, Gunay Goksu Ozdogan and Kemali Saybasili (eds.), p.68.

[76]In the early 1930s, 11% of the population of Sofia was composed of post-1918 refugees from Aegean and Vardar Macedonia.

were fleeing from Serbia to Bulgaria and not vice versa. Further evidence was the above-mentioned Serbo-Bulgarian Treaty of 1912 which defined the eastern and southern parts of Macedonia as unquestioned Bulgarian lands. But these dramatic developments did at least have one positive aspect and that was that the country did not have to face any serious internal minority problems apart from the Turkish one.

The Turkish minority was a natural heritage of Ottoman rule. The Turks constituted some 26% of the population in Northern Bulgaria prior to 1878, and after the Russo-Turkish war about 1.5 million Turks left the country. Although there was no centrally directed state policy against this population, the Bulgarians' attitude towards them was not as a rule favourable, especially after the uprising in April 1876. Their share in the population fell to 14% at the beginning of the century and to 10.5% in 1926, partly as a result of the territorial changes which took place after the second Balkan and the First World Wars. During the interwar period the Turkish minority problem was not a real issue as this segment of the population was largely made up of politically passive peasants, concentrated in two regions of the country. The real minority issue concerned the rights of the Bulgarian population living outside the country's borders, mainly in Greece (Western Thrace) and Serbia (Vardar Macedonia).

The ethno-national affiliation of these peoples is also a traditional point of political, but not linguistic or ethnographic, discussion and the issue itself was subordinate to quests for the territorial expansion of the Balkan states.[77] And the problem not only concerned Macedonia, but it was also shared by the entire Balkan group of satisfied states, all of which made attempts at intensive assimilation

---

[77]"In the nineteenth century, there was widespread agreement among European scholars that the Slav inhabitants of Macedonia were Bulgarians. However, the Serbs, who had achieved autonomy from the Ottoman empire in 1829 and had plans to expand their territory southwards, westwards and northwards, claimed Macedonia right down to Salonika on ethnic grounds, asserting that its Slav inhabitants were Serbs. The Greeks, who had achieved their independence in 1832 and had plans to expand northwards, based their claim to Macedonia on both historical and ethnic grounds." Christopher Cviic, Remaking the Balkans (London: The Royal Institute of International Affairs, 1992), p.37.

during the interwar period.[78] Not surprisingly, Bulgaria tried to resist these attempts and this was usually interpreted as proof of her revisionist attitude.

The minority issue was one of the Bulgarian government's most important fields of international activity. An attempt to solve the problem of the Bulgarian minorities in Greece[79] was made in September 1924 when a Bulgarian-Greek protocol was signed. This placed the Bulgarian minority in Greece under the protection of the League of Nations, thus recognizing de facto its existence. However, a harsh reaction by Serbia followed immediately. A Bulgarian minority inhabited the Greek part of Macedonia and recognition of this population as ethnically Bulgarian provided indirect support for an identical affiliation of the population in the rest of Macedonia. As a result of Serbian pressure, the protocol was not ratified by the Greek parliament, and in January 1925 Greece announced that it would not adhere to the provisions of the protocol and henceforth treated this minority as Greek. The same year a similar treaty was signed with the Kingdom of the Croats, Serbs, and Slovenes, converting the local

---

[78]One of the most consequentially minorities-discriminating legislation was passed by Turkey. It included: Law to Improve Turkish as an Official Language (1924); Law on Immovable Property of Non-Muslims (1924); Law on Settlements (1924); School Act of 1936 which required that students in foreign schools in Turkey hold Turkish citizenship; the Occupation Law of 1934 which prohibited a number of business areas from being occupied by foreigners. See Darina Vasileva, "Izselnicheskiat vapros i Balgaro-Turskite Otnoshenia" (English title: Immigrants' Issue and Bulgarian-Turkish Relations), in Aspekti na Etnokulturnata situazia v Balgaria (Sofia: CSD, FNST, 1992), pp.61-64. The Greek approach was similar. In 1926 a decree was passed that all Slavonic geographical names should be replaced by Greek ones. By the end of the 1920s all Bulgarian schools (19 in towns and 186 in villages with 320 teachers catering for 12,895 pupils in Bulgarian) were closed and the inventories destroyed. Also, all the icons in the Slavonic churches were repainted with Greek names. See World Directory of Minorities. Longman International Reference (London: Longman, 1990), p.116.

[79]This group is often defined as "Macedonians of Greece." The World Directory of Minorities gives Slavophone Hellens, Bulgarians as an alternative to Macedonians of Greece with the comment: "in common speech the Greek population referred to them as Bulgarians and the notion of them as a separate people, the Macedonians, only really came later in this century, especially after World War II and the founding of the Socialist Republic of Macedonia in neighbouring Yugoslavia." Ibid, p.115. After the names dispute between Greece and FYROM, since 1993 Greece has completely ruled out use of the word Macedonia and its derivatives in reference to anything other than Greece's own ancient history.

Bulgarian minorities into Serbs, but it was not ratified either.

This not only affirmed the attitude towards minorities as small change in geopolitical gambling, but also aggravated the impression that the only solution to the problem lay in ethnic cleansing, which was called population exchange in the 1920s. During and immediately after the Balkan wars some 15,000 Bulgarians left Greece for Bulgaria. After the Greek-Bulgarian convention of November 1919, 25,000 Greeks left Bulgaria for Greece and about 60,000 Bulgarians moved in the opposite direction. Even more dramatic was the population resettlement between Turkey and Greece as a result of which about 390,000 Turks left Greece after the Greek-Turkish war of 1920-1922 and over 1,200,000 Greeks left Turkey. Not all of them reached Greece and most of those who survived settled in Aegean Macedonia and Thrace.

This division dominated Balkan politics in the 1930s and, in particular, the four Balkan conferences which were held between 1931 and 1933, and was reflected in the Balkan Entente Pact which was signed by the satisfied states on 9 February 1934. Bulgaria's concern to solve the minorities' question was not taken into account and, in addition, Bulgaria feared that the Pact was inter-Balkan-oriented: "This fear was confirmed by a secret protocol annex which was made public in April 1934. The protocol annex declared that the Pact was not directed towards any great power and that its objective was to guarantee the security of the Balkan borders against any aggression on the part of a Balkan state."[80] By that time Albania was ruled out and the satisfied states did not even invite it to join the Pact, trading Italian support for its implementation against recognition of the Italian claims for a protectorate over Albania. The only Balkan state the Pact alluded to was Bulgaria.

As before World War I, this did not leave Bulgaria any option for defining its strategic orientation—the only option was Germany which not only supported politically Bulgaria's Macedonian dream but also provided economic assistance in the form of preferential treatment of Bulgarian exports to German markets, which was extremely important for the exhausted Bulgarian economy. Nevertheless, the Bulgarian government resisted pressures to enter the German-led coalition—one of the conditions for participating in the trilateral pact was Yugoslavia's

---

[80]Aurel Braun, Small-State Security in the Balkans (London: Macmillan Press, 1983), p.42.

participation in it. By the end of April 1941 the Yugoslav government had agreed to join the Pact and on 1 March 1941 Bulgaria joined the German-led coalition. On the same day, German troops entered the country but Yugoslavia withdrew at the last moment. As a result Bulgarian territory was used by Germany to attack Yugoslavia and Greece and Bulgaria was rewarded with significant territorial gains.

Bulgarian policy prior to and during World War II was therefore dominated by both national sentiments and revisionism, fitting into the general frame of the already established tradition whereby some kind of anti-Bulgarian alliance was formed whenever the prospect of unification between Macedonia and Bulgaria became even a theoretical possibility.

However, Bulgarian politicians were the prisoners of their Balkan background and the romantic dreams of a Greater Bulgaria. And national bitterness was easily transformed into the aggressive attitudes which emerged during World War II when Bulgaria once again found itself on the German side. The chain of events since the beginning of the century (and even after relations with Russia had been broken off in 1885 after Bulgarian unification) did not leave the country much choice. As in the case of Croatia, Hitler cleverly played on the Bulgarians' national feelings and allowed Bulgaria to govern the German-occupied Macedonian territory of former Yugoslavia. At the same time he consented to Bulgaria's occupation of the eastern portion of Greek Aegean Macedonia, with the exception of Salonika which was occupied by the Germans. In typically Balkan style, the Bulgarians imposed a heavy-handed and corrupt regime and succeeded in alienating a significant part of the local population, making the integration of the Bulgarian lands virtually impossible. Nevertheless, the Yugoslav partisan movement was least supported by the local population in Macedonia which still seemed to prefer heavy-handed Bulgarian rule to the restoration of the old Serbian one.

The new nation-states in the Balkans, Albania and Yugoslavia, came into being as a result of the collapse of the Ottoman and Habsburg Empires. But like most East European states between the two World Wars, they were in many respects geopolitically unstable and, in particular, they lacked firm guarantees on their borders.

In the case of Yugoslavia, as in other newly established nation-states in Eastern Europe, the problems inherited from the empire represented an additional source of instability, in particular minority problems. At the same time the new nation-states lacked the empire's means and traditions and the will to solve them. Designed to look like nation-states, they were in fact mini-empires, usually more oppressive towards their national minorities than the former empires had been towards them,[81] and local militant nationalism was one of the ways of overcoming the newly created nation-states' national inferiority complexes. This majority nationalism was common to both the satisfied and the dissatisfied nations but the difference lay in the latters' limited possibilities of applying it.

Attempts to solve the national and minorities' problems by creating a new collective identity, as in the case of the Kingdom of Yugoslavia, also failed. National affiliations turned out to be much stronger indicators of identification than expected and inevitably prevailed, either as a result of resistance on the part of the minority nations or of the temptation towards supremacy on the part of the majority.

The interwar experience showed the limited possibilities of legal solutions to the minorities' problem in the Balkans.[82] The existing legal framework under the structure of the League of Nations was a manifestation of wishful thinking and, in practice, had little in common with human and minority rights: "The principle of nation-statehood was held in indulgent abeyance for those nations allied to the victors, such as the Romanians, Poles, Serbs and Czechs, but was imposed punitively on those nations foolish enough to have allied with the vanquished, such as the Hungarians and Bulgarians... The Versailles-endorsed shift in the direction of the nation-state had the unfortunate effect of producing hybrid jurisdictions, neither dynastic empires accustomed to coping with heterogeneous populations nor nation-states that could assume homogeneous nationhood. The result was the worst of all

---

[81]"Versailles Europe embodied not the unqualified triumph of the principle of the nation-state but a convulsive geopolitical lurch from a select number of large empires to a large number of select empires... Although virtually all the successor states claimed nation-statehood, they were in reality mini-empires... Those few new jurisdictions that approximated nation-states did so out of necessity rather than choice, usually as a result of dictates imposed on the losers in the First World War." Raymond Pearson, "The Geopolitics of People Power: The Pursuit of the Nation-State in East Central Europe," Journal of International Affairs, Vol.45, No.2, Winter 1992, p.500.

[82]For further details see Boguslawa Bednarczyk, "Nationalism, Ethnic Minorities and Human Rights in Post-Cold War Central and Eastern Europe," Occasional Paper No.2, NATO Defense College, Rome, 1994, pp.11-14.

66

possible geopolitical worlds: newly concocted states living the lie of nation-statehood languished in a condition of permanent conflict both with their antagonized minorities and their territorially disadvantaged neighbours."[83] The logical outcome of this approach was easy to predict and as borders could not be drawn according to the minorities' distribution, the minorities were redistributed according to the established borders.

[83]Pearson, "The Geopolitics," p.501.

CHAPTER 4
MINORITIES AS BASIC FLASH POINTS
AFTER THE FALL OF COMMUNISM

Communist regimes did not and in fact were unable to solve minority conflicts, not only because of these regimes' political inefficiency but also because minority issues did not exist as such according to communist ideology. These conflicts were perceived either as secondary evidence of global super-power rivalry or as a sign of cultural or economic backwardness, and as national and ethnic harmony was expected to be the rule in communist societies any signs of conflict were treated as a form of deviation. Depending on the current political situation (and historical period), the reaction to any kind of deviation was its more or less violent, direct or indirect suppression, but since the actual issue had no right to exist the counter-measures were never consistent. Therefore, the latent development of ethnic tensions continued and finally exploded when the disciplinarian mechanisms of the communist state vanished since "the suppression of ethnic identities—particularly where there are inter-ethnic tensions—provides no long-term solution to those tensions. Eventually, and in various political, economic, and social ways, the tensions re-surface with, perhaps, more intensity because of the previous suppression."[84]

Although the evolution of the communist system and the reasons for its collapse are outside the scope of this monograph, it is worth mentioning that minority conflicts did exist during the communist period although they were not labelled as such. The approach varied from country to country but this did not alter the basic rule: the regimes were highly centralized and monopolized by the communist party so that political monopoly was the primary value and all others were subordinate to it.

In this respect, the Balkans provides us with two diametrically opposed examples. One is Bulgaria which was economically highly centralized and had a strong communist party with a dominating

---

[84]W. Harriet Critchley, "The Failure of Federalism in Yugoslavia," International Journal, Vol.11, No.8, Summer 1993, p.446.

national majority in which the minority issue was not a matter of life and death. The other is Yugoslavia which had a decentralized economy combined with a one-party system—a federation and a country without a dominating state majority and with constitutional solutions designed to meet all minority-based issues. Furthermore, the evolution of the Yugoslav constitutional system contained one concrete trend: more rights, more guarantees for the various nations and nationalities which, from today's perspective, represents a shift from a federation to a confederation.

The main topic of this monograph is not the system in the former Yugoslavia but minorities in the region **today** and their **current** impact on regional security. For that reason, the analysis will refer to the history of the former federation as a means of providing the necessary background. Today the Balkans is comprised of nation-states, all of which have a dominating majority and significant minorities. However, the creation and recognition of the post-Yugoslav states may not be the final stage of their evolution and minorities may play an active part in it.

In this Chapter, some of the basic minorities in Bulgaria and former Yugoslavia will be analysed from the point of view of their conflict-triggering potential. The analysis will focus on ethnic or national groups which may have grounds for secessionist claims. These groups are relatively compact, they are in open or latent conflict with the prevailing majority or with other minorities, and they may challenge the region's territorial integrity by claiming secession on the grounds of their right to self-determination, thereby sparking off conflicts which would have a serious impact on security. Since some groups have already utilized this opportunity and others seem to be seeking other ways of defending their collective rights, we may speak of two distinct models of post-communist transition.

Having presented the necessary basic **historical** overview of how and why nationalism evolved in the region, it is now possible to give more substantial answers to some **pertinent** questions, namely: how relevant are possible future claims for self-determination? How relevant were the claims which have already been excercised? Why and when does self-determination work? Is it the result of a group's internal evolution or is it imposed from outside?

What is most interesting for the purposes of the current analysis is the minorities' new situation and role as political actors in the emerging new system of international relations and security structures.

In short, the main change was the political emancipation of minorities who ceased to be the objects of government policies and became political actors or even political subjects. In fact, this period is reminiscent of a previous one and since 1989 minorities have been able to play the role which, theoretically and according to their declared intentions, they had been expected to play in 1919. But the context was completely different in 1989, with a trend towards the predominance of liberal values and the right to individual choice.

A minority is, in simple terms, a smaller part of a whole. Not only does this mean that the minority's possibilities to execute its rights are not equal to the majority's (a minority can always be outvoted on the grounds of formal democratic procedures) but also that the minority is doomed to coexist with the majority. In this respect, the relationship between the minority and the majority is asymmetric. The only alternative the minority has is to become a majority itself which is one of the generally accepted rights of minorities. As mentioned in Chapter 1, some of the Balkan minorities did make this choice after having exercised their right to self-determination through secession. Others preferred, or were obliged, to execute their rights, including the right to self-determination, through other, non-secessionist, strategies.

With respect to the various cleavage lines mentioned above, affiliation to the basic groups of nationalities is not an adequate criterion for classifying minorities in the Balkans. The real picture is much more complex and is aggravated by the fact that different types of distinctive criteria—ethnic, religious, denominational, cultural—are superimposed, thereby multiplying the possible lines of cleavage inside the existing communities. Within the nationally defined minorities, we have additional cleavage lines and vice versa: according to broader criteria, such as origin or religion, some communities spill well beyond national borders (see table).

For example, the whole region can be divided into two general blocs on the basis of religious affiliation—Christian or Islamic. The Christian bloc can be divided on the basis of Orthodox, Catholic, or Protestant denomination (Orthodox and Catholic being dominant), but there is no significant denominational cleavage among the Muslims, who are mostly Sunnites, although a potential conflict does exist on a linguistic basis (for example, whether Muslims can have Slav names). A potential conflict also exists on the basis of the growing influence of Shiite mullahs from fundamentalist Islamic countries on traditionally Sunnite communities. The division between Slav and non-Slav peoples on the basis of origin is also present, but a more relevant one would seem to be the culturally based division between Latin- (Western) and Slavic- (Eastern) rooted cultural heritage.[85] Czechs, Poles, Slovaks, Slovenes, and Croats are Slavs but are by no means Eastern in the sense of Byzantine. On the other hand, the Albanians and the Romanians are not Slavs but they are Eastern.

Therefore, the Christian community includes Bulgarians, Macedonians, Serbs, Croats, Slovenes, and Greeks, as well as a Christian minority among the Albanians in Albania and among the Turks and the Gipsies in Bulgaria; the Orthodox subcommunity would exclude the Croats and the Slovenes; the Slav community would include the latter plus the Bosnian Muslims but, on the other hand, would exclude the Greeks, the Albanians, and the Romanians; and the Islamic community includes Albanians, Bosnian Muslims, and Turks as well as Pomaks (Islamized Bulgarians) and Muslim Gipsies. The picture is further complicated by the significant numbers of mixed marriages, especially in the former Yugoslavia between representatives of the former Yugoslav nationalities.

For these reasons, the current analysis inevitably has to be limited to the main national, ethno-national, and ethnic minorities[86] which, as already mentioned, may have some grounds for secessionist claims. In accordance with this limitation, the main focal points will be the Albanians in Kosovo and FYROM; the Croats and the Serbs in Bosnia-Herzegovina; the Serbs in Croatia; the Macedonians in Bulgaria and Greece; the Pomaks in Bulgaria; and the Turks in Bulgaria. Although the Bosnian Muslims are not a minority in Bosnia, they will also be analysed as a separate group.

---

[85]The most striking idea of the continent's division on the basis of the Catholic/Orthodox cleavage was made by Milan Kundera who argued that the Eastern border of Europe corresponds in fact to the border between its Catholic (or in broader terms Latin-rooted culture) and Orthodox parts. For more details, see Milan Kundera, "The Tragedy of Central Europe," New York Review of Books, 26 April 1984. On the development of the concept of Central European identity, see Krishan Kumar, "The 1989 Revolutions and the Idea of Europe," Political Studies, Vol.40, No.3, September 1992, pp.439-461.

[86]The definitions of national, ethno-national, and ethnic groups as well as of other groups having a direct connection with the issue of nationalism were discussed in full in Chapter 2.

The Albanians in Kosovo

Kosovo is situated in the southernmost part of Serbia and is traditionally regarded as the cradle of the Serbian nation. In fact, this is one of the broadly televised historical myths and provides plausible grounds for Serbian nationalistic demands. Kosovo was part of the Serbian Empire for several decades in the fourteenth century, but the myth relates to the Battle of Kosovo Polje in 1389 in which the Ottoman Turks defeated the Albanian and the Serb army (see Chapter 1). By the same token this would imply that any European border can be called into question.

The next period of Serbian rule over Kosovo started after the Balkan wars in 1912-1913. As already mentioned, the formally declared nation-statehood principle was applicable only in cases where it was in the interests of the victorious nations. In this respect, a chain of precedents was set after World War I and the case of Kosovo was one of them. Their common feature was the contradiction between the status quo established as a result of military defeat (or victory) and the principle of self-determination. The province already had an Albanian majority and hardly qualified as Serbian territory on the grounds of self-determination.

Not surprisingly, during the interwar period there was a strong Albanian secessionist movement in the region and its members were persecuted by the Serbs. During World War II, both Kosovo and Albania were occupied by Italy. When the Yugoslav communists tried to organize a resistance movement there in 1941, many of the local Serbs responded but none of the Albanians did. According to one of Tito's envoys, even the name Yugoslavia repelled potential Albanian support. After the war the province was restored to the then-formed Yugoslavia, and in 1944-1945 an Albanian uprising broke out in Kosovo and was ruthlessly suppressed by the Yugoslav government although limited resistance continued until 1947.

In fact, the entire pre- and post-war period of Yugoslav dominance over Kosovo was characterized by attempts to colonize or assimilate the province. After 1918, World War I veterans (totalling about 40,000 Orthodox Slavs, mainly Serbs) were settled there as part of a state-sponsored programme. After World War II emigration to Turkey was encouraged and many Albanians took advantage of this opportunity. In line with Tito's concept of Yugoslavia as a multinational state, the Albanians were recognized as a national group and in 1946

Kosovo-Metohija was given the status of an Autonomous Administrative region, corresponding in fact to an administrative division of Serbia. In 1968, following the downfall of Alexander Rankovich, a Serb and the head of the State Security police with strong anti-Muslim prejudices, the status of Kosovo was upgraded to an Autonomous Province and the process of liberal reforms started, as in the rest of Yugoslavia after the Zagreb Spring.

Paradoxically, or perhaps simply according to the logic of decay that is inherent in oppressive regimes,[87] the 1968 reforms led to the first significant violent protest by the Albanians in Kosovo, lasting from November until March 1969. The demands included dropping "Metohija" from the official name of the province, its recognition as a republic, and the establishment of an independent university in Pristina. For the first time, slogans appeared calling for secession and unification with Albania. The government's response was a combination of force and dialogue. The organizers were imprisoned but all non-disintegrative demands were met: the Albanians were allowed to fly the Albanian flag; the province's name was changed to Kosovo; the branch of Belgrade University located in Pristina was transformed into an independent university which opened the way to its rapid Albanianization; and economic aid to the province was increased so that Albanians obtained better access to positions of authority. The process of liberalization continued so that in 1971, when the Kosovo constitution was amended, the province had in fact become a republic in all respects apart from name.[88]

---

[87]According to Crane Brinton, referring to Machiavelli, "collective cognitive dissonance" does not arise during sustained oppression but rather as a formerly oppressive regime begins to reform itself. Repression becomes definitely intolerable when reforms begin. See Crane Brinton, The Anatomy of a Revolution (New York: Vintage Books, 1965).

[88]The Albanians were a "nationality." Only "nations of Yugoslavia" had their republics. One of the reasons why Kosovo was not transformed into a "republic" and the Albanians into a "nation of Yugoslavia" was the provisions of three of the four post-war constitutions of Yugoslavia (those of 1946, 1963 and 1974) which guaranteed the right of the "nations of Yugoslavia" to secession. The threat of possible secession by Kosovo was a constant element in the Serbian approach to the issue—without Kosovo Serbia would no longer have been the biggest republic in the federation. Kosovo as a federal republic would also not have been a Slav one, thereby undermining Yugoslavia's perception of itself as a federation of Southern Slavs.

Further liberalization was, however, accompanied by more frequent outbursts of chauvinism—both by separatist Albanians and by integrationist Serbs. The community began to become increasingly polarized along ethnic lines, and at the beginning of the 1970s the first large-scale wave of emigration by Serbs from Kosovo took place. Another, indirect, sign of the intensifying ethnic conflict was increased Albanian emigration. According to the 1981 census, there were 18,172 less Serbs and 4,680 less Montenegrins in the province than there had been in 1971. This only deepened the Serbs' exclusive nationalism that was further aggravated by the next wave of serious riots in 1981, which were suppressed by the Serbian and Croatian armed forces. After the uncovering of a number of Albanian secessionist organizations in 1986, the Serbian authorities abolished Kosovo's autonomous status, thereby removing the possibility of solving the conflict by political means.

In 1981, Kosovo represented a turning point in the Serbian approach to ethnic conflicts. On the one hand, it reanimated respect and trust in strong-handed rule while, on the other, it revealed the primacy of ethnic identification and mobilization, at least in the Balkans. Whereas the "Serbs began to speak openly of the good old days when Rankovic was in charge of the security apparatus and claimed that it was time to put the Albanians of Kosovo in their place once and for all," the Albanians demonstrated that they "prefer to live under an Albanian despot rather than to remain part of Yugoslavia, however open the latter might be."[89]

Formulated in this way, the dilemma is unsolvable in terms of a consocietal approach. The Albanians have always been in the majority in Kosovo, and by the beginning of the 1990s they had become the prevailing majority. This was due to their birthrate which was the highest in former Yugoslavia, as well as to the Serbs' intensified emigration from the province. Today the province has roughly 2 million inhabitants of which the Serbs number less than 200,000. In the 1980s alone, some 50,000 Serbs left Kosovo for other Yugoslav republics. This Christian depopulation provided a good opportunity for Serbian intellectuals to launch a nationalist campaign, and in 1986 they produced a Memorandum by SANU (Serbian Academy of Science) in

---

[89]Pedro Ramet, <u>Nationalism and Federalism in Yugoslavia, 1963-1983</u> (Bloomington: Indiana University Press, 1984), p.167.

which they stressed Muslim genocide against the Serbian population of Kosovo.[90] Although there were important economic reasons for the Serbs to emigrate from Kosovo, emigration was interpreted purely in terms of ethnic conflict.

After obtaining the leading role in the Serbian Communist party in 1986, Slobodan Milosevic came to power in 1987 using the memorandum as an ideological basis for consolidating his power on a nationalistic basis, thereby enabling the party to be reincarnated as a militant nationalist organization and to survive after the system had collapsed (Milosevic launched his full-scale nationalistic campaign during the anniversary celebration of the Battle of Kosovo Polje in the province).

According to widespread opinion, the conflict in Kosovo may lead to a broader Balkan clash. In fact, there has already been conflict there since the 1981 riots and this is not just a conflict between Albanians and Serbs. Initially the other republics were rather reluctant to take sides with Kosovo, but when Serbian nationalism became offensive they also began to oppose it. They protested against the abolition of Kosovo's autonomous status, which also reflected on Vojovodina, and did in fact heighten the Serbs' suspicions and strengthen the position of Milosevic's nationalist lobby in Serbia.

The complexity of the situation leads to the conclusion that the Kosovo problem is probably the most complicated and most unsolvable issue. If we apply the liberal approach and the principle of self-determination, then the province should immediately become part of Albania but, according to the requirements of Realpolitik, it is not entitled to secession. However, the Albanians now have less and less to lose, and with unemployment affecting 90% of the population and the enforcement of martial law, secession and unification with Albania is becoming a more and more attractive option.[91] Although this will

---

[90]"Physical, political, legal and cultural genocide against the Serb population of Kosovo and Metohija is the severest defeat in the liberation struggle that Serbia led from Orasic (the Karadjorje uprising against the Turks) in 1804 to the (Partisan) uprising in 1941." Ivo Banac, "The Fearful Asymmetry of War: The Causes and Consequences of Yugoslavia's Demise," Daedalus, Vol.121, No.2, Spring 1992, p.150.

[91]According to an Albanian interviewed by Robert Austin, "When two similar businesses are facing bankruptcy, it sometimes makes sense that they merge." Robert Austin, "What Albania Adds to the Balkan Stew," Orbis, Vol.37, No.2, Spring 1993, p.270.

not change the disastrous economic situation, at least it will improve the Albanians' political status. And, vice versa, the prospect of secession can only be removed by other, more tangible, options.

The Albanians in FYROM

FYROM is a distinctly different state. In some respects, it is unique, particularly when viewed from the perspective of European reality at the end of the twentieth century but, at the same time, it is facing some of the problems which characterize the other former republics of the former Yugoslav federation.

The difference lies in its artificial nature since the republic, like the Macedonian nation, was created for purely political reasons so that it could be used as an instrument within the framework of broader competition with the neighbouring countries, especially Bulgaria. Of course, most of the world's nations and states were originally artificial, but in the case of FYROM this is an important factor since it presupposes the aggressive nature of Macedonian nationalism, although this is an understandable phenomenon for a new nation that is still in the process of nation building.

Similarities with the other former Yugoslav republics, especially Serbia, include the ethnic diversity of the republic's population and the existence of a significant minority with a different religious creed, in both cases basically Muslim Albanians. The combination of uniqueness, i.e. the militancy of Macedonian nationalism, and the inherited ethnic composition may trigger a broader Balkan confrontation which makes the Albanian problem in Macedonia even more dangerous than it is in Kosovo.

There are several similarities with Kosovo. First, the Albanians comprise a significant part of the republic's population—20% to 45% according to different estimates.[92] As these people live in compact territories on the border with Kosovo and Albania, this would make secession easy in technical terms, similar to the Albanians in Kosovo but unlike the Serbian or Croatian enclaves in Bosnia which are isolated from their kin-states. In addition, the Albanian population's

---

[92]The 1991 census was boycotted by the Albanians. According to the official data, the Albanians numbered 429,562 or 21% of the population. See Macedonia: Basic Economic Data (Skopje: Statistical Office of Macedonia, 1992). The Albanian leaders claim that 40%-50% of the population are Albanian.

unemployment and birth rates are the highest in the republic. But what is probably most important is that this minority's trend towards isolationism is becoming more and more pronounced, with these people living to an increasing extent in closed communities and avoiding any contacts with the official authorities. The difference is that the Albanian-populated territories represent a less important element in Macedonian historical myths than Kosovo does for the Serbs.

The conflict here is also rooted in recent history. The borders of the Albanian state, which were created in 1912 and modified after the Balkan wars in 1913, reflected, as is usually the case in the Balkans, the geopolitical concerns of the great powers rather than ethnic distribution, leaving significant segments of the Albanian population outside Albania—in Serbia and Montenegro, following the newly created Kingdom of the Serbs, Croats, and Slovenes in 1918, and in Greece, thereby laying the foundations for the (natural) dream of unification. During World War II, the Albanian-populated parts of Yugoslavia were incorporated into an Italian-administered Greater Albania. After the war the borders were redrawn, again in favour of the new Yugoslav federation, a member of the winning coalition, thereby repeating the overall territorial solution of 1913.

Although the Albanian problem in Macedonia was not as exposed as in Kosovo during the 1970s and the 1980s, according to the common Balkan rule, the local Albanians were perceived as a potentially alien population who could claim autonomous status or even secede at any time. For that reason, the Albanian-populated regions were usually subsidized economically but the minority was politically deprived. In 1967 the communist regime in the Republic of Macedonia even established a Macedonian Autocephalous Orthodox Church, one of its main tasks being to combat Albanian nationalism and to oppose the revitalization of Islam in areas with mixed populations. But, as a rule, up to the end of the 1980s, the problem with the Macedonian Albanians was overshadowed by the Kosovo problem within the all-Yugoslav context and by the ongoing linguistic, historical, and ethnological, albeit political, conflicts with Bulgaria within the regional context.

The real problem with the Macedonian Albanians arose in 1991 when the republic declared its independence. Secessions by the former republics from the Yugoslav federation were setting precedents, borders were being redrawn, and it had become really difficult to define any persuasive criteria for establishing which national communities were entitled to secession and which were not. The Albanian minority also had its own national intellectual elite, who were educated at the Albanian university in Pristina and were naturally susceptible to radicalization. This elite served as the driving force for political movements which were to demand more rights for ethnic Albanians, equal status with the Macedonian majority (for example, to end discrimination in employment), and broader education in Albanian, with the explicit demand to accord Albanian the status of an official language. Other demands were for Albanian autonomy or even secession from the Macedonian state and unification of the Albanian-populated territories.[93]

Some of these demands were grounded. The Constitution of the Republic of Macedonia reserves the status of a constituent nation for Macedonians only. Although it provides equal rights for all citizens of the republic, the remainder are treated as nationalities, similar to the provisions of the constitution of the former Yugoslav federation.[94] This alone is a sufficient basis for assuming that the Albanian part of the population can be treated as a minority and not as a fully equal constituency.

Since 1991, the Albanian population's interests have been represented at the political level by four ethnically-based political parties, the largest of which are the Party for Democratic Prosperity (PDP) and the National Democratic Party (NDP). After the 1990 parliamentary elections, this two-party coalition won 23 out of the 120 seats in the National Assembly (22 for the PDP, and 1 for the NDP). The PDP, which also had ministers in all the governments after 1990, was moderate although it did not automatically support the regime—it endorsed abstention by the Albanians in the 1991 referendum on independence, PDP deputies did not vote on the constitution, and the

[93]Robert Austin, "Albanian-Macedonian Relations," RFE/RL Research Report, Vol.2, No.42, 22 October 1993, p.22.

[94]According to the preamble of the Constitution, "Macedonia is established as a nation-state of the Macedonian people, in which full equality as citizens and permanent coexistence with the Macedonian nation is provided for Albanians, Turks, Vlachs, Romas and other nationalities living in the Republic of Macedonia." Ustav na Republika Makedonija (Kopije: NIP Magazin 21, 1991), p.3.

party encouraged the Albanians to boycott the 1991 census.[95] However, there was a certain amount of suspicion that the PDP's incorporation into the executive, usually on insignificant nominations, did not represent a means of integrating the Albanian population as a constituency with equal rights, but was rather a formal declarative act, as was the case with former communist regimes in Eastern Europe which were also formally constitutional and even multi-party since it was obligatory for partner parties to participate in communist governments.

On 12 February 1994, the PDP split into two factions. The split was partly precipitated by the AAA Affairs—the uncovering by the government of an underground group called the All-Albanian Army.[96] But the real reason was probably the struggle between the moderate (or conformist) and more extreme trends in the party and attempts by the Macedonian government to manipulate the PDP and, hence, the Albanian minority. This was probably one of the reasons why the moderate members of the Albanian political elite performed so badly in the October 1994 parliamentary elections in which the PDP won only 11 seats; one of the groups which split in 1994 received four seats and control over the key constituency of Tetovo; Arben Xhaferi, the chief ideologue of the Albanian radicals in Macedonia, also won a seat; and the traditionally more radical NDP won four seats.[97]

No matter how advanced the power sharing between Macedonian and Albanian parties is, there are few incompatible demands. First, from the Macedonian point of view, recognition of the Albanians as a constitutive nation and of Albanian as an official language is out of the question. The same applies to the demands by the Albanian-populated territories for autonomous status and for broader access to education in Albanian at all (and not only primary)

---

[95]For more details, see Duncan M. Perry, "Politics in the Republic of Macedonia: Issues and Parties," RFE:RL Research Report, Vol.2, No.23, 4 June 1993.

[96]"According to government sources, the AAA had collected a small arms cache of thirty-five automatic rifles, assembled a list of 21,630 names of potential recruits, established a chain of command and developed a strategy for mobilization that involved subverting the military." See Duncan M. Perry, "Macedonia," RFE/RL Research Report, Vol.3, No.16, 22 April 1994.

[97]Branko Gerosi, "Macedonia: Post-Election Jockeying," War Report, No.30, December 1994/January 1995, p.11.

levels. The Macedonians view these demands as opening the way to secession and the territorial disintegration of this fragile republic.

Nevertheless, in January 1992, after having boycotted the referendum on Macedonian independence, the Albanians held their own referendum on autonomy, in which the majority of the population took part and supported the demand. This was probably one of the turning points in the Albanian-Macedonian conflict. In a shooting incident in November 1992, the police injured three Albanians and, according to some reports, one was shot dead. The incident concerned black marketeers but it was interpreted in ethnic terms as the **Macedonian** police against **Albanian** black marketeers, and contributed to society's polarization along ethnic lines.

Hence the clashes that took place in February and March 1995 and led to at least one victim are the logical result of the process of building a Macedonian nation and nation-state at the expense of other national and ethnic groups. In fact, there is evidence that the FYROM political elite continues to adopt the Serbian approach to the ethnic problem and is generating a second edition of the Kosovo problem, the Tetovo case. The fact that one of the Albanians' basic demands in FYROM is the establishment of an Albanian university in Tetovo, like the demands for an Albanian university in Pristina, is just one additional detail of the common picture. The difference is that FYROM, unlike Serbia, has neither the economic nor the military resources to handle its own Kosovo, and the situation in this republic might trigger a dangerous Balkan conflict.

The Bosnian Muslims

This is probably the second unsolvable issue in the Balkans, but unlike the Albanian case in Kosovo and FYROM it has already erupted into war. As with the Albanian and Turkish minorities, the problems are aggravated by the possible interpretation of the conflict along religious cleavage lines, as a civilizational and religious clash between Christianity and Islam. The common Slav roots of the sides involved in the Bosnian conflict did not prevent war and this would seem to point towards the more general conclusion that religious affiliation is of greater importance in the Balkans than ethno-national affiliation.[98]

The Bosnian Muslims' national identity is one of the most contradictory and speculative identity problems. For centuries, it has been an established fact that they are a separate community, usually referred to as Bosniaks, and even under the Habsburg Empire they were treated as a separate entity and not as a national minority. The name Bosniaks had regional rather than ethno-national connotations, referring mainly to the population which inhabited Bosnia (similar to the Macedonian case), but the Empire was a multinational entity and the recognition of distinct minority groups was not in jeopardy. It only became so when the new nation-states were created after World War I. That is why nobody mentioned either the Bosnians or the Macedonians as separate peoples when the Kingdom of Serbs, Croats, and Slovenes was established in 1918. The same was true in 1929 when the kingdom was renamed Yugoslavia and the first serious attempts were made to create a homogeneous Yugoslav identity. The Bosnian Muslims were treated as Serbs by the Serbs and as Croats by the Croats.[99]

The basis of the Bosniaks' separate identity is the Muslim affiliation of the population of Bosnia. The first conversions to Islam took place in the sixteenth century, but unlike other regions in the Balkans the process here was gradual and conversion tended to be voluntary. One of the reasons was that a significant segment of the Bosnian population consisted of heretics, the followers of the Bogumil heresy which was a version of Manicheanism and persecuted by both the official Orthodox and Catholic churches.[100] Conversion to Islam offered the possibility of avoiding religious persecution and other forms of violence: "The disturbances and anarchy that had occurred during the pre-Ottoman period contributed first to the success of the conquest

---

[98]One of the advocates of this idea is Hugh Poulton. See Hugh Poulton, The Balkans. Minorities and States in Conflict (London: Minority Rights Publications, 1991), p.91.

[99]Vladko Macek, a leader of the Croatian Peasant Party, declared in 1936 that "The Croatian Peasant Party, as the political organization of the entire Croatian nation, considers the Bosnian Muslims the purest part of the Croatian nation, by origin, by history and by dialect." Ramet, Nationalism, p.8.

[100]It was called after its founder, Father Bogumil, who was born in Bulgaria. After the collapse of the Second Bulgarian Empire the heresy spread to today's Bosnia.

and later to the Islamization of the Bosnian peasants. The Catholic Church allowed the selling of heretics into slavery...The Bosnian peasants were given no protection whatsoever and had nothing to lose. They opened the way for the Ottomans and their religious ideology."[101]

Islamic affiliation was a significant enough element to modify the Bosnian Muslim community members' traditions and cultural identity but their ethnic affiliation remained Slav (both Serbian and Croatian) and the language they spoke was Serbo-Croat—or at least it was until former Yugoslavia fell apart and Serb and Croat became two separate languages. Until the end of the 1960s, the Bosnian Muslims did not have a separate and distinct ethno-national identity in the sense described in Chapter 2. This separation was a secondary result of the post-World War II territorial issue and, in this respect, Bosnia-Herzegovina is the second case of this kind after the Vardar Macedonia issue.

The problem to be solved was the status of what was then the historical and geographical area of Bosnia-Herzegovina. It could not be included in Croatia since it would have corresponded to the former Ustashi state and turned the republic into an overwhelmingly powerful economic unit. Nor could it be annexed by Serbia since this would have been seen by the other republics as Serbianization and obvious Serbian dominance. Finally, the area could not be partitioned between Croatia and Serbia, not because of the Bosniaks' separate identity but because this solution would have revived the 1939 precedent—probably the only case of unanimous Serbo-Croatian action in the mid-war period.[102] Under these circumstances, the status of Bosnia-Herzegovina was raised from a geographic and historical region to a federal republic.

---

[101]Antonina Zheliazkova, "The Penetration and Adaptation of Islam in Bosnia from the Fifteenth to the Nineteenth Century," Journal of Islamic Studies, Vol.5, No.2, 1994, p.191.

[102]"In 1939, a similar agreement on the carve-up of Bosnia had been reached between the then Yugoslav president Dragisa Cvetkovic and the Croat national leader Vlatko Macek with the blessings of the regent Pavlc of the Kingdom of Yugoslavia. The only determinant of the division was to be the relative majority of Serbs or Croats in a given area, with no consideration given to the existence of the Muslims. When questioned about the apparent oversight, the response of Cvetkovic and Macek was starkly simple: 'Let's pretend they do not exist.'" Rabia Ali and Lawrence Lifschultz, "Why Bosnia?" Third World Quarterly, Vol.15, No.3, September 1994, p.378.

It was precisely at this point that the problem arose of the identity of the republic's citizens. Initially, there were two competing theories, with the Croats insisting that the Muslims were descendants of ethnic Croats who first adopted the Bogomil theory and were later converted to Islam, and the Serbs insisting on the Serbian origin of both the Muslims and the Croats living in Bosnia-Herzegovina. At the beginning of the 1960s, a third theory was developed claiming that the contested population was of Turkish origin and that their roots were in Anatolia. In 1967, the first claim for a separate national Muslim status was raised.[103] A fierce discussion arose with appeals to national feelings, equality of nations, and the freedom of individual affiliation, but the problem was heavily politicized and manipulated. On the one hand, the discussion took place within the context of the first stage of the Croatian crisis of 1967-1972 when the federation was shifting rapidly towards the liberalization of interrepublican relations, and, on the other, by 1968 the Kosovo problem had already exploded with all its ethnic and religious connotations.

The instrumental approach to the issue of ethnicities was reflected in the post-war Yugoslav censuses. Probably the most reasonable approach was adopted in the 1948 census when a clear distinction between ethnic and religious affiliation was made. People of Muslim affiliation could choose between Serb-Muslim, Croat-Muslim, and ethnically undeclared Muslim.[104] The 1953 census forms did not provide a Muslim option as a subgroup of the two basic national groups and the ethnic and religious neutral Yugoslav option was only offered as an alternative to the Serbian and Croatian groups, which was chosen by 891,800 people (31.3% of the republic's population). In 1961, a census form containing an ethnic option, Muslim in an ethnic sense, in addition to the national options, Serb, Croat, and Yugoslav, was introduced and chosen by 842,247 people (25.7% of the republic's population). In the 1971 census forms, the Muslims were finally recognized as a nationality and 1,482,430 people (39.6% of the population) chose this option for national affiliation. By 1991, thanks

---

[103]For more details, see R.V. Burks, The National Problem and the Future of Yugoslavia (Santa Monica: Rand Corporation, 1971), p.26.

[104]The census registered 71,991 Serb-Muslims out of 1,136,116 Serbs (2.8% of the republic's population); 25,295 Croat-Muslims out of 614,123 Croats (1% of the population); and 788,403 ethnically undeclared Muslims (30.7% of the population).

to their higher birthrate, the number of Bosnian Muslims had grown to 1,905,829 (43.7% of the population).

However, the problem was not one of recognizing the cultural and religious distinction of those Muslims in Bosnia who did not feel that they were of either Serbian or Croatian nationality. The fact that, in 1948, 788,403 people, i.e 30.7% of the republic's population, chose to be ethnically undeclared Muslims meant that a significant part of the population felt that they belonged to a separate cultural community. The real problem was that the elevation of religion to a main ethnonational indicator led to a process of the community's confessional fragmentation. The fact that the Croat Muslims and the Serb Muslims, irrespective of their percentages, were deprived of the possibility of keeping both their national and religious affiliation forced people to take sides.

This became clear immediately after the 1971 census when the Muslim problem triggered a serious interrepublican crisis. Once again, however, for purely political purposes, the problem was interpreted within the broader framework of Serbo-Croatian rivalry. Each of the disputants advocated its own approach and addressed its particular interests. Ironically, from today's perspective, the Serbian party bought off the support of the Bosnia-Kosovo coalition in the struggle against the Croat liberals, fostering the idea that religious and cultural heritage provided a sufficient basis for the separation of national identity. This in fact was the basis for further self-determination demands based on Islamic affiliation.[106] It was thought—in general, quite reasonably but with serious doubts in this particular case—that the appropriate answer to the new challenges lay in the extension of the rights which had already been granted. The creation of a distinct Muslim nation was laid

---

[106]"Having emerged victorious... Muslim nationalists gained confidence and began to agitate for redesignating Bosnia as 'Muslim Republic' in the same way that Serbia is 'Republic of the Serbs' and Macedonia the 'Republic of Macedonians'... certain Bosnian linguists started toying with the idea that Bosanski, the language of the Muslims, should be recognized as a distinct language... The Muslim clergy, the ulema, had become increasingly active spokesmen for Muslim ethnic interests... in the late 1970s... a new generation, educated to think of Bosnian Muslims as a national group and encouraged by contacts with a renascent Middle East, began to look to Islam as a basis for political mobilization... the Muslims revived the dormant concept of Muslims as the 'only real Bosnians' and demanded the formation of separate Muslim national institutions in which the Muslim intelligentsia would gather and oppose the activity of Croatian and Serbian institutions." Ramet, Nationalism, p.153.

down in the new federal constitution of 1974.

The separation of the Muslim Slavs in Bosnia as a distinct national identity had both internal and external prerequisites: "Among the Bosnian Muslims themselves, as well as among the Serbs and the Croats, there are those who would argue that all Bosnian Muslims are simply Croats or Serbs who converted to Islam. This is the basis of the position that Bosnian Muslims are an artificial nation, which Tito created perhaps to contain Serb-Croat conflict in Bosnia and Herzegovina and certainly to serve the cause of Yugoslav non-alignment in the Middle East."[106]

From the constitutional point of view, the recognition of the new national identity was in line with the dominant concept of national relations based on a three-tier hierarchy. The top tier was the nation—a group with a national home in one of the six republics. The next two tiers were nationalities and other nationalities and ethnic groups. These were the groups with their national homes outside the federation. Affiliation to the second and the third tier was based on quantitive criteria but referred to recognized linguistic and cultural rights.

The status of nationality was granted to the Albanians, the Bulgarians, the Gipsies, the Czechs, the Hungarians, the Italians, the Romanians, the Ruthenians, the Slovaks, and the Turks. They had a variety of rights, including the right to autonomy (the Albanians in Kosovo and the Hungarians in Vojovodina, although these two examples are not symmetrical—traditionally the Serbs were a majority in Vojovodina, but not in Kosovo). In this respect, for years Bosnia-Herzegovina was somebody's national home and it was only after 1971 that that somebody was finally identified. It did, however, create a future problem, that that somebody was only a relative majority but a minority in absolute terms. Although they represented the biggest segment of the republic's population, the Bosnian Muslims as a nationality still constituted a minority and represented 39.6% of the population in 1971, 39.5% in 1981, and 43.7% in 1991.

Although the Bosnian Muslims' distinct ethnic and cultural affiliation prior to 1971 is obvious from the census data, the existence of a separate national consciousness is highly debatable. The process of national emancipation speeded up in the 1980s along with the decay

---

[106]Robin Alison Remington, "Bosnia: The Tangled Web," Current History, Vol.92, No.577, November 1993, p.366.

of centralistic ties and reached its peak after 1989. Moreover, we can only seriously speak of a separate Bosnian Muslim national identity after the war broke out in Bosnia in 1992. In this respect, the war played the role of a basic nation-building factor elevating the existing separate **ethno-national** identity to a distinct **national** one, according to the framework described in Chapter 2. It indicated clearly the opposing sides and provided the necessary aliens: for the Bosnian Muslims it was the Serb and later the Croat dream of Greater Serbia and Greater Croatia, and for the Serbs and the Croats it was Islamic fundamentalism. And current politics always provided sufficient evidence for the existing "ghosts."[107]

From this point of view the violence in Bosnia-Herzegovina is not something completely alien to the former Yugoslavia solution. The whole system was based on the assumption that differences between separate groups were more important than similarities, and the system's institutional leverages fostered and utilized these differences. In itself it was a potentially destructive element. However, this was inevitable since the whole federation was based on the concept of **de jure** autonomous and equal elements whereas **de facto** it was dominated by Serbia.[108]

Therefore, it may be assumed that the Muslim population of Bosnia-Herzegovina was in many respects **pushed** towards a separate national identity, with the external elements of the process of national emancipation (and even nation building) prevailing over the internal

---

[107]For example, the Bosnian president Alija Izetbegovic "was sent to prison for six years by the communists in 1946 for Islamic fundamentalism and reimprisoned in 1983 for having written and distributed an 'Islamic Declaration,' calling for the creation of a confessionally pure theocracy in Bosnia." Sabrina P. Ramet, "The Breakup of Yugoslavia," Global Affairs, Vol.6, No.2, Spring 1991, p.102.

[108]"During the war Tito's support was weakest in Serbia... Serbians... saw no advantage in Tito's revolutionary federalism... the unwritten agreement between Tito and Serbia, which permitted regime legitimacy in this key region, implied a backsliding from the denunciations of Serbian-dominated Yugoslavia that typified Tito's militant wartime position. Tito's part of the bargain was to dull the campaign against Serbian predominance through the espousal of centralism and Yugoslav unitarism—the ruling political and ideological antecedents that permitted the revival of Serbian influence. The bargain held until the early 1960s." Banac, "The Fearful," p.145. From the middle of the 1960s, when Tito's position had to evolve towards decentralization, Serbia's centralist orientation became more and more obvious and turned into one of the constant points of conflict in the federation.

quest for separation. Even when the collapse of the former federation
had become inevitable, Bosnia-Herzegovina was the last republic to
declare independence, not only because of the Serbian threat after the
Serbo-Croatian war of 1991 but also because of the obvious unviability
of a republic separated from a broader territorial, economic, and political
entity.[109]

The Croats and the Serbs in Bosnia-Herzegovina

At first glance, it would seem illogical to analyse these two
distinct, and often opposing, groups together. However, the reason for
this combination is pragmatic as the similarities in their situation in
Bosnia-Herzegovina are of greater importance than the differences.

As representatives of the two basic nationalities in former
Yugoslavia, the Croats and the Serbs have always tried to excercise a
constant and active influence in the region. Both groups claimed the
Bosnian Muslims as their ethnic kin and both perceived their own
national minorities outside the national homes and especially in Bosnia-
Herzegovina as important elements in their decade-long mutual rivalry.
For objective reasons—the nature of permitted conflicts in communist
societies—the discussions mainly focused on the economic sphere, with
the Croats taking the liberal, decentralistic approach and the Serbs the
traditionalist, centralistic one.

In 1981 the Croats in Bosnia-Herzegovina numbered 758,136
or 18.4% of the republic's population and the Serbs numbered
1,320,644 or 32%. In 1991, the figures were 755,892 (17.3%) and
1,269,258 (31.4%) respectively. Both Serbs and Croats are Christians
but of different denominations. The Croats are mainly Catholic and in
this respect they resemble the Poles—Croats also agree that "Good
Croat is Catholic." On that basis, the Croats, like the Poles, definitely
identify themselves with the Western cultural heritage, which is direct
evidence of their common Latin cultural roots. Also the Catholic Church
has played a significant role for both nations as an alternative basis for
collective identification, as opposed to the official one. The Serbs, who
are Orthodox, tend to identify themselves, on the grounds of historical
analogies, as the last Christian outpost against Islam.

---

[109]On the survivability of the post-secessionist entities, see Gertrude E. Schroeder, "On
the Economic Viability of New Nation-States," Journal of International Affairs, Vol.45,
No.2, Winter 1992, pp.549-574.

As already mentioned, their relations with the Muslim part of the population were rather pragmatic and for decades were based on the assumption that the Bosnian Muslims were in fact ethnic Croats or Serbs who had been converted to Islam. This developed into open hostility after the republic's secession from the Yugoslav federation and was a predictable result of the dispersion of Bosnia-Herzegovina's population, which in turn was a consequence of the population's migration within the framework of the Ottoman and Habsburg multinational empires as well as of the hardly distinguishable differences between the various ethnicities, or at least of the perception of these differences as insignificant until the middle of the twentieth century.

When the former republics of the Yugoslav federation began their gradual drift towards independence in 1990, the Croats and Serbs established their own ethnically-based political representations. The Croat Democratic Union of Bosnia-Herzegovina (HDZ-BH) is a local section of the HDZ in Croatia, while the Serbian Democratic Party of Bosnia-Herzegovina (SDS-BH) is an offshoot of a similar organization in Croatia, not in Serbia. The SDS also exists in Serbia proper but it is not the dominating one there and the leading political force is still the Socialist, ex-communist party. All this did not alter the fact that both parties closely coordinated their policies with the capitals of their home nations, Zagreb and Belgrade.

Both these Bosnia Herzegovina-based parties (HDZ-BH and SDS-BH) became the main rallying forces for their national groups' interests. Together with the Muslim Party of Democratic Action, it allowed them to mobilize the electorate along ethnic lines in the December 1990 parliamentary elections in Bosnia-Herzegovina. These elections provided an obvious example of ethnic identity which determined political behaviour and affiliation. As a result, the distribution of seats in the National Assembly between the three major political parties reflected the republic's ethnic composition: the Bosnian Muslims won 86 seats (36%) in the 240-seat Assembly, the Bosnian Serbs won 72 (30%), and the Bosnian Croats won 44 (18%). It in fact turned the elections into a census which had little to do with democratic free political choice, answering ethnological, cultural or historical questions, e.g. different groups' ethnic affiliation, rather than political ones such as the delegation of rights to a competent political elite.

The democratic nature of this proportional representation was highly dubious since it was used later as the basis for a majoritarian dictatorship at a time when there was a need for consocietal strategies.[110] Why such strategies did not achieve broader public appeal is still an open question but it was certainly not due to the lack of an alternative option to the ethnically based political representations since there was at least one supra-national party. The Alliance of Reform Forces of Ante Markovic was quite strong in the ethnically-mixed regions and in Sarajevo but by the beginning of the 1990s most of the Yugoslav nations no longer seemed to be interested in maintaining the federation's unity.

Croat and Serb minorities are both mainly concentrated near the borders with their home nations with the exception of the Serb enclaves in northern and central Bosnia, the biggest of which is Krajna on the border with Croatia or rather with the disputed territory of Kninska Krajna, regarded by the Croats as Croatian and by the Serbs as Serbian. In September 1991, the Serbian enclaves grouped themselves into four Serbian autonomous regions within the framework of Yugoslavia, based on the model of Kosovo and Vojovodina. The regions are: Bosnian Krajina, Romanija, Herzegovina, and Semberia. On 24 October 1991, the Serbian deputies in the Bosnian Parliament formed the Assembly of the Serbian People in Bosnia, and on 8 January 1992 Bihac was also declared an autonomous region.

On 9 January 1992, the Assembly proclaimed the association of the Serbian Autonomous regions, which came within the framework of what the Serbs saw as the still existing Yugoslavia and which had initially been called the Serbian Krajina republic in Bosnia-Herzegovina. After the recognition of Bosnia-Herzegovina as an independent state by the USA and the EC on 7 April 1992, the Assembly proclaimed the independence of the Serbian Republic of Bosnia-Herzegovina. On 24 September, the republic's leadership signed a cooperation protocol with the Republic of Serbian Krajina in Croatia and further unification of these units is probable.

Similarly, though on a smaller scale, on 3 July 1992 the Croat leaders in Bosnia declared the formation of the Croatian community in Bosnia-Herzegovina which included the territories under the military

---

[110]For more details on the consocietal approach, see Arend Lijphart, Democracy in Plural Societies. A Comparative Exploration (New Haven: Yale University Press, 1977).

control of the local Croatian armed forces.[111] In fact, the creation of two quasi state entities on the territory of Bosnia-Herzegovina implies either the republic's cantonization or the first step towards its partition between its two competing neighbours.

When the conflict deepened, both minorities organized their own more or less regular military troops. The most important Croat group was the Croatian Defence Council, HVO, which gradually incorporated the forces of the ultra-right Croatian Defence Union, HOS, of the Croatian Party of Rights, HSP. The HVO has about 40,000 soldiers, 40-60 tanks, about 500 artillery pieces, and about 150 portable air-defence weapon systems. The HVO operates in south-eastern and north-western Herzegovina and in central Bosnia. The Serbian forces are the successors to the former Yugoslav National Army (JNA) which split in May 1992 into the Army of the Serbian Republic (VRS) and the newly declared Yugoslavian Army (YA). The VRS is around 60,000-strong and has been reinforced by troops from Serbia (an estimated 20,000 men). It also inherited considerable quantities of armaments from the former Yugoslav National Army (over 300 tanks, 200-300 armoured cars, 500-600 pieces of artillery, and 35 aircraft, including 21 helicopters).[112]

The HVO is nominally allied with the Army of Bosnia-Herzegovina but, as already mentioned, relations between the two armies should be analysed within the triangle of interests between the Serbs, the Croats, and the Bosnian Muslims. In a few cases, the HVO has abandoned its nominal allies, as was the case with the Bosnanski Brod offensive, and has even practised ethnic cleansing, although to a far lesser extent than the Serbs (Croat actions in Prozor and Gorni Vakuf). In April 1993, open clashes, and atrocities, occurred between the HVO and the Bosnian Army in central Bosnia. Severe fighting also took place in Eastern Mostar which was shelled by the Croats at the beginning of 1994. The conflicting sides' attitudes changed radically after the signing of the Washington agreements in 1994 when the Bosnian-Croat confederation was created. However, it is still not clear whether, and how long, it will survive.

---

[111]For more details, see Bogdan Szajkowski (ed.), Encyclopedia of Conflicts, Disputes and Flashpoints in Eastern Europe, Russia and the Successor States (London: Longman Group, 1993), pp.138 and 376.

[112]Ibid, pp.18 and 90.

For the time being, it seems that the Serbo-Bosnian and Serbo-Croat contradictions are even more serious than the Bosnian Muslim and the Croat ones. This makes the Serbian armed forces' activities more clear-cut and since the Serbo-Croatian war of 1991 they have mainly been fighting against the Muslim forces, though occasional clashes also occur with the Croat military groups. Both sides also use the support of the various para-military groups from radical political, nationalist-flavoured organizations.

Although they are traditional rivals, the Croats and the Serbs have quite similar interests in Bosnia-Herzegovina: preserving their control over the inhabited and, in the Serbian case, occupied territories. However, since the Croats and the Bosnian Muslims fought against the Serbs for a certain period, the Croats have a different approach to the means of achieving this aim. That is why reports of ethnic cleansing and human rights' violations by Croats are rare. As a rule, there have always been two options for the Croats—a tactical and a strategic one.

The first option is taking sides with the Serbs and carving up Bosnia-Herzegovina, the precedent for which dates back to 1939, and the second option is joining the Bosnian Muslims against the Serbs. It seems that the main criterion for the current choice is the possibility of obtaining territorial gains.   Today the Croats still follow the second option mainly because their participation in the Bosnian-Croat confederation gives them important territorial gains and a positive international image.

However, this does not make them the Bosnian-Muslims' unconditional allies—the Croats and the Muslims have fought against each other as well as together against the Serbs. This triangle of interests will remain a constant possible source of tension and of loose, non-durable alliances until the territory of the Bosnian state is partitioned between the three conflicting factions in proportions which reflect the military and economic reality rather than moralistic wishful thinking. This is in both the Serbs' and the Croats' common general interest.

The Serbs in Croatia

The Serbs in Croatia, who can be divided into urban and rural populations, constitute the second largest segment of the population

(579,500 or 12.2% in 1991).[113] This urban/rural cleavage corresponds exactly to two distinct types of political behaviour. In general, the urban Serbs, representing approximately half the total Serb minority in Croatia, up to 100,000 of whom live in Zagreb, are integrated into Croatia's political life, have their own political representations, and endeavour to defend their rights within the framework of independent Croatia's political institutions. In contrast, the rural Serbs do not recognize Croatia's independence and have constituted themselves into a separate political, quasi state entity which is not recognized by any country, not even Serbia.

The rural Serbs number 140,000 to 160,000 people who mainly inhabit the regions of the so-called Kninska Krajina—the territories around Benkovac and Knin—where they constitute the majority of the populations. These regions are often treated in publications on the Yugoslav crisis as part of the so-called military frontier between the Austro-Hungarian and Ottoman empires (see Chapter 1). Although this is correct in respect of the northern parts of today's Kninska Krajina, the military frontier argument and the fact that Serbs have lived in these lands for centuries are used to motivate the claim that the territories belong to the Serbs. The fact is that the population around the Knin area became predominantly Serbian between the two World Wars and after World War II as part of the attempt to Serbianize Yugoslavia.

After the break-up of the Yugoslav federation and the first steps by the former republics towards independence, in 1990 the Serbian Democratic Party (SDS), and its later offshots in Bosnia-Herzegovina, was founded in Knin. After the 1990 elections had been won by the HDZ (the strongest Croatian party) following a strongly nationalistic campaign, Croatia's constitution was amended in May 1990 and Serbian citizens were granted the status of a national minority.[114] Although civil rights were guaranteed to all Croatian citizens, the change was a radical one for the Serbs who, under the old constitution,

---

[113]This number is far from accurate bearing in mind the impact of the Serbo-Croatian war in 1991 and the flow of refugees out of Bosnia-Herzegovina.

[114]Mark Thompson, A Paper House (New York: Pantheon Books, 1992), pp.279-280.

represented one of the constitutive nations.[115] The prospect of becoming a second-class stratum in the new nation-state further radicalized the Serbian population which had enjoyed the status of a nation in Yugoslavia and had been guaranteed special autonomous status even under the Habsburgs between 1578 and 1881.[116] After the HDZ victory, a strong process of Croatization was launched. Serbian domination in the police and the administration was sharply reduced,[117] and this was understandably perceived by the Serbs as jeopardizing the privileged status they had been granted by Tito as a reward for their support of his partisan guerilla (the Serbs in Krajina were among the most privileged and hence the most affected by Croatization).

However, there were also symbolic aspects to this change. An amnesty was granted by the Croatian authorities to certain figures and events in Yugoslav history which further deepened latent Serbian suspicions. The new Croatian flag with the old Shachovnca appeared, new uniforms were like the old ones from World War II, and a new (old) currency, the Kuna, was issued. All this resembled too closely the Ustashi period.[118] The ultranationalistic wave was in addition

---

[115]The change was significant: being a constitutive nation, the Serbs "had a say in any political changes made to the structure of the Yugoslav state. With their new legal position, the Serbs are regarded by Zagreb as having no right to contest Croatia's independence or its territorial integrity." Stan Markotich, "Ethnic Serbs in Tudjman's Croatia," RFE/RL Research Report, Vol.2, No.38, 24 September 1993, p.28.

[116]Here an analogy with Serbo-Croat relations in the early 1920s is inevitable (see Chapter 3).

[117]According to some estimates, "immediately prior to the elections in April 1990, Serbs made up 40% of the Croatian Communist Party, eight out of 12 senior editors in Radio Zagreb and 60% of the police." Poulton, Balkans, p.24.

[118]The question concerns the Croatian puppet-state, created in 1941 by Hitler after his occupation of Yugoslavia. He cleverly used the Serbo-Croatian animosities and in fact most of the atrocities to Serbs during World War II were committed by Croats, members of Ustashi groups. The Ustashis also ran the death camp in Jasenovac, where some 60,000-80,000 people were killed, most of them Serbs. But throughout the whole postwar period the Jasenovac syndrome was effectively used by the Serbian political authorities as a check against possible Croatian nationalism. Naturally, the number of victims was exaggerated in Serbian publications—as many as 700,000 Serbs murdered in Jasenovac. For more details, see Ljubo Boban, "Jasenovac and the Manipulation of

combined with the removal of Cyrillic signs from Croatia where the Latin alphabet is in use, driving many moderate-minded Serbs to extremist attitudes which made interethnic dialogue and cooperation increasingly improbable. Hence, it is hard to deny that "the Croatian government failed to show even a modicum of understanding for the growing anxiety of the Serbs in Croatia, regardless of the real motive behind their fear and whether this fear was founded or not. On the contrary, the Croatian government, from the top to the bottom of the pyramid, has been feeding this anxiety with its every move."[119]

In late July 1990, the unofficial parliament of the Serbs in Croatia—the Serbian National Council—declared autonomy for the local Serbs. A referendum on this issue was held in Krajina between 19 August and 2 September in which 567,127 people were reported to have voted for and 144 against "Serbian autonomy on the ethnic and historic territories populated by the Serbian people within the existing borders of the Republic of Croatia, as a federal unit of SFRJ."[120] As a result, the Serbian Autonomous Region of Krajina's autonomy was legitimized on the basis of the right to self-determination and by popular vote although it was not recognized by either Croatia or any other state. In June 1991, the Serb-populated territories in eastern Slavonia constituted themselves into the Serbian Autonomous Region of Slavonia, Baranja, and Western Srem (until the recognition of Croatia's independence, they were autonomous regions within the framework of the Yugoslav federation). On 26 February 1992, the two regions united

---

History," East European Politics and Societies, Vol.4, No.3, 1990, pp.580-592. On the radicalization of the moderate Serbs, see also Misha Glenny, The Fall of Yugoslavia: The Third Balkan War (London: Penguin, 1992), pp.92-93. One of the reasons for the different figures is the confusion about the victims in Jasenovac and the total number of Serbs murdered in Croatia. "Between May and October 1941 it is estimated that the Ustashi killed between 300,000 and 340,000 Serbs." In response, "when the Croatian army finally surrendered in May 1945... Serbs marched several 'death columns' across the country on foot, denying their prisoners either food or water... The exact number of Croats who died is uncertain, but it is estimated at about 100,000." Andrew Bell-Fialkoff, "A Brief History of Ethnic Cleansing," Foreign Affairs, Vol.72, No.3, Summer 1993, p.117.

[119]Davor Glovas, "The Roots of Croatian Extremism," Mediterranean Quarterly, Vol.5, No.2, Spring 1994, p.45.

[120]Poulton, Balkans, p.26.

into the so-called Republic of Serbian Krajina. However, since they are separated from each other by Croat- and Muslim-populated territories, unification is virtually impossible without actually dismantling Bosnia-Herzegovina and Croatia.

It is almost impossible to determine which side was the first to break the rules of ethnic tolerance. Furthermore, each party to the conflict has its own rationale. The Croatization campaign, which was condemned by the Serbs, was a logical reaction to years of Serbianization of the Yugoslav federation. An important instrument of Serbian dominance in the republic was the Serbianization of the state administration, and its Croatization was an inevitable step along the road to independence. On the other hand, the memory of the Ustashi period was still vivid among the Serbs and action on the part of many Croats provided grounds for concern.

The threshold was crossed, however, when the Serbo-Croatian war broke out after Croatia's declaration of independence on 25 June 1991.[121] What is extremely important to note here is the new role of the Yugoslav National Army (JNA) whose officer corps was dominated by the Serbs. As the federation started to fall apart, the JNA became more and more of an independent political actor in the deepening conflict and was obviously taking the Serbian side. The remains of Serbo-Croatian confidence were broken after the war in 1991, destroying the fragile and limited possibilities which existed for multinational cooperation so that any guarantees of national interests had to be sought within the framework of the nation-states. Bearing in mind the incompatibility between the Croat officials' and the Serbs' approaches to the issue of the status of Krajina, a prolongation of hostilities in terms of a mini-cold war is probable. A feasible solution to the problem lies in the possible trading of issues within the Croatia-Bosnia-Serbia triangle.

The Macedonians in Bulgaria

The Macedonian issue is the oldest and the most obvious example of the instrumental treatment of national problems. Everything connected with the question of Macedonia and the Macedonians is

---

[121]For more details on the war, see Norman Cigar, "The Serbo-Croatian War, 1991: Political and Military Dimensions," The Journal of Strategic Studies, Vol.16, No.3, September 1993, pp.298-317.

strongly politicized and any debate on the subject, be it historical, geographical or linguistic, is in fact a camouflaged political debate.

As a geographical area, in ancient times Macedonia was inhabited by different ethnicities. The first recorded and longest civilizational presence was that of the ancient Greeks who hellenized the region. The rise of the Roman Empire and the subsequent Slav invasion after A.D. 600 marked the end of the ancient Greek period in Macedonia's history. Later the region was an object of rivalry between Byzantium, Bulgaria, and Serbia which all occupied the territory at different periods (see Chapter 1).

Following the Ottoman conquest of the Balkans, the next largest ethnicity, the Turks, began to settle in Macedonia. But, until the end of the eighteenth century, it is highly speculative to speak of the existence of nations as such in the Balkans because nations in this region were a product of the nineteenth century (see Chapter 2). The term Macedonians, which was then in use, had purely geographic connotations and referred to the inhabitants of the region of Macedonia who belonged to different ethnic or ethno-national groups. The majority of the inhabitants were Slavs who, especially after the re-establishment of the Bulgarian Exarchate, identified themselves as Bulgarians[122]—they spoke Bulgarian and shared common historical myths. Other significant groups were the Greeks, the Turks, the Albanians, the Serbs, and the Jews.[123]

At the beginning of the twentieth century the struggle for the liberation of Macedonia from Ottoman rule developed within the framework of the existing European balance-of-power system, organized by the Bulgaria-based Internal Macedonian Revolutionary

---

[122]"Gradually, the emergence of the 'Macedonian Question' as a problem of European concern drew the attention of diplomats and journalists to the plight of Macedonians, the name by which foreigners came increasingly to identify native-born Bulgarians of Macedonia in order to distinguish them from Bulgarians of the Bulgarian state. Such identification became particularly necessary when Bulgarian Macedonian revolutionaries...proceeded to develop their own political program for an autonomous Macedonian state." Evangelos Kofos, National Heritage and National Identity in Nineteenth- and Twentieth-Century Macedonia (Athens: Hellenic Foundation for Defence and Foreign Policy, 1991), p.12.

[123]For more details of the ethnic composition of Macedonia, see Stefan Karastoyanov, "Macedonia (An Ethno-Geographical Profile)," Bulgarian Military Review, Vol.2, No.2, 1994, pp.55-84.

Organization (IMRO). Some of the leaders of the IMRO clearly understood that Macedonia's unification with Bulgaria would be strongly opposed by the Balkan countries as well as by the Great Powers and they therefore opted for liberation through independence. Other IMRO leaders opted for the direct annexation of Macedonia to Bulgaria. As a result a split occured in the IMRO at the beginning of the twentieth century and two trends emerged within the organization. Nevertheless, liberation from the Ottomans was perceived as a priority and the liberation movement continued. In 1902 the Gorna Djumaya uprising broke out, followed by the Ilinden uprising in 1903. Both were unsuccessful and the region was not liberated from the Ottomans until the end of the two Balkan wars which represented a kind of threshold for the Macedonist movements.

During the Balkan wars of 1912-1913 and World War I, the Bulgarian Macedonian revolutionaries "put aside their autonomist slogans and actively joined the ranks of the Bulgarian army to fight for the liberation of Macedonia from Ottoman rule and its unification with the Bulgarian fatherland."[124] Nevertheless, Bulgaria was the definite loser in the war and the disputed territory was partitioned between Bulgaria (approximately 10%), Serbia (approximately 41%), and Greece (approximately 49%). Until 1913 nobody questioned the Macedonian-Slav population's Bulgarian affiliation and although many distinguished representatives of this population identified themselves as Macedonians, in most cases this did not imply affiliation to a distinct Macedonian nationality.[125]

The real (contemporary) Macedonian question did not arise until after the two Balkan wars when the satisfied group of states had to integrate the newly gained territories into their state entities. In fact, the Macedonian question is a territorial one and can be formulated in

---

[124]Kofos, National, p.12.

[125]"The men of the IMRO certainly considered themselves Macedonians, not by nationality, but as part of a larger multinational region... As for the nationality of the Macedonian Slavs, they did not question its Bulgar character." Ivo Banac, The National Question in Yugoslavia: Origins, History, Politics (Ithaca: Cornell University Press, 1984), p.326. It is probably not by accident that the first compilation of regional folk songs, published by a Serbian Croat, Stefan Verkovic, in 1864, was entitled "The Folk Songs of the Macedonian Bulgars." The collection of regional poems published by Dimiter Miladinov was entitled "Bulgarian Folk Poems." In the editions published in Skopje after World War II they were entitled "Macedonian Folk Poems."

the following way: who is entitled to the territory of Macedonia? Since the answers to this question were based on the principle of peoples' right to self-determination, the question was reworded to read, what nationality inhabits the region? Bearing in mind that the national affiliations of the Greek, Turkish, and Albanian segments of the population were clearly defined by linguistic and religious criteria, the final formulation of the question was, what is the ethno-national affiliation of the Slav population of Macedonia? Is it Bulgarian, Serbian or is it a distinct Macedonian nationality?[126]

The answers vary according to the analysts' political and national attitudes. With four different, interested sides we have four different approaches to the problem—a Bulgarian, a Greek, a Serbian, and a Skopje approach. The Greek approach has always denied the existence of Macedonian nationality. The Serbian and Bulgarian approach treated the issue in an instrumental way, sometimes recognizing a distinct Macedonian nationality and at other times denying it, depending on the demands of the current political and territorial debate. At the beginning of the twentieth century the Serbs treated Macedonia as South Serbia and the Slav population in the region as Serbs. The main task of the Serbian campaign was to eliminate the Bulgarian association from the history and the affiliation of the Macedonian territory's population.[127] Finally, at the end of World War II when Serbianization was seen to have failed, a more effective instrument for alienating the Macedonian Slavs from their Bulgarian roots was found in a distinct Macedonian nationality.[128] This

---

[126]The commonly used formulation, Slav-speaking population, verges on incompetence. There is no Slav language; there is a group of Slav languages and every Slav speaker speaks some concrete language from the group of Slav languages.

[127]"...since it could hardly contest the Bulgarian character of the majority of the population under its control, Serbia attempted, with little success, both Serbianization and colonization. Without trying to prove the Serbian character of the population and yet not admitting that it was non-Serbian, either, Serbia sought to prove that the Macedonians were not Bulgarians." Symeon A. Giannakos, "The Macedonian Question Reexamined: Implications for Balkan Security," Mediterranean Quarterly, Vol.3, No.3, Summer 1992, p.38.

[128]The theory of the Macedonians as a separate people was advanced in 1906 by Jovan Cvijic, a Macedonian Serb. It was however rejected by the Serbian government which at that time hoped to Serbianize the region. For more details see George B.

98

approach was developed after World War II, following the setting up of the Socialist Republic of Macedonia within the framework of the Yugoslav federation and the launching of an intensive process of nation building.

Since one of the most important and generally recognized ethno-national indicators is language, the primary phase in the Macedonian nation-building process was the creation of a separate Macedonian language. Until 1945, no such thing had existed as the population spoke a Bulgarian dialect. In 1945, the Macedonian alphabet and orthography were approved and the first Macedonian primer appeared in 1946. A Macedonian grammar appeared in 1952 and the Institute of the Macedonian Language, Krste P. Misirkov, was founded in 1953.[129] The future language was based on a Bulgarian dialect and in fact Macedonian still retains all those characteristics of Bulgarian which distinguish it from the other Slav languages.

It would be unfair to put all the blame for this conversion process on the Serbs and the later Macedonists because the Bulgarian communists also played a significant part in it. They supported the Comintern's policy in the 1920s of the recognition of a separate Macedonian nation as the first step towards broader Balkan federation. After World War II, the issue of the Balkan Federation was raised again between Bulgaria and Yugoslavia. Following Bulgaria's repeated failure to coopt Macedonia during the occupation, the Bulgarian Communist Party again supported the idea of a Macedonian nation in the belief that this would be one step towards the future unification of the Bulgarian population and territories via a federative supra-national structure.[130] Within this framework, the creation of a Macedonian republic based on the newly invented Macedonian nation was contingent upon the lessening of Serbian dominance within the future federal entity.

In line with this idea, at the end of the 1940s the Bulgarian communists enforced Macedonianization, including Pirin Macedonia. Yugoslav teachers of the newly created Macedonian language were

---

Zotiades, The Macedonian Controversy (Salonica: Institute for Macedonian Studies, 1961), p.25.

[129]Poulton, Balkans, p.50.

[130]This assumption was based on the Bled agreement of 1947 between Tito and Dimitrov.

invited to replace the Bulgarian ones, the Macedonian press was distributed throughout the region, and the population was forced to declare its affiliation to Macedonian nationality during the 1946 census.[131] This typically modernist (in its communist edition) attempt to enforce upon society some kind of rational project—in this case a nation-building project—culminated in 1948 in a symbolic gesture of goodwill by the communists who authorized the transfer of the tomb of Goce Delcev (a Macedonian Liberation hero) from Sofia to Skopje, marking the communists' voluntary refusal to identify Bulgaria with the liberation struggle in Macedonia.

Not surprisingly, this Utopian Balkan federation did not work and when relations between the USSR and Yugoslavia began to deteriorate in 1948, the issue of the Macedonian nation became the basis of Yugoslav claims against Bulgaria: the supposed existence of a significant Macedonian minority in Bulgaria. The 1956 census recorded 187,789 people who declared themselves as Macedonians (over 95% of the Pirin region) but in 1965 the figure dropped to 8,750, which provided the Yugoslav authorities with serious grounds for alleging that Bulgaria was suppressing the Macedonian minority. However, according to the Bulgarian explanation which seems to be the more probable one, in 1946 and in 1956 people still did not perceive Macedonian affiliation as excluding and opposing Bulgarian affiliation. In fact, many of them identified themselves, as they had done for decades, as Macedonian Bulgarians. It was only after the conflict intensified in the 1950s that its political and ideological connotations became obvious to the public. At the same time, the Yugoslav authorities vigorously rejected the right of the Bulgarian population in Macedonia to declare their Bulgarian affiliation.[132]

---

[131]Its results were never made public but according to estimates some 250,000 people declared themselves to be Macedonians.

[132]"The Yugoslav communists declared the Slavic inhabitants of the Yugoslav portion of Macedonia to be 'Macedonians,' although the people considered themselves, and had been considered by most ethnographers for a hundred years, to be Bulgarians. In their census data the Yugoslavs have been very careful to show statistically that these 'Macedonians' are not Bulgarians. In the 1948 census, the Yugoslav Republic of Macedonia had a population of 1,152,986. Of this number, 789,648 (68.5 per cent of the republic's population) were Macedonians and only 899 (or less than 0.1 per cent) were Bulgarians. The Yugoslavs have found a population of over 60,000 Bulgarians living in Yugoslavia in each of the three post-war censuses. However, about 55,000 of these

The reason why Skopje was desperately pushing for a completely distinct, historically-rooted Macedonian nationality was simply that it was this separate nationality which provided the sole justification for Macedonia to exist as a separate republic in former Yugoslavia. And it is still one of the basic sources of legitimacy of the newly created Macedonian state. The problem does not lie in the newly created nationality as a source of legitimacy but in the retroactive application of that argument. Certainly, after five decades of nation building, a separate national identity already exists today in FYROM. On this basis, however, the Macedonists are making revanchist demands, claiming that it has **always** existed, or at least since the time of Alexander the Great, which inevitably leads to the expropriation of Bulgarian and Greek history which started several decades ago.

Another important aspect of this retroactive policy is the problem of Macedonian minorities in Bulgaria and Greece. If Macedonian nationality did in fact exist in distant history, it did so not only in the FYROM territory but also in Macedonia as a geographical and historical **region**. Hence, after the division of Macedonia, the Macedonian nation was also divided and its segments remained as Macedonian minorities in Bulgaria and Greece. This is only one step away from claims for reunification.[133]

Of course a Macedonian nation exists today. But the distinct **present-day** Macedonian nation is the result of an enforced process of nation building over a period of five decades which took place only in the former Republic of Macedonia of the former Yugoslavia. There was

---

live in the Serbian republic, in territories along the Bulgarian border which were ceded by Bulgaria to Serbia after World War I. Part of the territory ceded in 1920 was the city of Strumica and its surrounding area, which is now part of the Macedonian republic. The population of this area, since it is part of Macedonia, is overwhelmingly 'Macedonian.' Apparently the border regions which were ceded by Bulgaria in 1920 can have a Bulgarian population if they are in Serbia, but not if they are in the Macedonian republic." Robert R. King, Minorities under Communism. Nationalities as a Source of Tension among Balkan Communist States (Cambridge: Harvard University Press, 1973), p.98.

[133]Article 49 of the Republic of Macedonia's new Constitution states that "the Republic cares for the status and rights of those persons belonging to the Macedonian people in neighbouring countries." See Constitution of the Federal Republic of Macedonia (Skopje: NIP, 1991). Macedonia's parliament passed an amendment in January 1992 that Macedonia "will not interfere in the internal affairs of neighbouring countries" but Article 49 has not yet been abrogated.

no such process in Greece and Bulgaria so that there simply could not be any Macedonian minorities in these two countries.[134] Although Macedonian minorities do not exist as such in Bulgaria and Greece, they do in fact pose a very real and serious problem there simply by virtue of the fact that a tradition already exists in Skopje for a retroactive approach. These possible claims are probably the real reason for Greece's refusal to recognize the Macedonian state and nation and Bulgaria's opposition to the Macedonian nation. And political declarations of non-interference are not sufficient when the entire political and intellectual context is dominated by irrational nation-building euphoria.

There is a solution and that is to recognize the real historical logic of events: the Macedonian nation as it exists **today** is a newly created branch of the Bulgarian nation, separated in the middle of the twentieth century. This was the essence of the Bulgarian proposal to Skopje in 1978. On the basis of this assumption, a mutuallly acceptable interpretation of the common history of the two nations could be worked out, but the idea was rejected—understandably because the Macedonian nation is really a new one and new nations' nationalisms usually lack persuasive arguments for their own existence which makes them extremely militant.

From today's perspective the idea still seems to be vital and there are at least three sources of optimism. First, the economic embargo imposed on the FYROM by Greece proved that the newly established country needs close contacts and normalized relations with all its Slav neighbours and probably most of all with Bulgaria. Second, the actual and aggravated tensions with the Albanian minority may weaken the intensity and the importance of the Macedonian-Bulgarian rather than the historical quarrel. Third, the aforementioned Albanian problem makes the idea of the reunification of the former Bulgarian territories less appealing to the Bulgarians and this may further reduce the existing tensions between the two countries.

---

[134]Moreover, bearing in mind also that the conversion process of nation building was taking place only in part of the territory of Macedonia as a geographical and historical region, it is doubtful whether the newly created nation in the former Republic of Macedonia of the former Yugoslavia can claim the name Macedonian, thereby depriving the other nationalities inhabiting that region of their traditional affiliation to the historical region.

The Pomaks in Bulgaria

The Pomaks, who are also called Bulgarian Muslims or Bulgarian Mohammedans, are a religious community. According to the World Directory of Minorities, "they are Slav Bulgarians who speak Bulgarian as their mother tongue but whose religion and customs are Islamic."[135] In this respect, they used to share many similarities with the Bosnian Muslims until the latter were upgraded to the level of a nation in 1971. The Pomaks share the same religion as the Bosnian Muslims and were also converted to Islam during Ottoman rule.[136] They do not have a distinct language and their customs and traditions resemble their Bulgarian kin traditions, providing a fascinating mixture of Muslim and Christian rites. But the basic similarity lies in the Pomaks' role in the country's political life: as a minority group they are often treated instrumentally by the political actors, both the state authorities and parties, acting on their behalf.

The Pomaks number about 250,000. They mainly inhabit regions in the Rhodopa Mountains, along the Mesta River valley in Pirin, and some areas around Lovech. The regions are mountainous which for centuries made them virtually inaccessible. This is one of the reasons for a certain degree of isolationism on the part of the Pomak communities and for the strong traditionalist attitudes within their social organization. In fact, modernization only really started under communism when the industrialization of the country was accompanied by attempts to secularize social life. However, the regions remained

---

[135]World Directory, p.118.

[136]The question "were converted" or "converted" is also an object of political interpretation. For a long period in Bulgarian historiography the myth of totally enforced conversion was dominant. There is considerable evidence of violence in this process during the Ottoman period but it cannot be treated as a general rule. "If considered objectively, the Islamization of the Rhodope Bulgarians is not a unique phenomenon, nor is it the result of some deliberately organized assimilation campaigns of the Sublime Porte. It was the effect of serious and various political and economic factors, which affected all European provinces, and does not give sufficient grounds to Bulgarian historiographers to emphasize it in a more specific or dramatic way than this is done in the histories of other nations. This is all the more so if we bear in mind that the Bulgarian Muslims in the Rhodopes, like the Albanian Muslims, have preserved their language and national affiliation." Antonina Zeliazkova, "The Problem of Authenticity of Some Domestic Sources on the Islamization of the Rhodopes Deeply Rooted in Bulgarian Historiography," Etudes Bulkaniques, No.4, 1990, p.111.

highly underdeveloped and the majority of Pomaks are still mainly employed in the agricultural (tobacco production), construction, and mining sectors. After 1989, these last two sectors were severely hit by economic collapse, and unemployment in the above-mentioned regions is extremely high.

Identification of the Pomaks is one of the underlying causes of potential conflict (identification and not self-identification because in this respect the Pomak issue is generally used for political purposes by political actors outside the Pomak communities). For centuries they were looked upon with suspicion by both the Bulgarian and the Turkish communities. The former considered that the Pomaks had abandoned their native faith, while the latter considered that they were not true believers. But attempts by the two above-mentioned national groups to coopt the Pomaks started when the self-determination of peoples received some serious, and not purely declarative, attention in the Balkans. That is probably why the Bulgarian government launched its assimilation campaign against the Pomaks in the 1970s, influenced to a certain extent no doubt by the Helsinki process (and probably it was the most pervasive answer by the communists to the issue of human rights in general and minority rights in particular). Instead of recognizing the minorities and their rights, an attempt was made to wipe the minorities off the political landscape, exactly according to the Stalinist rule of "no man, no problem." As far as the Turks were concerned, attempts to coopt the Pomaks into the Turkish minority on the basis of their common religion began in 1990 when the Turkish minority party, Movement for Rights and Freedoms (MRF), was founded.

The Bulgarian state mainly applied administrative methods of assimilation. In the new identity cards issued at the beginning of the 1970s the item "nationality" was missing. The Greek and Turkish approach was adopted which treated all citizens of the state as presumably belonging to that state's nationality. The only formal ethnic or national indicator was the name and that is why the Pomaks, as well as Gipsies and Turks with names of Arab origin, were compelled to change their names into Bulgarian ones. The other aspect of state activity was to secularize social life as much as possible. But, as in the case of the Bulgarian Turks, it was not an entirely directly enforced process. Some of these changes were part of the gradual and, vis-à-vis the conditions in the Balkans, understandable process of assimilation. In view of the suspicious attitudes adopted towards them by ethnic Bulgarians (under communist rule, one can hardly speak of the Christian majority), many Pomaks and Turks preferred to change their Arab names into Slav-sounding ones, seeing this as the inevitable price to be paid for the possibility of social advance. In many respects the regime did succeed—by the 1980s the Pomaks' Islamic affiliation had been preserved although it had become less dominant.[137] This process was reversed in 1984 when the regime started to enforce assimilation, and more particularly after 1989.

Irrespective of communist attempts at secularization, the Pomaks did preserve their religious attitudes. This was just further evidence of their closed communities' autarchic potential which helped them to resist all kinds of assimilation, even by the Turkish population during Ottoman rule. The Pomaks continued to keep their seperate identity although Islam remained a strong criterion of self-identification and is still a potential basis for quests based on the notion that the Pomaks are part of a more broadly defined Turkish community.

In fact, this was the second attempt in twenty years to assimilate the Pomaks, this time not on an administrative but on a confessional basis. There is strong evidence that Bulgarian elements prevail in the Pomaks' amalgamated cultural identity—the Pomaks speak Bulgarian; they did not take part in the 1989 exodus of Muslim Turks to Turkey; Pomak traditional habits and national costumes very closely resemble Bulgarian ones, etc. Nevertheless, they are often treated as Turks by the authorities at the local level in the regions where the MRF won the local elections. During the 1992 census, there were reports of Pomaks being pressurized into declaring Turkish affiliation, and in two villages the census data was contested after the holding of parliamentary hearings on the issue.[138]

---

[137]"Until 1984 feelings of ethnic separateness and the strength of religious conviction were declining to such a degre that Muslims, for example, regarded Islam as relatively unimportant in terms of their identity." Ivan Ilchev and Duncan M. Perry, "Bulgarian Ethnic Groups: Politics and Perceptions," RFE/RL Research Report, Vol.2, No.12, 19 March 1993, p.41.

[138]Immediately after the census, "instances of 'pressure' were reported by Duma and some other newspapers to have occurred in the Pirin region and the areas of Smolyan and Kardzhali, where large numbers of ethnic Bulgarian Muslims live. According to these reports, MRF members in senior local positions were very active just before the census was taken... In one case some 2,729 —23% of all schoolchildren in that area—had claimed to be Turkish, whereas in 1991 none had. In another area, 1,174 out of a total of 1,721 schoolchildren identified themselves as Turks... Duma suggested that the census

Another source of potential tension is the second edition of the names issue. Prior to the 1990 elections, the then acting parliament passed a law on Bulgarian names allowing Muslim names to be restored through a court procedure. Later, the MRF began to push for, and in November 1990 succeeded in changing the act in order to simplify the procedure from a court to an administrative one but its efforts were interpreted by Bulgarian nationalists as further Turkization. As a result, mutual accusations between activists of the MRF and the Bulgarian nationalist parties increased and the new procedure for name changes was not only made easier but it also put more leverage into the hands of the local authorities where the MRF was often in office.

Another aspect of the names issue was the pressure that was exerted on those who preferred to keep their Bulgarian names. It led to local tensions in 1993-1994 when an increasing number of hodjas refused to perform religious funeral rites for Pomaks with Slav names. In 1994 the question as to whether a Muslim can have a non-Muslim name was seriously debated among the Muslim authorities in Bulgaria. The dispute is closely related to the frequent cases of conversion to Christianity which have occurred in the last two years, strongly opposed by the Muslim authorities, the MRF, and even representatives of the Islamic countries in Bulgaria. This opposition in turn provoked a violent reaction from Bulgarian nationalists.

This is the real problem with the Pomaks: too many sides claim them as their kin and use the Pomak community for their own particular interests. With the exception of the recognition that Pomaks are ethnic Bulgarians which has generally been accepted for generations, suppositions about their origin vary from claims that they are the descendants of the Turks who settled there before the Ottoman period and who, as a result of stress, have forgotten their original language, to the version of their having Arab roots originating in Egypt. No matter how insubstantial such suppositions may be, they are perceived by the Bulgarian majority as a direct attack on Bulgarian identity, especially when such theories are put forward by foreign scholars and politicians.

---

results might have to be invalidated for the municipalities of Yakoruda, Satovcha, Garmen, and Gotse Delchev, contending that respondents there had answered the questions about their native language while under pressure from MRF activists and that as many as 40,000 Bulgarian Muslims had been forced to say that they were Turks." Rada Nikolaev, "Bulgaria's 1992 Census: Results, Problems, and Implications," RFE/RL Research Report, Vol.2, No.6, 5 February 1993, p.60.

106

In 1994 there were also two direct attempts to provide scientific arguments for the Pomaks' supposed distinct ethnic origin. One was reported to be an analysis of the Pomaks' genotype on the basis of blood tests and the second was a research based on anthropological measurements and the detection of specific features in the Pomaks' cranium. Both studies were to be carried out by foreign researchers which fuelled a violent reaction in the Bulgarian media.[139]

Closely related to the issue of the Pomaks' ethnic affiliation is that of language. The MRF insists on introducing Turkish as a compulsory language into regions with a Turkish population as a means of preserving the ethnic homogeneity of the Turkish-populated regions. However, the party is also pushing for Turkish to be compulsory in Pomak-populated regions and treats this population as Turkish, and this provides additional arguments for Bulgarian nationalists.

The denominational issue is also potentially explosive. Most Bulgarian Muslims are Sunnites but growing numbers of Shiite activists from Iran and Middle Eastern Islamic countries are reported to be visiting Pomak regions. Closely related to this is the threat of Islamic fundamentalism. The fact that young people are being offered grants to study at Islamic universities in Saudi Arabia, Libya, Egypt, and Syria and that over ninety people took advantage of this opportunity in 1993-1994 provide the basis for the argument that the Muslim communities are being fundamentalized. On the other hand, education in Islamic universities is often the only way to advance, bearing in mind the extent of the economic crisis in the Pomak region.

The real problem, however, is not confessional education as such but the biased equilibrium between the state and the religious authorities. Unlike the 1960s and the 1970s, the state is on the defensive, not least because of the state administration's deepening atrophy, the inevitable result of prolonged political instability in the country and of the general distrust of all kinds of power, especially the police which is often identified with the political police. The periodical changes in the ruling elite during the transition phase is also a significant source of executive weakness. As a result, the centres of power have shifted towards the local level, giving the local religious authorities incomparable and uncontrollable influence. This influence

<hr>

[139]No independent confirmation of these attempts was found by the author but the fact that such issues are broadly televised is an indication that the problem is a serious one.

increased even further with the switch from Sunnite to Shiite denomination, the latter being traditionally active not only as a spiritual but also as an administrative and legal authority.

In this context, the Pomak issue may become an explosive one. Unfortunately, the similarities between this issue and the Bosnian Muslim one since the 1970s are becoming too numerous. In both cases, the population was pushed towards a separate identity, in both cases it is being used instrumentally in political gambling, and in both cases there are external (out-of-community) political actors which depend on and are interested in deepening conflicts. The basic difference is that Bosnia was a political and administrative entity long before the federation fell apart. It is also true that the final impetus for Bosnian independence was provided by the Serbs' attacks.

And this is probably the answer to the question as to what the possible development of the Pomak issue may be. It may become a problem if the Pomaks are pushed towards deepening autonomy and radicalized by some kind of attack—in this case against their identity. Attempts at assimilation at the state level are absolutely impossible, not least because at that level there is a clash between political and economic, but not ethnic, interests.[140] But at the local level these contradictions are translated into ethnic ones in the shape of a clash between ethnic elites so that the Pomaks may become an object of rivalry and this would have a serious impact on ethnic stability.

The Turks in Bulgaria

The Turks mainly inhabit two parts of Bulgaria—the regions around Kardjali in the Rhodopa mountains and around Razgrad. They are descendants of Turkish peasants who settled in the Balkans during Ottoman rule. Until the 1989 crisis, they numbered about 900,000. After attempts by the Bulgarian government to change their names into Bulgarian ones, some 250,000 emigrated to Turkey, some 40% of them returning to Bulgaria at the beginning of the 1990s.

This was not the first emigration wave of Turks from Bulgaria nor was it the first assimilation campaign. As mentioned in Chapter 3,

---

[140]On the eve of the 1994 parliamentary elections, Pomaks from two Rhodopa villages sent a petition of protest to the President of the Republic against the use of their enforced Bulgarian names in the electoral lists. This case is proof of the deepening decay of the state bureaucracy rather than evidence of a state-run assimilation campaign.

all the Balkan wars were followed by stronger or weaker Turkish emigration, starting with the Russo-Turkish war in 1878 when Bulgaria was liberated and about 1.5 million Turks left Bulgaria. The Turks constituted about 26% of the Bulgarian population in Northern Bulgaria in 1876 and by the turn of the century the percentage had dropped to 14% to become 10.5% in 1926. The next significant wave of emigration took place after World War II: some 250,000 left Bulgaria between 1949 and 1951; about 155,000 at the beginning of the 1950s; and between 55,000 and 130,000 (Bulgarian and Turkish data differ) between 1968 and 1978.

Attitudes towards the Turkish minority were a strange mixture of two extremes: complete recognition of their rights with preferential treatment even, and total rejection of the very existence of minorities. Preferential treatment was for years part of the Bulgarian state's policy for incorporating this population into society which in itself was an indirect sign that this minority was perceived as an alien body. Preferential treatment was, however, mainly conducted in the economic field through higher prices for the traditional product from the Turkish-inhabited regions—tobacco—and susidized prices. Direct evidence of this treatment is the fact that, "according to incomplete data from the State Savings Bank (the largest savings institution in Bulgaria), in 1989 regions with compact Muslim populations held between 1.2 and 1.5 times more savings than the rest of the country."[141] Preferential treatment was a rather constant element in the Bulgarian landscape after World War II.

This was not the case with political attitudes towards the minorities and in particular the Bulgarian Turks. The regime hesitated between recognition of their status and rights and total rejection of the very idea that minorities existed which was the ideological basis of the forceful assimilation attempts. The 1947 Constitution guarantees the rights of national minorities but the 1971 constitution mentions only citizens of non-Bulgarian origin (Article 45). This was how the official attitudes evolved: until 1970, Turks could study in Turkish schools, Turkish-language newspapers were published, and Radio Sofia broadcast in Turkish. In the middle of the 1970s, this attitude drastically changed and the Turkish minority was perceived as a

[141]Krassen Stanchev, "Can Economic Reforms Overcome Ethnic Tensions?" Paper, Institute for Market Economics, Sofia, 1994, p.5.

potential secession-oriented group whose very existence threatened the country's integrity.[142]

From today's point of view, things do not look that clear-cut but the fact is that the perceived threat was a strong enough motive for action. As in the case of the Pomaks, it was undertaken through a forceful change of names of Arab origin which once again proved that one of the basic problems in the Balkans was that of questioned identities, both collective and personal.[143] The campaign was cynically labelled a renaissance process since the official version of assimilation was that it was a voluntary process on the part of the Turkish population, which in fact is not Turkish but ethnic Bulgarian converted to Islam during the Ottoman rule and which, by the middle of the 1980s, had become conscious of its Bulgarian roots. The name changes were also voluntary from a procedural point of view—people had to sign a standard form stating their wish to change their names. It completely blurred the difference between those who were forced to change their names (the majority) and those who did it voluntarily (a number of Turks as well as Pomaks preferred to use names of Slav origin for the reasons already described).

Forced assimilation was too naive as an attempt to change the Turkish minority's identity. For that reason, the change of identity was more probably not the real aim but just the camouflage for a smarter project. According to one of the many surmised reasons for this abrupt change in the regime's strategy, enforced assimilation and changing names of Arab origin were designed as a means of antagonizing

---

[142]The conflicts in Lebanon and Cyprus were used by the political establishment as a point of departure for building similar scenarios for Bulgaria. The fact that Turkey was a NATO member and perceived as potentially hostile was of somewhat secondary importance—the perceived hostility was present also in the 1950s and the 1960s.

[143]"One might say that a name is an indisputable sign of personal identity. So it seems natural to have a right to choose one's name. But, in the Balkans, even personal names are contestable. One picks a name to transmit information about one's more general identity (whatever it means). On the other hand, others try to influence the choice of a name for the same reason. In the Balkans, authorities often get involved in the name choosing process, usually trying to achieve cultural and political assimilation. So there are cycles of contests over what is a proper name in a certain community. Moreover, there are legal and other repressive mechanisms that are devised not only to influence the choice of personal names, but there are campaigns of name changing." Vladimir Gligorov, "Balkanization: A Theory of Constitution Failure," East European Politics and Societies, Vol.6, No.3, Fall 1992, p.299.

110

Bulgarian society along ethnic lines in order to lay the ground for the nationalistic mobilization of the Bulgarian majority under the auspices of the communist regime.[144] According to this scenario, communism would play the role of the Bulgarian nation's redeemer. From today's perspective and following the development of events in Serbia in the second half of the 1980s and the 1990s, this explanation for the ethnic conflict in Bulgaria in the 1980s now seems to be the more reasonable one.

Assimilation attempts and especially reactions by the Bulgarian majority in 1989 revealed the real dimensions of the Turkish minority problem in Bulgaria: the problem does not lie with the minority but with the majority. It is based on the division between those Bulgarians who regard Turks (and, in broader terms, Muslims) as citizens with equal rights and those who opt for the Bulgarians' privileged political status. It is not surprising that after 1989 the latter group found itself concentrated mainly around the Bulgarian socialist party, the former communist one, which was playing a patriotic card with nationalist overtones although on a far lower scale than the Serbian one.

The totally pragmatic approach that was adopted in this respect was obvious from the Bulgarian Socialist Party's (BSP) attitude towards the MRF. The MRF was registered in 1990 thanks to the support of the BSP, and it was thanks to the BSP that it took part in the 1990 parliamentary elections. The aim was to split the non-socialist vote and this was achieved: the MRF took 7% and entered parliament, and the Union of Democratic Forces (UDF) came second. Later, when the MRF started supporting the UDF at the parliamentary level, it was the BSP which raised the issue of the unconstitutional character of the MRF since it was perceived as an ethnically-based party and the new Bulgarian constitution adopted in 1991 forbids the existence of such organizations. The issue was addressed to the Constitutional Court and the MRF won by a majority of one vote. The BSP, however, continues to use the Turkish problem for nationalist-based mobilization.

The assimilation campaign of the 1980s had a crucial effect on both the Turkish minority and Bulgarian society. The Turkish minority was the real winner in the long term. Thanks to the attempt to enforce assimilation, the prevailing part of this population started to identify itself along ethnic and national lines. Secondly, for the first time

---

[144]Stanchev, Can Economic, p.7.

probably in a century, the Turkish minority was emancipated and for the first time it felt the obvious support of its kin state.

In a paradoxical way, the dramatic events of 1986-1989 enforced the future democratic process in the country. Thanks to them, a Bulgarian opposition was formed in the context of the minority issue and became extremely sensitive to it. The small-scale conflict in 1989 was a necessary experience in order to prevent a nationalist clash on a broader scale. But what is more important is that the Turkish minority itself turned into a rational political actor so that the problems it faces can now be solved at the political, parliamentary level. Although many issues are still disputable (such as the nature of the constitutional limitation forbidding the existence of ethnically-based parties, which will be discussed in Chapter 5), it is now part of the political landscape just as the Turkish minority is part of the Bulgarian one.

The ethno-national composition of the Balkans is extremely complicated. The population can be rearranged into different subcommunities depending on the cleavage criteria—ethnic, cultural, religious—which are the result of different historical experiences.

These groups often found themselves in conflict with the prevailing majority. They were not invented after democratic changes began. Minority conflicts in the Balkan countries in fact preceded the systematic collapse of communism there and were the first signs of its decay. They exposed the weaknesses of the communist state in its final period of existence, the ineffectiveness of direct violence, the increased role of public opinion, and the tangible influence exercised by the international community and the international context on internal developments in the East European countries.

The intensive process of minorities' consciousness in the region was not launched in 1989. In fact it had already started in the 1970s when attempts began to liberalize communist regimes. In the case of Bulgaria, because of the absence of other significant national minorities, it mainly affected the Turkish population and to a lesser extent the Pomaks. Least affected were the Gipsies, probably because of their ability to adapt, or because they were simply ignored as significant political actors. In both cases, however, the question of minorities' rights and freedoms was not elevated to the level of self-determination through secession. The option was the Turkish exodus in 1989 which had a tremendous impact both on Bulgarian society and on the Turkish population itself. In fact the assimilation attempt had a modernization impact on this population and turned it into a political community. On the other hand, thanks to the small-scale ethnic conflict in 1989, Bulgarian society and its future political elite became extremely sensitive to the national issue.

The case of Yugoslavia was the opposite. Although the federal system was designed to meet the minorities' challenge, the last two decades have been marked by a constant demand for more rights and guarantees, often to the extremes of sound reasoning. This paradox is easily explicable from today's perspective: the former Yugoslav federation was built as an enforced incorporation of its parts into a common state. Who actually enforced it—the Serbs, Stalin, or concrete post-World War II circumstances—is of secondary importance. Of primary importance is the fact that it was imposed from above. It was not the result of the exercising of free choice by the peoples inhabiting the various parts of the future federation in the same way that its binding element was not the will and the interest to stay together but the imposed obligation to do so. The process of democratization which took place after 1974 gradually removed the obligation but did not replace it with a reason for staying together rather than apart.

As a result, since the dramatic changes of 1989, the political map of the Balkans strongly resembles that of 1919 at least in one respect: the existing minorities are again active participants in big politics and the states are again facing the prospect of their emancipation, the first and simplest way of achieving which is self-determination. The problem lies in what the limits to minorities' self-determination are and what form this process may take.

CHAPTER 5
MINORITIES AFTER THE COLLAPSE OF COMMUNISM:
THE TEMPTATION OF SELF-DETERMINATION

After the euphoria had evaporated surrounding the democratization and the romantic "refolutions"[145] in Eastern Europe, some of the darker aspects of these events began to emerge. A new metaphor was also born: Europe is back to 1919. This Chapter is an attempt to develop this idea and to explain the reasons behind it: what are the similarities and the differences between the situation after World War I and the one following the Cold War?

In general, both periods marked the end of a serious war and an emerging patchwork of ethnically heterogeneous states in Eastern Europe. In both periods we have a trend towards self-determination as an emanation of democracy and human and, in this case, collective rights, as well as the questioning of external and internal borders. In both periods the difference between external and internal borders was blurred, with the internal ones often treated as potentially external. But one of the most striking similarities between 1919 and 1989 is the machinery which was used in former Yugoslavia, but which was also applied elswhere in the Balkans, for solving the minorities' issue, mainly on the grounds of the mechanically applied right to self-determination through secession. And the logical consequences of this are population exchanges, forcible assimilation, and the violation of basic rights.[146]

Of course, there are significant differences between 1919 and 1989, the major one being the aggravated division of the European

---

[145]The term, introduced by T.G. Ash, which is used to describe the nature of the change in Eastern Europe as reforms with a revolutionary depth.

[146]Ernest Gellner's description of the new nation-states established after 1918 in many respects corresponds to the situation in the 1990s: "They were just as minority haunted, but they were smaller, unhallowed by age and often without experienced leaders, while the minorities whose irredentism they had to face included members of previously dominant cultural groups, unused to subordination and well-placed to resist it." Ernest Gellner and E.H. Carr, "Nationalism Reconsidered," Review of International Studies, Vol.18, No.4, October 1992, p.288.

continent into a Western and an Eastern part. This division had existed
for centuries at the cultural level but it was not that obvious at the
beginning of the twentieth century. However, by the end of the 1980s
it had already been elevated to a qualitatively different level so that the
terms Eastern and Western became some kind of civilizational markers.

As a result, the European continent was torn between different
types of tendencies. The societies of the so-called Western countries
have entered their post-modern phase of evolution, the industrial
revolution there has been followed by the information revolution, and
inter-state rivalry is being replaced by closer integration. The societies
of the East, on the other hand, are still solving problems which are
often typical of the eve of the industrial phase of development—and
building from its bases a democratic framework for dealing with
minorities' issues was one of them.

That is why the whole process of transforming the system in
Eastern Europe is in some way related to the issue of minority rights.
If we assume that the legitimacy of the communist system was the first
issue to be challenged at the beginning of the transition to democracy,
the second one was the legitimacy of external and internal borders
precisely because they did not coincide with ethnic divisions. Although
the reasons why they did not coincide have already been discussed in
Chapters 3 and 4, it should be mentioned in passing that the actual
procedure for drawing these borders was also open to question. Most
of the existing borders (82%) were established as a result of
geopolitical compromises reached "at postwar international conferences
rather than by bilateral agreement (only 18 percent) and thus were
often perceived as having been imposed by the Great Powers. As the
international environment changes, we are witnessing a delegitimation
of existing borders between states but also within states."[147]

In accordance with the spirit of democratization, these problems
were solved on the basis of people's right to self-determination and, in
extreme cases, the right to execute self-determination through
secession. This subissue emerged as a dominant one in the Balkans
and, in some cases, as in the former Yugoslavia, turned the problem of
democratic change and minority rights into unsolvable disputes and
conflicts.

---

[147]Jacques Rupnik, "Europe's New Frontiers: Remapping Europe," Daedalus, Vol.123,
No.3, Summer 1994, p.99.

However, the status quo in Eastern and Southeastern Europe, as it was established after the fall of communism and the collapse of the Soviet empire, was not the restoration of the status quo which had existed before the outbreak of World War II and in many respects it brought modern European history back to the point at which it had actually begun—in 1919. Although the circumstances have changed and Europe has changed too, the Balkan region is still submerged under the old problems of mutually claimed territory, newborn nation-states, and numerous minorities. The question is, first, whether the hysteria for nation building based on secession was the only or even real implementation of the right to self-determination, and, second, whether this hysteria was an isolated episode which took place only in former Yugoslavia or whether it may have a broader application.

Secessionist Self-Determination as a Substitute for Democratic Change

The right of minorities to self-determination through secession is not an established norm of international law despite the fact that it is widely practised and has been internationally recognized since 1992 in the case of the Balkans. Furthermore, its moral grounds are not as clear as they may appear. For decades it was one line of the intellectual argument and in fact it is only in the last fifteen years or so that a theoretical approach has begun to develop towards the issue of secession. It took quite some time to overcome prejudices to the obvious revolutionary potential of the secessionist act.[148] This potential was probably one of the reasons why "in earlier times, East Europe's ethnic mosaic contributed to the rise of communism just as it now threatens to inhibit the reconstruction of the old communist system."[149]

---

[148]"To accept the right of self-determination in blanket fashion is to endow social entities which cannot be identified in advance with a right of revolution against the constituted authority of the state, and even to obligate the state to yield to the demands of the revolutionaries... As W.K. Hancock adroitly put it... 'The apostles of secession have unfettered freedom as nationalists, but they will be shot as revolutionaries.'" Cited in Emerson, From Empire, p.297.

[149]Stephen R. Bowers, Ethnic Politics in Eastern Europe (London: Research Institute for the Study of Conflict and Terrorism, 1992), p.8.

Secession is a unilateral attempt on the part of the population of a distinct region within an independent state to separate (secede) from that state and become an independent entity according to the terms of international law. It is "a special kind of territorial separatism involving states. It is an abrupt unilateral move to independence on the part of a region that is a metropolitan territory of a sovereign independent state."[150] Usually, as in the case of irredentism, the territory is inhabited by an ethnic minority. Though in both cases (irredentism and secession) we have an attempt to redraw existing international borders, the difference lies in the subject laying the claim. In the case of secession, unlike irredentism, the object and the subject of the conflict coincide, the claim comes from inside, and is much more defendable since it is based on the right of peoples to self-determination.

The juridical basis for this type of claim is provided under Article 1, para. 2 and Article 55 of the UN Charter, as well as UN Resolution 1514 which was passed in 1960.[151] It was on this basis that an overall functional and effective system was developed for dealing with the issue of decolonization at the international level. In order to prevent the erosion of the existing state order based on the principle of state sovereignty, Resolution 1514 and the later reports to UN Commissions treated this approach as a right of existing states to determine their internal affairs free of outside intervention, but not as a right to create states. After a series of UN resolutions interpreting self-determination as a right which does not include secession, the Friendly Relations resolution (UNGA 2625) was adopted in 1970 which directly condemns any action aimed at partial or total disruption of the "territorial integrity or political unity" of any other state or country.

Hence self-determination did not mean the right to redraw existing international borders, and the process of decolonization was to take place within the colonies' existing boundaries and, therefore, took no account of ethnic and national distribution. Self-determination was

---

[150]Alexis Heraclides, The Self-Determination of Minorities in International Politics (London: Frank Cass, 1991), p.1.

[151]Paragraph 2 of Resolution 1514 states that "all peoples have the right to self-determination." However, this is a significant departure from the original nineteenth- and early twentieth-century concept of self-determination advocated both by Wilson and Lenin, who spoke of the right of nations, not people, to self-determination.

to be, and in fact was, applied to state (i.e. administrative) and not to ethno-national (usually regional) entities. As a result, when the decolonization process had by and large been completed at the beginning of the 1970s, a large number of nations and ethnicities found themselves divided by borders which had been drawn by accident. The few attempts at regional self-determination based on ethnicity were not treated as legitimate in terms of international law. The only exception was Bangladesh,[162] which was motivated by purely humanitarian reasons.

As decolonization progressed and the issue of human and minority rights obtained wider appeal, the problem of secession began to receive closer attention and the complexity of the issue provided many arguments in favour of separatist and secessionist acts. For example, Anthony D. Smith analysed the evolution of discontent in an ethnic community through ethnic revival to a separatist ethnic movement, provoking the government's reaction.[163] According to Lee C. Buchheit, a secession not only can be legitimate, but it also depends on whether the ethnic minority is capable of an independent existence and whether a greater degree of world harmony would exist after secession. Buchheit also analyses in detail the legal and non-legal arguments against secession. Most of the latter directly correspond to the situation in the Balkans today: "the threats of Balkanization; the fear of indefinite divisibility since secessionist territories are rarely homogeneous; the establishing of non-viable states doomed to rely on international aid; trapping other minorities within the seceding state with a similarly deprived situation but without the possibility to secede

---

[162]The most serious attempts in that direction were the cases of Congo-Katanga in 1960 and Nigeria-Biafra in 1967. The creation of the new states of Senegal (separated from the Mali Federation) and Syria (from the United Arab Republic) were accepted by the parent states and cannot be treated as secession understood as a unilateral act. It was rather a partition of the existing states which is one of the five ways in which new states can be legitimately created (by granting of independence; by acknowledgement of de facto existing independence after dissolution of empire or federation; by merger of two or more units; by partition based on mutual consent; and by seizure of independence). For more details see Heraclides, Self-Determination, pp.24-26.

[163]See Anthony D. Smith, The Ethnic Revival (Cambridge: Cambridge University Press, 1981).

in their case."[154]

The real problem arose when communism collapsed and the process of democratization exploded. However, the problem was not the unfreezing of old national contradictions which had been frozen by communist regimes—the refrigerator metaphor was quite popular in 1990-1991. No matter what the ideological basis of an autocratic regime in multiethnic societies is, its democratization inevitably leads to ethnic diversity since the collapse of centralized autocratic power, coupled with the issue of self-government, immediately gives rise to the problem of the new rulers' **selves**. In ethnically diverse territories this inevitably leads to ethnically motivated competition, which further fosters the emergence of new ethnic and national consciousness.[155]

In the Balkans, this took the extreme form of secessionist self-determination although it was in fact a revolutionary act and, from a formal point of view, in contradiction with international law. This often gave rise to ambiguous political responses which were interpreted differently by the opposing parties. On the one hand, we have the principle of state sovereignty and the inviolability of state borders which are the basis of the 1975 Helsinki Agreement,[156] and on, the other, we have the above-mentioned arguments which recognize the legitimacy of separatist movements as subjects of international law and their right to secede under certain conditions. Although recognition of a compact ethnic or national group's right to secede on the basis of its

---

[154]Lee C. Buchheit, Secession. The Legitimacy of Self-Determination (New Haven: Yale University, 1978), pp.20-30 and 228. Other authors, including James Crawford, Anthony Birch, Michael Walzer, also argue in favour of the legitimacy of the secessionist act under certain conditions.

[155]For more details on the effects of democratization on ethnic conflict in a multiethnic society, see Renée de Nevers, "Democratization and Ethnic Conflict," Survival, Vol.35, No.2, Summer 1993, pp.34-43.

[156]This principle was in itself a compromise between the Soviet Union's desire for unchangeable borders as a guarantee for the territorial changes after World War II (especially in respect of the existence of the GDR) and the West's desire to keep the issue if not open, at least not closed. Inviolability of borders was not closing the issue; it did not mean that borders could not be changed but meant that they could not be changed by force. But in the 1970s it was translated and interpreted in slightly different ways by the various parties. For the Soviets it meant unchangeability since, in the context of the bloc divisions, a non-violent change was unthinkable; for the West it meant an open door for the non-violent change which began in 1989.

right to self-determination was not covered by international law, the secessionist approach has tended to prevail, mainly because it fitted perfectly into the surrounding euphoria of democratization and was enhanced by the expectations of a future spring of nations.

In spite of its internal contradictions, this philosophy was the natural continuation of the liberal tradition of respect for basic human rights. On the one hand, it was a liberal and humanitarian approach to the right to self-affiliation and, on the other, it promoted collective, as opposed to individual, identity, to be imposed on members of a community and not chosen by them. But this contradiction did not become obvious until the second phase of the East European "refolutions." During their first phase, national self-determination, especially in the Balkans, and democracy were treated as synonyms, both by the local political actors and the international community. The logic was misleadingly simple and attractive: national self-determination was directed at the dismantling of empires, and, since empires were totalitarian and communist, national self-determination was anti-communist and, finally, since anything anti-communist was democratic, national self-determination was an emanation of democracy.

Hence, there was full support for national self-determination activities and an underestimation, initially, of the real danger and possible scale of local ethnic conflicts. The whole atmosphere, which was seeped in idealism, overwhelmingly resembled the 1919 period. The dominant assumption was that an era of humanitarian liberal democracy was beginning,[157] that a civilized will to respect human rights existed, that nations' territories could be defined by borders, and that the inevitable contradictions could be solved through mutual agreements applying conflict-resolution strategies within a reformed legal system.

None of these assumptions turned out to be true in the Balkans. Nationalism re-emerged as an exclusive and militant attitude, nations' rights still prevailed over internationally recognized human rights, and intermingled minorities provided a constant basis for claims for the redrawing of borders. Growing mutual suspicion blocked dialogue and even when a normative system for the defence of minority rights existed, as in the case of former Yugoslavia, it was either a declarative

---

[157]Francis Fukuyama's sensational essay was just the most prominent manifestation of the dominant expectations. See Francis Fukuyama, "The End of History," The National Interest, No.16, Summer 1989.

one or it was suspended as soon as open conflict erupted.[158] In addition, once the process begins, it tends to become endless: the self-determination of one minority as a means of defending its collective rights usually reaches the point of secession and contradicts respect for individual human or even the collective rights of another community which has the misfortune to be a subminority within some newborn majority (a former minority which has seceded and attained self-determination).[159]

In fact it is the disputable problem of which subjects are entitled to secession. The problem itself has a long history, and the solution was usually motivated by practical reasons biased by current political interests.[160] This was true in the case of Bosnia-Herzegovina where

---

[158]"Ethno-national groups are essentially collectivities that have found themselves dominated by the moral-cultural agendas of other, larger groups by having been included in nation-state formations where their relative weight is small... While a range of legal and even constitutional provisions can be made for ethno-national minorities, these do not solve the attendant difficulties once mobilization along the ethno-national cleavage has begun... As the severe restraints of communism vanished, all ethno-national collectivities began to mobilize, to identify the new limits of political action and, in the process, to come up against other similar groups. The added difficulty is that during the communist period, most forms of identity other than the national one were weakened, leaving nationhood with functions that it is not necessarily well placed to meet." George Schopflin, "Nationalism and National Minorities in Eastern and Central Europe," Journal of International Affairs, Vol.45, No.1, 1991, p.58.

[159]"It is impossible to sustain the notion that every ethnic group can find its expression in a full-blown nation-state, fly its flag at the United Nations... the process of ethnic separation and the breakdown of existing states will then never be exhausted. Many countries in the world continue to contain numerous ethnic enclaves. Even within those enclaves, further ethnic splinters exist. Moreover, new ethnic 'selves' can be generated quite readily, drawing on fracture lines now barely noticeable. Subtle differences in geography, religion, culture, and loyalty can be fanned into new separatist movements, each seeking their own symbols and powers of statehood." Amitai Etzioni, "The Evils of Self-Determination," Foreign Policy, No.89, Winter 1992-93, p.27.

[160]A good illustration is the evolution of Abraham Lincoln's approach to the issue of secession. In 1848, in reference to the Mexican war, he said: "Any people anywhere being enclined and having the power have the right to rise up and shake off the existing government, and form a new one which suits them better. This is a most valuable, a most sacred right—a right which we hope and believe is to liberate the world. Nor is this right confined to cases in which the whole people of an existing government may choose to exercise it. Any portion of such people that can may revolutionize and make their own so much of the territory as they inhabit." Confronted with the threat of secession by the

the problem was solved entirely along the lines of the old decolonization assumption that the process should take place within administrative and not regional dimensions and the reasons for this reversal were both practical and political. At the practical level it was really difficult, if indeed possible, to proceed with a "velvet divorce" between the different parties involved in mutual conflicts long before the collapse of the former Yugoslav federation. But probably more important were the political determinants of the decolonization approach: if the modern interpretation of the issue of self-determination and secession had been applied, then the case of Serbian secession in Croatia and Bosnia-Herzegovina should have been treated on equally legitimate grounds whereas it was generally ruled out on moral grounds—to a considerable extent because of the non-democratic approach in executing this right adopted by the Serbian side.

In accordance with this approach, "the Arbitrarian Commission established by the Peace Conference on Yugoslavia ('the Badinter Commission') rejected a submission that the Serbian minorities in these republics also possessed the right to self-determination."[161] Hence such a right should be applicable to federal units but not to communities within such units, and this is highly disputable. First, the main argument is based on the assumption that the former Yugoslav republics had the right to leave the federation as guaranteed by the post-World War II Yugoslav constitutions. Formally, they really did have the right but since the divorce had to be approved by all the republics, this made it a virtually hypothetical possibility. Second, in no way did it answer the question as to whether the Serbian self-proclaimed territorial entities in Croatia and Bosnia-Herzegovina should have the legitimate, internationally recognized right to secede the day after they had joined (as they were invited to do) the Bosnian-Croat Federation which was formed in 1994.[162]

South, he stressed in his first Inaugural that "plainly, the central idea of secession is the essence of anarchy." Cited in Emerson, Empire, pp.304 and 450.

[161]"Strategic Policy Issues. The Challenge of Self-Determination," in Strategic Survey 1992-1993, p.26.

[162]Hence, the questions raised by Michael Lind address a very sensitive issue: "If east Germany can join west Germany, by what reasoning can the 90 percent majority of ethnic Albanians in Kosovo be denied accession to Albania, if they choose and can make their

No hard and fast rule can be laid down to answer the question as to who is entitled to secede, but it would seem unwise to declare that this right applies to any communities which can make their choice effective since this replicates the revolutionary aspects of secession and there will always be a significant number of votes in favour as justification. The problem is in fact unsolvable and can be defined in the following way: how to translate a revolutionary act into democratic language?

Another difficulty arises from the fact that all the conflicting parties have their rational motives and, what is more important, all of them interpret their actions in terms of democratic change. And this is the most significant element in the Yugoslav case: when the federation started falling apart (in fact, after adopting the new Constitution in 1974), the nationalistic idea turned into a comfortable basis for new political attitudes. In the general atmosphere of anti-communist euphoria which prevailed throughout Eastern Europe in 1989-1990, the existing historical prejudices between different minorities, which had been suppressed during Tito's rule in accordance with the concept of national homogeneity, evolved into a substitute for the idea of anti-communist democratic change. As a result, the latter became identified with claims for national self-determination on a secessionist basis. Once this process had exploded, it began to create established facts in a far from democratic way, albeit in accordance with democratic procedures, and this in turn determined the response.

Legitimacy, Minorities, and Majority Rule

The issue of legitimacy—both the legitimacy of the process of transforming the system and the legitimacy of the political elites—was the next crucial one after the collapse of communism. In both cases, one generally acknowleged source of legitimacy was the popular vote. However, the Balkans provides one of the most blatant examples of what is known in political theory as democratic majoritarian dictatorship which refers to a situation in which a minority, which would have been outvoted anyway, faces the choice of either becoming subordinate at

---

choice effective? How can compact populations of Bosnian Croats be forbidden by the international community from voluntarily merging with Croatia (the very international borders of which are recent and fluid)?" Michael Lind, "In Defense of Liberal Nationalism," Foreign Affairs, Vol.73, No.3, May/June 1994, p.98.

its own expense or of violating democratic procedures.[163]

According to traditional democratic procedures, which recognize the popular vote as the sole source of legitimacy, the formally democratic act of having a referendum, or winning a parliamentary election after a strongly nationalistic campaign, is sufficient to legitimize the subordination of a minority.[164] But the act of secession in ethnically-intermingled regions always leads to the creation of another subminority which will most certainly be outvoted. All the secessions which have occurred in former Yugoslavia were legitimate from the procedural point of view. In a plebiscite held on 23 December 1990, 88.5% of the participants voted for a sovereign and independent state of Slovenia. Slovenia was the most ethnically homogeneous republic and the plebiscite did not provoke ethnic strife. But a precedent had been set that was mechanically applied in two other republics which had a much more complex ethnical composition.

Following the same majoritarian pattern, a referendum was held in Croatia in May 1991. An overwhelming majority of the eligible voters—86%—took part and 94% of them voted for independence. The fact that the prevailing majority of the Serbian minority (12% of the republic's population) boycotted the referendum was a detail of secondary importance.[165] A similar referendum was held in Bosnia on

---

[163]"The principle of majority rule prescribes that in choosing among alternatives, the alternative preferred by the greater number is selected... If a deadlock occurs in a choice between two alternatives that are very highly ranked by the respective partisans, then violence and civil war may well result... Hence, in any case where citizens are split into roughly equal groups, each preferring its own alternative and the rejection of the other group's alternative to such values as social peace, avoidance of violence, national cohesion, etc., no solution compatible with the rule is possible. For in this case deadlock—the only formally compatible condition—will not be accepted, and one side will seek to impose its preferences on the other by any means at its disposal. Thus the majority principle would have to be set aside." Robert A. Dahl, A Preface to Democratic Theory (Chicago: The University of Chicago Press, 1956), p.37.

[164]See, for example, Charles R. Beitz, Political Theory and International Relations (Princeton: Princeton University Press, 1979), pp.112-114.

[165]Not all the Serbs in Croatia boycotted the referendum—part of the urban Serbs took part in it, possibly expecting some economic advantages from an independent Croatian state. But it was not the case for the Serbian minority as a whole and especially for the rural Serbs. The boycott was the only democratic option for them since they would have been outvoted at the republican (later state) level anyway. However, participation in the

1 March 1992, which was also boycotted by the Serbs. And the holding of these referenda, especially the one in Bosnia-Herzegovina, was even recommended by the EC as a means of providing a legitimate basis for recognizing the new states. So, from the formal juridical point of view, the problem was completely solved and nobody really cared that the referenda (especially the Bosnian one) had been overwhelmingly boycotted by the future (new) minorities. But, from the formal point of view of the majoritarian approach, it did not make the results any less legitimate;[166] it only made them illegitimate from the point of view of consensus-building strategies.

This is one aspect of the majority rule trap. The other aspect is connected with the nature of plebiscitarian mechanisms. The problem is that, historically, the principle of self-determination, as implemented through a plebiscite in the form of a referendum, is a political instrument for dissolving broader and complex social entities into smaller but more homogeneous segments. Any kind of plebiscitary approach divides the community, destroys existing ties, capsulates the different ethnic groups, and forces their members to choose the right side from one of the two or more opposed sides in a political or other kind of conflict. A plebiscite highlights the differences at the expense of the similarities. Since a referendum is a perfect, i.e. formally democratic and legitimate, means of splitting a multiethnic community, it has very little to do with democracy when applied to such issues as nation building. It is a democratic instrument applicable to constantly changing political processes (for example, changing a government or even a political system) or in cases where it is aimed at establishing existing attitudes. A referendum can be a dangerous tool if its results are used as a basis for justifying decisions which have been taken, especially in the domain of ethnic relations where the period of the effective influence of such decisions is measured not in years but in generations.

---

referendum would have legitimized its results.

[166]The Bosnian case is strong evidence of the above-mentioned evolution of the approach to self-determination: "The basis of self-determination today is no longer ethnic or cultural but rather territorial, to which has been added, for good measure, the classic majoritarian principle, which does not address the disturbing question of the 'tyranny of the majority.'" Alexis Heraclides, "Secession, Self-Determination and Nonintervention: In Quest of a Normative Symbiosis," Journal of International Affairs, Vol.45, No.2, Winter 1992, p.404.

Another aspect of the majority rule trap is the ability of a newly created state to execute the majority's choice. Winning a referendum is only the first step; the next step is implementing the decision. As a rule, a referendum is held, first, when a government is sure that it will win (precisely the case in Croatia and Bosnia), and, second, if it has sufficient power to enforce the results. The latter requirement is especially important in cases of referenda for independence. In some respects, the Croatian government—bearing in mind the impossibility of solving the Kninska Krajina problem—but in particular the Bosnian government could not fulfil this requirement.

This makes the process of further national self-determination dependent on constant external participation, which in turn raises the question of the survivability of the newly created states, not only economically but politically and militarily too. Are these states based on any real grounds or are they artificial, quasi, and phantom states? Can they survive in the long term without a constant external presence? If not, are the moral arguments sufficient justification for their constant external support? In broader terms, it simply means that the proliferation of states on the basis of secessionist self-determination may lead to the collapse of the existing international order.[167] Of course, this was not a new phenomenon; it was known from the experiences of many post-colonial states. But the fact that it was taking place in Europe, in countries at a presumably high level of civilizational development, made the issue that much more shocking.

From today's perspective it is obvious that support for the majoritarian approach and quests for independence were determined by international influences although this does not alter the point about the inadequacy of the motives for such responses. After the first steps in this direction had proved to be successful, the existing precedents were

---

[167]"Self-determination, in fact, was given more attention than long-term survivability... fundamental to the notion of decolonization was the idea that people could best govern themselves when free from shackles, or even the influences, of foreigners. The idea, then, that states... could be simply unable to function as independent entities was... offensive to the notion of self-determination... The disintegration of the Soviet Union and Yugoslavia over the last two and a half years has created almost 20 new states... One hopes that most will succeed, but lack of experience in government, weak civic institutions, limited economic prospects, and ethnic strife will inevitably reduce some to helplessness—a condition in which Bosnia, with its civil war, now finds itself." Gerald B. Helman and Steven R. Ratner, "Saving Failing States," Foreign Policy, No.89, Winter 1992-93, p.4.

themselves justification for claims.[168] But the real problem was that secession-oriented self-determination on the basis of majority rule did not implement the basic aim—the real, as against the declarative, defence of human rights, both individual and collective.

The next subtopic—the legitimacy of the elites—is also closely related to the minorities' issue and mobilization based on nationalism. The problem is that when the transition to democracy begins, all the political actors are equally illegitimate—the representatives of the old elites because they had previously never been elected by popular vote as well as the new emerging elite because it has not yet been elected by popular vote. Like the communists in the 1940s, their only source of legitimacy is their historical right. The first free elections legitimized the new elites, but they also complicated the problem by legitimizing a significant part of the old ones too.[169] However, at the end of the 1980s, they all had limited possibilities for choosing from among different bases of mobilization, both for electoral purposes and for post-electoral support. Nationalist-based mobilization was not only the cheapest and easiest but also the only feasible one in view of the devastated economies.

The massive use of nationalist or patriotic appeals was the final element in the evolution of the process of democratic change into

---

[168]"What has changed after the series of 'velvet' revolutions is not the release of the genie of nationalism out of a tightly capped bottle but essentially two things: the language of the discourse where it is no longer necessary to pay lip-service to the dominant jargon and, much more importantly, the international status quo where an attempt can be made nowadays... to realize the claims articulated in this discourse... The Yugoslavs watched closely the developments in the Baltic, and the bewilderment of Croat and Slovene secessionists was sincere when they asked why they should not be recognized if Estonians, Lithuanians, and Latvians could be." Maria Todorova, "Ethnicity, Nationalism and the Communist Legacy in Eastern Europe," East European Politics and Societies, Vol.7, No.1, Winter 1993, p.149.

[169]The second and the third wave of parliamentary elections complicated the picture even more, bringing back to power (this time by popular vote) the former communist parties and raising the difficult question as to whether the old regime was so totally imposed from above without any support from below as it was generally perceived. This also created some confusion about what policies to support—institutionalized parliamentary democracy (together with the possibility of leftist parties gaining power) or quasi revolutionary right-wing or nationalistic, reaching out for historical, not procedural, sources of legitimacy. On these new confusions, see Anne Applebaum, "The Fall and Rise of the Communists," Foreign Affairs, Vol.73, No.6, November/December 1994, pp.8-12.

secessionist self-determination.[170] Since it was a means of dissolving empires, secessionist democratization initially won Western governmental support, and any idea or personality opposing communism—according to the clear-cut scheme, also declaring the aim of national self-determination which was perceived as an alternative to totalitarian communist internationalism—was automatically launched into political orbit. The result, and at later stages in the conflict one of its causes, was the deepening of cleavage lines and the fragmentation of multiethnic societies. Naturally, the different ethnicities' elites played according to the rules and had to accept the tempting strain of self-determination in order to ensure their own political survival.[171]

Non-Secessionist Self-Determination and the Limits to Minority Rights

The Yugoslav option which has just been discussed was in many cases unique, at least for the historical reasons which have already been mentioned. However, since it was widely televised it became the symbol of a possible form of post-communist disintegration. Thus the former Yugoslav experience was a contribution, although a tragically expensive one, to Europe's awareness of ethnic potential. The less televised approach was that of Bulgaria, defined by Secretary of State Eagleburger at the time as an "island of stability."

In the Bulgarian case, historical experience also played an extremely important role. As already mentioned, the country had

---

[170]"Nationalism, an uncomplicated ideology with which the masses can easily identify, has been used by populist politicians to fill the ideological void. Just as in the late nineteenth and early twentieth century... in the late 1980s independent political movements... were able to incorporate nationalist values and symbols into their programs and, on balance, have proved to be quite capable of mobilizing the masses." Zoltan Barany, "Mass-Elite Relations and The Resurgence of Nationalism in Eastern Europe," European Security, Vol.3, No.1, Spring 1994, p.169.

[171]"Increasingly, governments tended to rely on ethnic nationhood for legitimating their power. This signified that although they had achieved power through popular election, the nexus between the rulers and the ruled was regarded as too weak to carry them through the harsh problems of creating markets and facing the criticism that accompanies competitive politics. Unfortunately, making governments ethnic tended to make the states ethnic, which promoted collectivist, anti-individualist values; it made it that much more difficult to establish genuinely legitimate institutions." George Schopflin, "Postcommunism: The Problems of Democratic Construction," Daedalus, Vol.123, No.3, Summer 1994, p.138.

minorities, and hence minority problems, living outside its borders. The only relatively contentious issue was that of the Bulgarian Turks but in this case too the perceived threat was more serious than the real one. Nevertheless, the perceived threat, in this case self-determination and secession, did bias Bulgarian politics and did in fact lead to assimilation attempts during the 1980s.

As mentioned in Chapter 4, these attempts represented a small-scale ethnic conflict which was to shape the future policies of both the state and the minority communities. Both sides joined the transition process with incomparably higher sensitivity to the minority rights issue and the concrete manifestation of this sensitivity was the fact that secession—the reason for the perceived threat in the 1980s—was simply ruled out as an option. Thus, from the very beginning, both sides set certain invisible limits to the minority issue.[172]

The second aspect of the problem was the mutual understanding of the opponents' rationales. The majority's representatives in the democratic political elite had a kind of a guilt complex as a result of the violation of Turkish and Bulgarian Muslim human rights in the 1980s and so they were willing to cooperate. The minorities' representatives were aware of the Bulgarian public's sensitivity to the state integrity issue and their strategy was based on the assumption that this integrity should be maintained. What is more, as citizens of the Bulgarian state,[173] in many cases they felt they were Bulgarians.

The invisible limits were obvious in the debate on the legitimacy of ethnically- and religiously-based political parties. After serious discussion, the registration of such parties was forbidden, and that is

---

[172]Such a "limitation" fits into the existing tradition or even system of ethnic coexistence in the ethnically mixed regions which are still preserved and can be characterized as "a necessity imposed by the reality of establishing linking lines which would overcome the closed nature of the religious and ethnic communities in their everyday life." Tsvetana Georgieva, "Coexistence as a System in the Everyday Life between Christians and Muslims in Bulgaria (Ethnological Study)," in Relations of Compatibility and Incompatibility between Christians and Muslims in Bulgaria, Antonina Zheliazkowa (ed.) (Sofia: International Centre for Minority Studies and Intercultural Relations' Foundation, 1995), p.163.

[173]This is obvious from all the basic documents of the Turkish minority party, the Movement for Rights and Freedoms (MRF), where the integrity of the state and the affiliation to the common fatherland—Bulgaria—is stressed.

one of the reasons why the MRF is registered as a Movement. But, at the same time, the Turkish minority party does exist and for over a year was practically a ruling party—MRF deputies' votes were decisive for the survival of the government which had been formed on the MRF ticket.

The explanation for this paradoxical situation is in fact quite simple: it demonstrates existing de facto consensus that national and religious minorities (in this case—Turkish) exist, that their interests should be represented and their rights defended at the **political** level but within the framework of the existing multinational community, defined as the Bulgarian people. Hence, ethnic tensions are translated into political language which rationalizes ethnic conflict and makes it much more manageable. Of course, "...the potential for violence is always present, and its prevention requires continuous surveillance and management by public authorities. This approach to conflict management is essentially political. Its initial presumption is that the ethnic disputants are behaving as rational actors, deploying their resources to promote and defend group interests that are real, not illusory."[174]

This was not a model that was introduced but rather the result of a peculiar set of circumstances. From today's point of view, however, it is already an existing and functioning model of a non-violent approach to ethnic conflicts. Its core comprises, first, recognition of the inevitable invisible limits to minority rights and, second, the primacy of the multi-ethnic community's integration. In other words, the formula "democracy, i.e. self-determination in a multiethnic state," was treated as inapplicable in the Bulgarian case and the chosen option was "democracy, i.e. constitutional guarantees of minority rights in multiethnic communities." The issue of self-determination was interpreted as "entitling a people to choose its political allegiance, to influence the political order under which it lives, and to preserve its cultural, ethnic, historical, or territorial identity."[175]

---

[174]Milton J. Esman, "Political and Psychological Factors in Ethnic Conflict," in Conflict and Peacemaking in Multiethnic Societies, Joseph V. Montville (ed.) (Lexington: Lexington Books, 1990), p.61.

[175]Morton H. Halperin, David J. Scheffer, Patricia L. Small, Self-Determination in the New World Order (Washington: Carnegie Endowment for International Peace, 1992), p.47.

The issue of invisible limits or, to put it more concisely, limited minority rights, may sound provocative and discriminating. However, the basic assumption is that in every multiethnic community there are some collective, not individual, minority rights which are inevitably limited by definition, due to the fact that they **are** minorities. Especially in intermingled communities with existing historical prejudices (as in the Balkans), this seems to be the only realistic option. Having to choose between full respect of collective and individual minority rights it seems more reasonable to choose the latter.[176] The ideal—absolute equality of collective rights including the right to territorial self-determination through secession—seems on the surface to be advantageous, but in fact it is not. First, it can usually only be executed at the expense of the majority's collective rights and, second, it may turn into an unrealistic promise since attempts to implement this Utopia may lead to violations of minority rights which go beyond the invisible limits.

The basic limitation in this respect concerns the right to secede which is, in fact, part of an agreement between the minority and the state.[177] This agreement elevates the integrity of the multiethnic community to a higher level of priority. It also means that other minority rights should be applicable depending on their impact on the integrity of the broader community. Minority language status is a good case in point. Elevating it to the status of an official language is more than questionable since this may be a direct step and a powerful tool for alienating minorities, a real obstacle to their integration into societies

---

[176]It seems to be true also as a basis of foreign policy: "The unbridled assertion of collective rights, most often expressed as an aspiration to national self-determination, has become a major threat to global stability... The United States should resist the trend toward expanding collective rights. A policy based on American support for collective rights, including political self-determination, will inevitably fail. First, it would tend to put the United States increasingly in the position of arbiter among conflicting claims to a particular homeland... Second, it would inevitably be applied selectively... Third, the expansion of internationally recognized collective rights could lead to conflict with American domestic policies." Robert Cullen, "Human Rights Quandary," Foreign Affairs, Vol.71, No.5, Winter 1992-93, p.85.

[177]"There are two sides to the coin. One is... tolerance and indeed respect for cultural diversity. The key here is for a state to perceive cultural-ascriptive diversity as actually enriching society... The other side of the coin is that various distinct regionally-based groups would, for their part, not question—let alone threaten—the territorial integrity of the state concerned." Alexis Heraclides, "Secessionist Conflagration. What Is to Be Done?" Security Dialogue, Vol.25, No.3, 1994, p.288.

and a far cry from their assimilation. As a result, such an approach may foster the capsulating of the minority which would lay the ground for the dissolution of the multiethnic entity.

The language issue is probably the best illustration of the inevitable limits of minority rights: "in the context of language rights, equal rights for equal individuals would mean that each individual can use in all situations his or her own language. This would, of course, be impractical, and would go beyond actual minority claims."[178] Hence, the only reasonable approach seems to be the guaranteed possibility, but by no means the obligation, to use or study a minority language. Otherwise majority or smaller minority groups' rights (as in the case of the Pomaks) may be violated.

However the problem of limited rights is not that clear. Minority and majority status are usually asymmetrical. Sides which are deprived in some respects are often privileged in others. One of the advantages minorities usually have is access to a distinct culture (that of the majority) which, in broader civilizational terms, means an additional possibility for individual development. A case in point here is the uniqueness of the Pomaks' tradition as a result of their location on the border between Islam and Christianity. Another advantage is the broader political rights of national minorities with recognized dual citizenship, as in the case of the Bulgarian Turks who emigrated to Turkey and participate in parliamentary elections in Bulgaria.[179] This group is also privileged in economic respects—e.g. having the opportunity to receive their pensions in Turkey and still use the Bulgarian health service free of charge.

Another example of the enhanced rights of minorities is the situation where they have the right to choose—the case of national minorities with their own nation-state outside the disputed community. The idea, which is a very rational one, is that the right to secede must

---

[178]Tibor Varady, "Collective Minority Rights and Problems in Their Legal Protection: The Example of Yugoslavia," East European Politics and Societies, Vol.6, No.3, Fall 1992, p.274.

[179]On the eve of parliamentary elections on 18 December 1994, the possibility of significant support for the MRF from Bulgarian Turkish voters in Turkey was strongly debated in the Bulgarian media. Their number is estimated at 150,000 eligible voters. The main question was whether citizens with dual citizenship and who were not resident in Bulgaria had the right to influence Bulgarian internal politics.

be recognized after certain procedural or economic obstacles have been overcome and this may be a test of determination and the real need for secession.[180] However, it would seem reasonable to apply this approach only in cases where a minority has no other possibility of becoming a majority except via secession. When the possibility to choose exists, as in the case of minorities with a national home outside the existing state borders, secession should be ruled out. This is the case with most Balkan minorities that have a right to choose, which majorities do not.[181]

However, there is also a problem with the option of choice since it is based on the assumption that complete freedom of movement, in political as well as economic terms, does exist. As experience of the consecutive migration waves from Bulgaria to Turkey shows, the recipient country is often unable to absorb all the immigrants. Lower population mobility in Europe vis-à-vis the United States also has to be taken into acount. All this makes the choice option less realistic than the consensus-oriented, invisible limits approach.

The application of the principle of self-determination in the Balkans provides direct evidence not only of its complexity but also of its inevitable limitations. The two countries—the former Yugoslavia and Bulgaria—demonstrate completely different approaches to the issue so that we can speak of two models of post-communist handling of the minorities' self-determination problems.

The first model—the former Yugoslavia—is an attempt to realize a consecutive Utopia of absolute equality in the field of minority rights.

---

[180]"The point of erecting inconvenient but surmountable obstacles to secession is not to make secession impossible, but to avoid making it too easy. A second approach, which might or might not be used in conjunction with the first, would be to impose special exit costs, a secession tax as it were, over and above whatever compensation secessionists are required to pay to state or private individuals who will lose property as a result of secession." Allen Buchanan, "Self-Determination and the Right to Secede," Journal of International Affairs, Vol.45, No.2, Winter 1992, p.362.

[181]In fact, this is the approach to minorities' rights in Latvia, to mention an example from another region of Eastern Europe. They are limited on the assumption that "any representative of the other ethnic groups living in Latvia, in case he is not satisfied with the Latvian legislative provisions regarding treatment of non-Latvians or disagree with insufficient representation in the structures of power, they have an option, being able to return to their respective national States where they can exercise their ethno-political rights of self-determination not attainable in a foreign ethno-state." Juris Bojars, "Human and Minority Rights and Policy in Latvia," Research Paper, Riga, 1994, p.11.

It promotes ethnic differences, stressing elements of common affiliation at the expense of the various individual identifications.[182] The inevitable conflicts between loyalty to the group and loyalty to the individual are solved in favour of the group.[183] Its inevitable and logical result is the fragmentation of the existing communities and the atrophy of the social fabric.

The second model—the Bulgarian one—can be defined as non-secessionist, a model which opts for realistically limited and thus defendable minority rights. In some respects it resembles Lijphart's idea of consensual democracy[184]—de facto it is close to the grand coalition model without the possibility of mutual veto and proportionality but with elements of segmental autonomy. This is also indirect evidence that ethnic conflict in the civilized world is more metaphorical than real. Bulgaria has reached (or retains) the level at which "contention and competition are better characterizations of the dynamics of ethnic relations," on which "peaceful contention for status and resources is usually channeled through legitimate political activity, legally sanctioned cultural expression, and acceptable political behavior."[185]

---

[182]"Under normal circumstances, most human beings can live happily with multiple identifications and enjoy moving between them as the situation requires. Sometimes, however, one or another of these identities will come under pressure from external circumstances... Conflict between loyalty to a national state and solidarity with an ethnic community, within or outside the borders of that state, may lead to accusations of 'dual loyalties'... For the individual, or at any rate for most individuals, identity is usually 'situational,' if not always optional... Collective identities, however, tend to be pervasive and persistent. They are less subject to rapid changes and tend to be more intense and durable... This is especially true of religious and ethnic identities, which even in pre-modern eras often became politicized. It is practically true of national identities today." Anthony D. Smith, "National Identity and the Idea of European Unity," International Affairs, Vol.68, No.1, 1992, p.59.

[183]Such a legal structure "that privileges the members of one ethnically defined nation over the residents in a particular state" is defined by Robert M. Hayden as "constitutional nationalism." Robert M. Hayden, "Constitutional Nationalism in the Formerly Yugoslav Republics," Slavic Review, Vol.51, No.4, Winter 1992, p.655.

[184]Lijphart, Democracy, pp.25-44.

[185]Martin O. Heisler, "Ethnicity and Ethnic Relations in the Modern West," in Conflict, Montville (ed.), p.27.

All secessions in the Balkans have led to the creation of a new minority which obtains the same rights to repeat the precedent. This means that the solution to the problem of minority rights does not lie in atomizing existing communities but in providing constitutional guarantees for these rights and giving priority to the communities' integrity. The highest priority should be given to the preservation of multiethnic communities even at the expense of certain rights—on a larger scale the balance will be in favour of the minorities' situation.

Hence, self-determination in multiethnic communities can only be viable if secession on the grounds of the majoritarian approach is not considered as an option. The existing borders should be treated as an inviolable framework within which an optimum number and degree of minority rights should be guaranteed. The criterion for that optimum is the survivability of the multinational or multiethnic entity as a social body.

This does not mean that the former Yugoslav federation should have been kept at all costs. It does mean, however, that any dismantling of the existing state entities or changes to existing borders should be preceded by the development of the corresponding legal basis. A separate issue is whether it would have been possible to achieve this in the conditions under which democratization virtually exploded in Eastern Europe. Probably it would not have been, which does not however make the result of the trial and error change any more justifiable.

The delay in amending the legal framework to coincide with the dynamics of the events inevitably led to the equally justifiable but conflicting rationales of the different parties to the conflicts. For the Croats, the Slovenes, the Macedonians and the Bosnian Muslims, the actions on the part of the Serbian authorities were already a violation of the constitutional agreements between the republics significant enough to nullify the federation itself, as in the case of the "Great Bank robbery" in 1990.[186] On the other hand, until 1992, the Serbs' actions had a certain, albeit dubious, degree of justification as they were at least formally in line with the preservation of the then still

---

[186]Before the December 1990 elections in Serbia, the Serbian government empowered the National Bank of Serbia to rediscount the equivalent of US$ 1.7 billion in bank loans. The money was used to pay salaries and pensions and this created an extremely positive image of Milosovic and his party which won the elections. But the "Great Bank robbery" blocked the stabilization programme initiated by Ante Markhovic.

existing **de jure** Yugoslav Federation. In this ambiguous situation, it was inevitable that the moralistic approach was adopted as the basis for explaining and justifying the different parties' actions. Moralism alone, however, is a questionable basis for policy making.

CHAPTER 6
THE CONFLICTS IN THE BALKANS
AND THE INTERNATIONAL COMMUNITY

The evolution of the crisis in the Balkans has been a stubborn process of shedding illusions. The ease with which the communist system in Europe collapsed together with the spectacular, surgical, US-led operation in the Iraqi desert created the illusion that local crises were easy to manage. But this has now been completely dispelled by the long-lasting bloody conflict in the former Yugoslavia and those in Russia where the case of Chechnya is just one blatant example.

The basic reason for these illusions was the explosion of democracy, but the political and security community was not conceptually prepared for the rapid change and the new political challenge following the collapse of the communist system and the USSR. Hence, decisions on newly emerging problems have been taken on the basis of the current process of trial and error and it has already become clear that many of these decisions were miscalculated. As a result, during the last four years, serious mistakes have been made in managing crises. These miscalculations have predetermined current West European and American moves and today's decisions are a kind of justification for those former mistakes. In many cases, these miscalculated moves now preclude the possibility of taking any action even assuming that there is the willingness to do so.

In this respect, the Balkan crisis also highlighted a serious conceptual gap. On the one hand, it was a result of the momentum of the bipolar logic which reduced the number of political actors to the two constellations dominated by the two super-powers, so that all possible contradictions, including ethnic ones, were subordinated to the dominant global political and ideological conflict. On the other hand, all institutional solutions and security structures were designed to meet the needs and requirements of this bipolar logic and these structures were not capable of tracing and responding to other types of contradiction especially ethnic ones. Hence, the miscalculation of the danger ethnic conflicts, to which the Balkans is extremely susceptible, was a certain extent preordained, as were the possible approaches solving them.

The Participants in the Conflicts and their Interests

The first significant change in the international environment in the Balkans, as highlighted by the Yugoslav crisis, was the multiplication of the participants involved in ethnic and minority conflicts. They now consist of two significant groups of political actors, local and external ones. The group of local participants includes:

- local communities (ethnically-motivated electorates);
- local elites (usually the local leaderships of ethnically-based political organizations);
- local administrations (including the governments of newly proclaimed, ethnically-based independent entities);
- local Mafia structures which were built up as a result of economic and arms embargoes (comprising both local and external participants).

The group of external participants includes:

- external Mafia structures;
- foreign governments of the new Great Powers (in the Yugoslav case, the United States, France, Great Britain, Germany, and Russia);
- foreign governments of the new local powers (Greece, Serbia, and Turkey);
- international organizations and alliances.

Unlike the bipolar era, all these participants currently have distinct terests which create a complicated network of motivations.

The interesting point, however, is that these motivations have n been thought up ad hoc, that is to say that the policy priorities set not before but in the process of policy making in response to quirements of events on the ground as and when they occurred. In addition, the decision making was often not based on proper of the current situation but was deeply rooted in historical es and prejudices.

ese historical prejudices were also broadly used for n by the media which often constructed a biased picture of orresponding to the expectations of both the publics and tes. The most evident examples in this respect—although different reasons and produced under completely ons—were the media policies, which were strongly enophobic in Serbia and contained a clear pro-Muslim bias in the United States.[187]

In some respects the various participants' interests are coherent, but the impression of clear-cut cleavages between them is misleading since it is not that obvious which parties to the conflict are interested in solving it in a peaceful manner and which are not. The clear-cut approach (the victims who want to stop the conflict and the aggressor who does not) is biased by secondary political interests, and these contradicting attitudes conceal parallel, if not similar, attitudes.

One particular similarity of interests—between the Serbs and the Croats in Bosnia-Herzegovina—has already been discussed. Another is between the Bosnians in Bosnia-Herzegovina and the Croats in Croatia. In general, given Serbian ambitions, both the Bosnian Muslims and Bosnian Croats are interested in preserving the existence and integrity of the newly created nation-states and in fostering the process of nation building which is probably the best evidence that, as Charles Tilly puts it, "war made the state, the state made war, and both together made nationalism."[188] This general interest is sufficiently strong to help overcome mutual claims and distrust. But, as experience has already shown, the Bosnian-Croat alliance is still quite fragile. The same ambiguous similarity of interests is true of the Croats in Croatia and the Croats in Bosnia-Herzegovina: the latter have a traditionally more secessionist attitude and are the main supporters of Bosnia-Herzegovina's truncation between Croatia and Serbia. That is why, in many cases, the interests of the Croats in Croatia are closer to those of the Muslims in Bosnia than to those of the Croats in Bosnia.

---

[187]The case of Serbian manipulation is broadly explored. The interesting case in this respect is the media policy in the Western democracies. One of the few books on this issue, and probably the only one in the West so far, is a collection of articles published in Berlin in 1994. As related by Jacques Merino in his interview with the director of the Radar Fin public relations agency, the image of the Serbs as unquestioned evil and of the rest as unquestioned victim was consciously constructed without taking into consideration the objectivity of the information. See Klaus Bitterman (ed.), Serbien muss Sterben. Wahrheit und Lüge im jugoslawischen Bürgerkrieg (Berlin: Edition Tiamat, 1994). Peter Brock also questions the professionalism of some prominent journalists reporting from the former Yugoslavia who already had a clear-cut picture of the events before exploring them. One of them, the Pulitzer-winning Ray Gutman, even declared that "he had abandoned strict objectivity in his coverage in order to pressure governments to act." Peter Brock, "Dateline Yugoslavia: The Partisan Press," Foreign Policy, No. 93, Winter 1993-1994, p.165.

[188]See Charles Tilly, Coercion, Capital and European States (Oxford: Blackwell, 1990).

Separation of ethnically-motivated electorates as a distinct interest group from the local elites is an indicator of the differences (or at least lack of similarities) between the two. These differences derive from the elites' widely used opportunities to treat and use minority groups instrumentally. The problem is not just limited to the sources of the new elites' legitimacy (discussed in Chapter 5), but it is also linked to the propagation of these sources, the question of renewing the status quo which determines the very existence of these already formed elites. In this respect, the case of the Bosnian Muslims is most evident and the obvious interest of the people (the electorate) lies in stopping the war. However, from the point of view of the local elites and the warlord structures which have already been formed, the conflict is a brutal, bloody but reliable means of integration on a nationalistic basis.[189] Moreover, it is the most effective instrument of nation building. Each new victim substantiates the internal grounds for the Bosnian nation's legitimacy and hence contributes to the formal, external, sources of legitimacy which predominated in 1992-1993 mainly in the form of international recognition of the republic as an independent state. Before the war, for political purposes—first Tito's and subsequently the local politicians'—religious identification was given the status of national belonging. Since the war religion is no longer the only source of that belonging.[190]

Again, in a very paradoxical way, the Bosnian elite's interests are quite similar to those of the local Serbs—they too need the war. The conflict had already structuralized the communities and created new social roles, corresponding directly to a state of war. There are already whole strata within the social hierarchy (not necessarily Mafia structures) which derive their political importance from the conflict.

---

[189]"In a warlord system, military chiefs follow a spatial strategy of acquisition. Each chief struggles to obtain exclusive control over a body of people and their belongings by carving out and securing against competitors the territory in which they live. A distinguishing feature of a warlord system is the effort by political-military enterpreneurs to secure for themselves a populated territory and its inhabitants by offering protection against rival lords and roving bandits." See Henk Houweling, "Peacekeeping After State Collapse," in Peacekeeping Challenges to Euro-Atlantic Security, Ernest Gilman and Detlef E. Herold (eds.) (Rome: NATO Defense College, 1994), p.93.

[190]When the conflict in Bosnia-Herzegovina erupted, Henry Kissinger wrote that "Bosnia is not a nation in any except a geographic sense." But it would be more precise to use the past tense—it was not before the war.

Without the war, the local Serbs would have had two options—being a minority in a Muslim state or a minority in a greater Serbian one. In neither case would they have been the subject of big politics and a sufficient number of people in the political elite realize that. The economic level—feeding the already emerged Mafia structures and supplying all parties to the conflict—is only the most obvious element in this respect.[191]

The interests of the Serbs in Serbia are also three-tiered (electorate, elites, Mafia structures) and as a rule correspond to the general map of interests, but with one important difference—the Belgrade regime's interests are defined much more over the longer term. That is why it would be a serious mistake to identify the Belgrade regime's interests, or, in broader terms, those of the Serbs in Serbia, as corresponding to the interests of the Serbian minorities outside Serbia. The idea of a Greater Serbia is of secondary importance in comparison with the new roles and identities of the different communities structured by the war.

For many reasons, including international isolation and the severe economic difficulties resulting from the embargo,[192] the Serbs in Serbia are much more inclined to participate in some kind of peace agreement. It was Belgrade that started to push for signing the peace plan in 1993 and it was the local Serbian parliament which rejected it. Probably the Belgrade regime understands that in the long term it is impossible for the state to exist outside the international framework and in total isolation.[193] Direct evidence of such attitudes was the pressure and embargo imposed on the Bosnian Serbs by Belgrade in 1994 in return for easing international sanctions against rump Yugoslavia.

---

[191]The existence of such structures gives reasonable grounds for the rumours, which abounded in November 1993, that "Serbian arms and ammunition were at least partly responsible for the emergence of the Muslim-dominated Bosnian army as a real fighting force in the course of the year." Patrick Moore, "Croatia and Bosnia: A Tale of Two Bridges," RFE/RL Research Report, Vol.3, No.1, 7 January 1994, p.115.

[192]On the effect of the embargo on the Serbian economy, see M.R. Palairet, "How Long Can the Milosevic Regime Withstand Sanctions?" RFE/RL Research Report, Vol.2, No.34, 27 August 1993, pp.21-25.

[193]For more details, see Marie-Janine Calic, "The Serbian Question in International Politics," Aussenpolitik, Vol.45, No.2, 1994, pp.146-155.

At the same time, Belgrade has a strategic interest in dragging out the war as a source of legitimacy for the regime. As already mentioned, from the very beginning the nationalistic conflict was a way of absorbing former communist power (and probably also structures such as the army and intelligence) into the new post-communist environment. The attitude to the sanctions is also somewhat paranoid: the Serbian economy is really suffering from the embargo but, on the other hand, the embargo is a comfortable excuse for incompetent management. Furthermore, a centralized economy, like the Serbian one, is relatively efficient only in extraordinary situations such as a state of war.

After its consequent engagement on the Bosnian side, the US Administration, together with the Europeans, did in fact save Milosevic's post-communist or, rather, crypto-communist regime, thereby creating new sources for its legitimacy. The nationalist legitimacy of the Belgrade regime was augmented by the active image of the external threat. An external enemy was what the Serbian post-communists needed most of all—and they got it. The question is how long this motivation will prevail over the day-to-day difficulties facing the devastated Serbian economy and at what point it will be possible to build a new self-identification.

The external enemy turned out to be the final link in the chain of a new Serbian identification—together with religion (Christianity versus Islam)—and it still remains sufficiently strong. Although the conflict in Yugoslavia did not start out as a religious one, it has now become one. It was not even, or at least in the beginning it was not, an ethnic one—the sides were defined on an ethnic basis but they were not in conflict. The realization of ethnic belonging was not the reason for the conflict but it provided a camouflage. It was mainly a political conflict with territorial and economic overtones rooted in historical prejudices, but it was presented as a purely ethnic and religious conflict in order to conceal the real aims of its participants.[194] As soon as the conflict was translated into ethnic terms all attempts to solve it through

---

[194]Along these lines, "Samuel Huntington, in order to reassert the importance of cultural factors in international politics,... turns liberal and Marxist reductionism on its head, arguing that cultural differences have become the primary facilitator of international conflict rather than one basis (among others) for conflict mobilization." Richard E. Rubenstein and Jarle Crocker, "Challenging Huntington," Foreign Policy, No.96, Fall 1994, p.121.

the application of rational strategies were doomed to failure, simply because "ethnopolitical conflicts are fought not just about resources or power, but about protecting group status, culture, and identity. Identity and belief are non-negotiable...Ethnopolitical movements can energize group members for sustained collective action but have little capacity for political control."[196]

The Great Powers and their Response

In many respects, the interests of the external participants also have an identificational basis. The United States role as the sole military super-power after the collapse of the Soviet Union was challenged by the conflict and in this respect the interests of the United States are two-tiered. The first tier consists of direct military options and possible threats to stability in the region and, in a broader sense, the impact of conflicts on relations with the new democracies in Eastern Europe and especially with Russia. The second tier of strategic American interests concerns the image of a military super-power and its credibility as such.

The American approach to the conflict evolved through several phases. Switch-on, active periods were followed by switch-off periods of reluctance and lack of initiative. But all the time the Balkan conflict was a point of secondary importance and this is understandable given the traditional dominants of US strategic interests. By the middle of 1991 the US Administration had cut its options to appeals for reasonable unity although it understood that this was impossible to combine with the strain for extreme self-determination.

The core idea was in fact to stake on the possibility of limited satisfaction to the various Yugoslav ethic groups' claims for independence which resembled too closely the communist solution under Tito. And for that reason these appeals for unity were neither particularly dramatic nor decisive. It would now seem that the US Administration viewed emerging nationalisms as less of a threat than the possible disintegration of the Soviet Union, and this was the next miscalculation. Or at least this is the conclusion that may be drawn from the disregarded CIA warning which predicted precisely the later bloody disintegration of Yugoslavia and suggested that the United

---

[195]Ted Robert Gurr, "Peoples against States: Ethnopolitical Conflict and the Changing World System," International Studies Quarterly, Vol.38, No.3, September 1994, p.365.

States should exert energy and influence to encourage the bloodless break-up of a decaying totalitarian regime.

As a result the American position was extremely ambiguous. This ambiguity was determined in many respects by the fact that the Yugoslav crisis could be interpreted as a possible precedent for an approach to the Soviet case. It would now seem that the policy was constructed according to the logic of a fire extinguisher so that the priorities were changed to meet the currently prevailing bigger threat. In 1991 the bigger threat was the uncontrolled dismantling of the Soviet empire, as if a controlled one were possible; hence, the quest for unity was the first priority on the agenda.[196]

When Croatia and Slovenia began to drift towards independence on 26 June 1991, the first change was made in the American attitude and interests in the region: instead of unity, priority was given to some kind of peaceful, negotiated outcome. When this also turned out to be impossible, the next phase occurred—recognition of Croatia and Slovenia on 10 March 1992 and of Bosnia-Herzegovina on 7 April 1992. At this point first-tier American interests became closer and even similar to those of the other West European countries. At their core is the need to prevent the conflict from spilling over into Kosovo and FYROM and reaching the point at which two NATO member countries, Turkey and Greece, may not only become directly involved, but involved on different warring sides. This means that European and United States interests are also similar to those of the Albanians in Kosovo and FYROM and to those of the Bulgarians and of the Macedonians in FYROM, although this did not do very much to assist with the rapid recognition of the Republic of Macedonia as an independent state. These interests are not however that similar to the Bosnian Muslims'—it is hard to disagree that "an independent Bosnia has nothing to do with US national interests in the general sense that chaos anywhere is a potential enemy. Fighting for Bosnian independence would mean a wrong-headed and nasty war that would merely bring greater instability to the region and more civilian casualties. An indirect approach of constraining the Serbs by putting political and military pressure on Serbia's borders, on the other hand,

---

[196]This is the only explanation for President Bush's statement in his speech in Kiev in August 1991, in which he rejected support for "those who promote a suicidal nationalism based upon ethnic hatred." Cited in US Department of State Dispatch, Vol.2, No.32, 1991, p.596.

would set an example of multilateral European and American commitment to stability."[197]

The second tier of American interests relates to the long-term consequences for the United States image. It is hardly possible to evaluate the effects of this, but loss of credibility in the Islamic world is quite likely and this could create some problems in the future. It is highly probable that the United States will pay a long-term price in relations with its traditional Middle East allies for its failure to intervene on behalf of a Muslim minority. From that point of view, its inability to solve a serious conflict in a vital strategic region or even to formulate consistent pragmatic policy may turn into a long-term failure for the current Administration or at least into a serious challenge for the United States role as the leader of the democratic world. Or maybe this Administration has simply demonstrated a higher degree of isolationism than the previous one; maybe it was the result of a strong desire to concentrate on domestic issues. Whatever the reason, in strategic terms, it resulted in the creation of a vacuum, with the notion that, from the very beginning, the Clinton Administration did not possess the authority that is required to be the sole military super-power.

Another possible explanation is that the Bosnian problem and that of possible involvement were highly dependent on domestic issues, and for that reason periods of activity and eagerness to do something tend to correspond to the intensity of the internal political debate rather than to the conflict itself. Of course, this did not only apply to America. All the Great Powers' responses to the former Yugoslavia issue have, to some degree, been a reaction to their own domestic issues or to distinct historical myths.

Germany's unilateral recognition of Croatia and Slovenia in December 1991 was, on the one hand, a result of the complex relations in the German-Serbo-Croat triangle involving the phantoms of World War II (the German-Croat alliance against the Serbs), which was the basis for allegations for some new edition of these relations at Serbia's expense. On the other hand, recognition was a symbolic gesture—it was a response to the need to have an issue of major importance for

---

[197]Michael G. Roskin, "The Bosnian-Serb Problem: What We Should and Should Not Do," Parameters, Vol.22, No.4, Winter 1992-1993, p.31.

Germany's first foreign policy initiative after reunification.[198]

The French reactions were also deeply rooted in the World War I and II experience with Serbia as a traditional ally, although the spectre of Islamic fundamentalism had a much stronger impact for purely internal reasons. The same applied to Britain—its experience in Northern Ireland inevitably biased its attitude towards the conflict in Bosnia-Herzegovina. At the collective level—that of the European Union—top priority was given to the approval of the Maastricht Union Treaty by Germany and this seems to have been somehow traded against recognition of the two republics on 15 January 1992 by the other EU members. But, despite the differences in their approaches, the Europeans had a clear interest—and a much more tangible one than the Americans—in the former Yuglslavia: keeping the conflict inside the existing borders and preventing any possible elements of destabilization being exported to the EU.

Right up to the very moment of recognition, it was clear that both these new-born states were a long way away from meeting the necessary criteria of statehood. First, they were not in effective control of their own territory, or in this case the territory claimed by them. Second, the grounds for these claims—the internal borders inherited from the former Yugoslavia—reflected a compromise but it was a compromise between completely different requirements to the ones which were now needed. These boundaries reflected the idealistic expectations of the brotherhood of the Yugoslav people and not the real correlation of power in the region. In itself it was potentially capable of producing nationalistic clashes and human rights violations, and this represented the third source of concern.[199] When the EC was directly

---

[198]Up to the beginning of 1992 the United States was seeking possibilities for avoiding the uncontrollable break-up of the Yugoslav federation, attempting to delay official recognition of the new post-Yugoslav states, which, by the way, had not at that time met the conditions of recognition as such. However, "when Bush called Kohl to request delaying German recognition of Slovenia and Croatia, his call was never returned." Paula Franklin Lytle, "U.S. Policy Toward the Demise of Yugoslavia: The Virus of Nationalism," East European Politics and Societies, Vol.6, No.3, Fall 1992, p.313.

[199]According to the British approach, "These countries were recognized as independent states at a time when they manifestly did not fulfil the criteria of statehood that the United Kingdom has always insisted upon for recognition... This premature recognition, in subservience to German pressure, has been an unfortunate example for a common EC foreign policy." Rosalyn Higgins, "The New United Nations and Former

confronted with the issue, this was the reason why it decided to enhance the recognition criteria with respect to human rights, both on a practical and a legal (constitutional) basis. On 17 December 1991 a set of criteria was formulated, including tests of human rights guarantees and guarantees for minorities and arms control, and it was agreed that if the republics passed these tests the EC states would recognize them in January 1992.

However, Germany did not wait and officially recognized Croatia and Slovenia on 23 December: "The Germans maintained that they did not need to wait to see if the EC tests had been passed as they had had assurances from the Croats and the Slovenes."[200] The reason for Germany's persistent pressure to recognize the newly created states was not just its quest for a spectacular beginning to reunited Germany's foreign policy. The German approach was diametrically opposed to the French one and it may well be that differences over recognition presage the beginning of future competition between the two countries over EU leadership after Maastricht.[201]

In addition, Germany had solid reasons to be much more seriously concerned by the conflict and these reasons were not purely historical as is often suggested. By 1991 it was obviously a local high-intensity conflict and its possible impacts could affect most of the neighbouring countries. Germany was the only neighbouring country among the Great Powers and already had problems with its Croatian immigrant community. The prospect of a massive flow of refugees was not inviting and, hence, the attempts to solve the conflict by changing its legal definition as a civil war into its definition as an international one in order to establish a legal basis for engaging international institutions in its resolution.

Yugoslavia," International Affairs, Vol.69, No.3, 1993, p.470.

[200]Trevor C. Salmon, "Testing Times for European Political Cooperation: The Gulf and Yugoslavia, 1990-1992," International Affairs, Vol.68, No.2, 1992, p.253. However, later it turned out that only Slovenia and FYROM met the EC human rights conditions for recognition and that Croatia did not.

[201]On the Franco-German quarrel over recognition, see Pia Christina Wood, "France and the Post Cold War Order: The Case of Yugoslavia," European Security, Vol.3, No.1, Spring 1994, p.131.

From today's perspective, recognition of the newly created states did not help to solve the conflicts but at least it made the picture look simple. The war was perceived in different ways by its participants: from the point of view of the supporters of the united federation, secession was an attempt to change borders by force and thus the war was a means of defending state integrity, a typical civil war; from the perspective of a predominant ethnic group in a secessionist republic, it was a means of defending an independent state; and seen through the eyes of a minority member in a secessionist republic, secession was perceived as an attempt to create a monoethnic state which would threaten the minority's ethnic identity, and the war as a form of resistance for defending this identity. Thus the conflict was civil or international depending on the size of the ethnic group and its geographical location, and the recognition issue was in fact a way of supporting one or another side to the conflict, thereby blurring important nuances in the conflict.

Recognition opened the way to international involvement in the Yugoslav crisis and to NATO's military involvement. Although it was probably not intentional, the prospect of its involvement, which arose after recognition, provided additional arguments to the discussion about NATO's future following the dissolution of the Warsw Pact (WP). The problem was actively debated in 1991-1992 in an atmosphere of post-cold war stability illusions. Additional arguments in the discussion were purely European initiatives which highlighted the increasing degree of re-Europeanization of security matters on the continent—the creation of a Franco-German corps, the revitalization of the Western European Union, and the provisions in the Maastricht Treaty for establishing a common foreign and security policy.

All this probably created a certain notion of allies' alienation, leading, in the case of the Balkans, to disagreement over the methods although an agreement on the aims was reached.[202] In this context the United States recognition of Croatia and Slovenia in April 1992 was

---

[202]"The Americans are beginning to face in the defense field what they have grown accustomed to in the economic sphere—pre-cooked, non-negotiable European positions. In the defense and security arena, European and American views should not often diverge; but, as policy toward the Bosnian arms embargo showed, that cannot be guaranteed. When the Europeans have to choose between giving primacy to NATO or to EC considerations... the EC usually wins out." Jonathan Clarke, "Replacing NATO," Foreign Policy, No.93, Winter 1993-94, p.27.

probably motivated not only by the idea of internationalizing the conflict but also by the need to maintain some sort of consensus within NATO. The only shocking part of that move was the recognition of Bosnia-Herzegovina too, which, least of all the former republics, responded to the criteria of an independent state and was the most evident example of the above-mentioned brotherhood compromise. If it was a purely moralistic act, it would have serious political consequences, and if it was a gesture to the US allies in the Middle East, it was a half-way solution.

Russia had a completely distinct set of interests. From the very beginning of the Balkan crisis, the USSR, and later Russia, was present, directly or indirectly—indirectly as a constant concern of the Bush Administration in respect of the possible implications of the collapse of Yugoslavia as a precedent for the USSR with all the attendant threats to security and stability. Later, after the collapse of the empire, the case of Yugoslavia could be treated as a precedent again, this time both in respect of Russia's approach to its minorities in the near abroad and to the issue of secession in its autonomous regions.

This precedence predetermined Russia's questionable approach to the conflict. It could neither support the right of the Croats, the Bosnian Muslims, and the Slovenes to secede because it would have opened the way for its own non-Russian minorities to do so, nor could it fully support punishment of the Serbs because this would have destroyed its own options to act on behalf of Russian minorities living outside its borders.[203] In this case, the historical ties are of secondary importance and they were in fact used later as a justification when Russian policy became more pro-Serbian-oriented—as a result of both the Americans' Bosnian bias and of Russia's gradual orientation towards a tougher policy on secessionist issues.

The Balkans is a unique region in which different sets of interests meet and often collide. The former Yugoslavia crisis is the most evident example as it outlined the extremely complicated network

---

[203]"A related reason for many people in Moscow to oppose the use of international peacekeeping forces in Bosnia against the will of Serbia is fear that a similar fate could await Russia. Russians have frequently drawn parallels between the collapse of the USSR and the breakup of Yugoslavia, and the prospect of UN-sponsored Blue Berets streaming into the Dniester republic or South Ossetia does not appeal to Russia." Suzanne Crow, "Russia Adopts a More Active Policy," RFE/RL Research Report, Vol.2, No.12, 19 March 1993, p.4.

of interests of the potential participants (both internal and external) in the conflict. It demonstrated at least that neither NATO nor other international institutions can act as a super-power if only for the lack of a monolithic coherent interest. Each party to the conflict can usually find some kind of support among the outside actors, and the latter have their own rationales which correspond both to their historical experience (including deeply rooted prejudices) and to their current political and economic interests. The result is hesitation and reluctance to do anything concrete to stop the war. Working out a common, unanimously approved approach to the conflict turned out to be a Utopia and each step is some kind of a compromise which is inevitably perceived and treated by the participants as inconclusive.

This is the reason why, after the outbreak of war in the former Yugoslavia, the minorities' issue in the Balkans took on completely new dimensions. Since the rights of some majorities are still open to question, the minorities' issue is impossible to solve out of some broader security network efficient enough not only to regulate the existing tensions but also to prevent the development of ethnic competition into open conflict and clashes.

CHAPTER 7
THE MINORITIES' ISSUE IN A SECURITY FRAMEWORK

What kind of policies can be built into such a fragmented and multi-tiered map of interests in a region like the Balkans that is so susceptible to historical myths? In general, it is true that conflict in the Balkans was a "typically nineteenth-century Balkan-style problem which cried out for a nineteenth-century concert-style solution in which the great powers imposed solutions on the lesser powers, recognizing the military balance on the ground, to be sure, but making clear to the victor that no more fighting would be tolerated."[204] Similar is the approach according to which the problem could be solved by Western intervention at the first stage of the conflict.[205] But in the case in question it was impossible—not least because nobody was willing to pay the price. It is also important that "the qualities of Western societies that lead to public pressure to do something also put severe limits on Western abilities to translate words into practice...Western cultures...find it hard to understand codes of behaviour based on fanaticism, machismo and paranoia, as well as political structures based on ethnic loyalties."[206]

The other and probably more important reason for Western inertia was the lack of a broader concept of European security after the dissolution of the WP and the collapse of communism. Any regional

---

[204]Harvey Sicherman, "Winning the Peace," Orbis, Vol.38, No.4, Fall 1994, p.532. The possibility of building a new European post-cold war security order based on the nineteenth- century principle of the Concert of Europe, consisting of the United States, the (then) Soviet Union, Britain, France, and Germany was proposed by Charles A. Kupchan and Clifford A. Kupchan in "Concerts, Collective Security, and the Future of Europe," International Security, Vol.16, No.1, Summer 1991, pp.151-161.

[205]On the possible steps and limits to the engagement of the West, see Sabrina P.Ramet, "The Yugoslav Crisis and the West: Avoiding 'Vietnam' and Blundering into 'Abyssinia'," East European Politics and Societies, Vol.8, No.1, Winter 1994, pp.202-203.

[206]Pierre Hassner, "Beyond Nationalism and Internationalism: Ethnicity and World Order," Survival, Vol.35, No.2, Summer 1993, p.60.

commitment could only take place against the background of a broader framework of priorities, and this is still missing. Located in a region that is complex in security terms, the Balkan countries' security concerns are so closely linked together "that their national securities cannot realistically be considered apart from one another."[207]

In the existing security vacuum, these concerns can only be approached within a broader regional framework extending beyond the Balkans. This brings us to the broader issue of the possible institutionalization of East European security, of which the Balkans is part. However, the problem is not just an East European one since European security is indivisible and an unstable Eastern part of the continent is a major threat for the Western part too. But does the indivisibility of European security necessarily imply a common European security structure? If so, is such a structure feasible in a still divided Europe? And is such a structure a necessary condition for the final success of the democratization process in the Eastern part of the continent or a consequence of this process?

Filling the Security Vacuum: The NATO Option

Before answering these questions, the threats to European security must be defined.[208] In general, there are two sources of potential threats. The first is the danger of a Russian imperial revival after the possible failure of democratic reforms and a nationalistic renaissance. The second is the possibility of high-intensity local conflicts on an ethnic or national basis in the former WP countries, including Russia.

Hence, two hypotheses may be formulated: first, any European security solution has to deal with two different sets of problems and, second, different problems require different instruments for their solution. The first set of problems is closer to the paradigm of deterrence while the second one is closer to the balance of power. However, it is doubtful whether a security structure meeting both

---

[207]Barry Buzan, People, States and Fear: An Agenda for International Security Studies in the Post-Cold War Era (New York: Harvester Wheatsheaf, 1991), p.190.

[208]For a detailed analysis of the possible threats, wars, and the responses to them, see Charles L. Glaser, "Why NATO is Still Best. Future Security Arrangements for Europe," International Security, Vol.18, No.1, Summer 1993, pp.5-50.

requirements is at all possible.

But what is more important is that by engaging one type of instrument this inevitably leads to the simulation of an environment corresponding to these instruments, which initiates its evolution towards what has been anticipated from the point of view of the applied approach characteristics. Of course, there is a good deal of reason in the assumption that "the prospect of Visegrad Group's membership in NATO will threaten Russia only when she defines her interest in terms of restoring her control over the territory of the former USSR, which, at the next stage, will also imply efforts to establish control over East-Central Europe. Thus, assuming the interests of Russia and the West are in conflict, exclusion of the Visegrad Group from the Western security arrangements becomes a victory for Russia."[209]

This may be exactly the case when building a security strategy on the assumption that a Russian threat has to be faced, but it is oversimplifying matters to narrow the field down to the possible revitalization of Russian nationalists in response to some sort of closer cooperation between Western and Central and Eastern Europe. The difficulty is that the first paradigm—deterrence—is a logical consequence of the possible, and actively debated, redrawing of the European map. It is built up on the assumption that Russia is a real threat to the former WP allies and that at least the Visegrad Four (Poland, Hungary, the Czech Republic, and Slovakia) should be given security guarantees against falling into the Russian sphere of influence. The difficulty however is, first, who should get the guarantees and what should happen to the others? If some countries join NATO, which is the requested form of guarantee, the Alliance's new Eastern border will immediately turn into a new demarcation line across the continent. The countries beyond this line "would fall back into the Russian sphere of influence... the Russian empire would again take shape. An extensive enlargement of the Western alliance to Russia's frontiers for its part

---

[209]Antoni Kaminski, "East-Central Europe between the East and the West," European Security, Vol.3, No.2, Summer 1994, p.311. But, to put it another way, if Russia does not define her interest... (as above) and hence will not perceive the Visegrad Group's membership in NATO as a threat, then what is the reason for that membership?

would neither be acceptable to Moscow nor to Washington."[210]

In other words, the question as to whether to extend NATO eastwards or not can only be answered after solving the problem of whether there are vital Western interests to justify a new deterrent strategy. The answer seems to be in the negative. Since most wars in the East would not directly threaten Western security, from the Western point of view "consequently, extending security guarantees in these cases would not be justified by standard security concerns. The key exception appears to be wars launched by Russia to re-establish the subjugation of Central Europe. This line of argument suggests that the West might offer conditional security guarantees to some of the countries of Central Europe—the West would offer to protect them against Russia, but not each other."[211]

However, the idea of enlargement has many supporters and not just among the East Europeans. The latters' interest in entering the sole existing and effective collective defence alliance is understandable, especially after the dissolution of the WP and in the face of the security vacuum which now exists. The arguments in favour of NATO membership are numerous and in fact promote the obvious idea that it is better to be healthy and rich than ill and poor. At the same time, however, there is no clear idea as to how to achieve it. On the other hand, the major concerns of Western advocates of NATO enlargement are primarily Western, not Eastern, security concerns and NATO's future after the end of the Cold War. In broader terms, Western security really depends on the stability of the democratic transition in the Eastern part of the continent and any support of this process is in favour of Western security. However, it is still an open question as to whether security guarantees via NATO membership would provide a stable framework for democratization or, rather, whether the unstable political situation of the possible new NATO members would affect the Alliance's integrity and effectiveness. One of the approaches in favour of NATO's enlargement refers to the membership of former dictatorships in the Organization and points out that "NATO membership helped stabilize democracy and stem authoritarian backsliding in Portugal, Spain, Greece and Turkey...the need for a stable

---

[210]Lothar Ruehl, "European Security and NATO's Eastward Expansion," Aussenpolitik, Vol.45, No.2, 1994, p.121.

[211]Glaser, "Why," p.14.

security framework is greater when democracy is most fragile and threatened..." The conclusion is that "if NATO does not address the primary security challenges facing Europe today, it will become increasingly irrelevant. NATO must go out of area or it will go out of business."[212] But the ongoing disputes between Turkey and Greece over the Aegean Sea provide arguments to the contrary.

Notwithstanding these open questions, in January 1994 the United States initiated NATO's Partnership for Peace (PfP) programme, but, as is often the case with compromises, the United States confused the issue instead of clarifying it. The real problem is that the PfP programme tries to satisfy all sides' expectations which are partly incompatible, allowing the various countries to decode identical mesages in different ways. For the East European countries which have opted for NATO's fast extension eastwards, it is an introduction to their future membership.[213] From the NATO point of view, PfP "is not a security measure designed to enhance defence but a political compromise aimed at appeasing those who want to join NATO."[214] Or, in other words, it is a huge, unachievable promise, bearing in mind that Eastern Europe expects everything to be in concrete form: a concrete list—who; a concrete schedule—when; a concrete prescription—how. And the extraordinary thing is that, officially, nobody dares to say that NATO's extension to the East is unrealistic, at least as an idea, because it would be ineffective as a possible solution to the East European countries' real problems.

In fact, the advocates of this idea submit it without even really understanding what NATO is, how the Alliance functions, and what possible problems would emerge after enlargement. A closer look into the problem, however, reveals several reasons which make NATO's enlargement a distant Utopia. First, every organization possesses some critical mass in respect of its size, beyond which any extension undermines its ability to fulfil its functions. Although this has not yet

[212]Ronald D. Asmus, Richard L. Kugler, and F. Stephen Larrabee, "Building a New NATO," Foreign Affairs, Vol.72, No.4, September/October 1993, p.30.

[213]An interpretation confirmed by President Clinton in his Prague 1994 statement that it is not a question of whether but when NATO should enlarge.

[214]James H. Brusstar, "Russian Vital Interests and Western Security," Orbis, Vol.38, No.4, Fall 1994, p.617.

proved to be so in practice, it is quite probable that NATO has already reached the limitations of its critical mass.

Second, since the NATO member countries are the Western democracies, this means that any decision (political or military) has to be endorsed by the electorates of the member countries. If there were to be an extension to the East, it might be extremely difficult to explain and justify in a persuasive manner to taxpayers, say, in Spain or Holland why they should bear the burden of a probable and possible commitment on behalf of the future East European NATO members: "in the absence of threats to vital perceived interests, it is extraordinarily difficult for democratic states to sustain domestic support for distant and risky military operations overseas even when governments may wish to do so."[215] As experience from the Yugoslav conflict shows, it is easy to mobilize public support as long as it does not require anything more than a moral commitment. The real problem arises when the issue of commitment boils down to the question of who is going to pay.

In fact, this type of question concerning NATO is a new one. As a collective defence structure designed to meet the challenge of a concrete and specific antagonist, the question of costs was a hypothetical one. The possible conflict with the former Warsaw Pact was expected to be a global one, or at least a global outcome was seriously taken into consideration. This conflict was perceived as a threat to the existence of Western civilization and in fact it was an all-or-nothing game. The costs of this commitment, no matter how high, were always justifiable in the face of the other option. For that reason, during the Cold War the question was not one of whether certain costs should be incurred but of how to allocate the inevitable costs in the most effective way. After the Cold War, and especially in the case of possible East European membership, it is not the allocation but the costs themselves which are disputable.

The third reason against NATO's enlargement is the nature of the conflicts in Eastern Europe and the former Soviet Union, excluding the above-mentioned possible strategic Russian threat which would bring NATO back to the era of the all-or-nothing option. NATO's competitiveness derives from its defence, not from any conflict-

---

[215]Gareth Evans, "Cooperative Security and Intra-State Conflict," <u>Foreign Policy</u>, No.96, Fall 1994, p.18.

prevention or conflict-resolution capabilities. Membership in NATO keeps existing conflicts (in the case of Greece and Turkey) within the limits of a sustainable political dispute but does not have the power to solve them. There is no evidence that a future enlargement of NATO would improve these conflict-resolution capabilities and this is the essence of the issue: as a defence structure, NATO is capable of providing security guarantees against threats from **outside** the Alliance. Unfortunately, most of the threats that the PfP countries are facing come from within these countries.

Another serious misunderstanding of the issue results from identifying the Alliance solely with its defensive aspects. From today's perspective, it would seem that the more important impact of NATO has been its ability to provide an institutional framework for building codes of understanding and mutual dialogue between different national mentalities, cultures, and interests. In this respect, NATO is one of the important pillars of future West European integration. However, this means that membership in NATO is qualitatively similar to membership in the EU—a problem which cannot be solved by a political decision alone.

Reasonable legal doubts about NATO's enlargement also exist. The problem is how the security guarantees would be met and what it would mean in terms of operational planning. Would it mean that NATO troops would have to be forward-deployed on the territory of the future NATO members and how does this relate to the Conventional Armed Forces in Europe (CFE) Treaty? If not, "would not NATO have to develop a substantial offensive capability, above and beyond that already envisaged for NATO's Rapid Reaction Force? Moreover, to extend NATO's nuclear umbrella... would cause enormous political controversies in a number of West European countries, particularly Germany".[216]

And probably the most important argument against NATO's extension eastwards is that it is simply not in the vital interests of Western Europe and the United States. The primary issue presupposing all others is Russia and its continuing pursuit of a non-threatening policy towards the rest of Europe, mainly its Western part. If one assumes that NATO's extension would resurrect Russia's imperial agenda, then

---

[216]Adrian G.V. Hyde-Price, "After the Pact: East European Security in the 1990s," Arms Control, Vol.12, No.2, September 1991, p.295.

the outcome to the dilemma over enlargement is obvious.[217]

Filling the Security Vacuum: If not NATO, then what?

The answer to this question can be given only after specifying the needs and the tasks. What Eastern Europe needs is a working security structure, security guarantees. The tasks consist of detecting sources of potential threats and working out possible solutions which have to correlate with the general approach to the issue of security, according to which "the great powers form a kind of global security complex among themselves, taking the whole planet as their region" and "lesser states will usually find themselves locked into a regional security complex with their neighbours. The particular character of a local security complex will often be affected by historical factors such as long-standing enmities... or the common cultural embrace of a civilizational area."[218]

This approach seems to fit the Central and East European case. Seen from the perspective of four years of post-communist development, the East European countries often face similar, if not identical, sets of problems in the security field. These are the dubious legitimacy of internal and external borders; potential irredentist or secessionist claims raised on behalf of or by minorities; the blocking of the reform process by self-fulfilling prophecies of strategic insecurity; and lack of security guarantees against falling back into the sphere of a re-emerging Russia as a Great Power with its understandable, though not excusable, imperial ambitions.

If we agree with Zbigniew Brzezinski that "Russia can be either an empire or a democracy, but it cannot be both" and that "the current objectives of Russian policy are if not openly imperial, at the very least proto-imperial," then it is highly probable that in the prevailing Russian

---

[217]"If Russian intentions towards Europe remain non-threatening, then the United States major security interest in Central and Eastern Europe is that of making sure this region is free of military forces threatening to the West... Moreover, incorporation of the countries of Central Europe into the Western defence alliances... would decrease Western security because Russia would then adopt a much more confrontational stance." Brusstar, "Russian," p.618.

[218]Barry Buzan, Morten Kelstrup, Pierre Lemaitre, Elzbieta Tromer, and Ole Waever, The European Security Order Recast. Scenarios for the Post-Cold War Era (London and New York: Pinter Publishers, 1990), p.15.

thinking about Central Europe the region is explicitly designated as "an area of special Russian interest and influence."[219] But in any case it is part of the historical destiny of Eastern Europe to be an object within a broader framework of geopolitical gambling, and hypothetical membership in NATO is unlikely to radically change this situation. Hence, complaining about it cannot be a serious basis for pragmatic policy.

Bearing in mind the existing conditions, two possible options may be put forward. The first is the revitalization of the concept of collective security which was largely discredited by the League of Nations.[220] However, this is quite improbable since it implies one necessary condition: the existence of mutual understanding and a consensus on basic values and problems of common concern. As the former Yugoslavia crisis shows, a consensus on even obvious matters of a political and moral nature is difficult to achieve—it is true that "NATO does not remotely resemble a great power with well-defined interests over a range of issues and a well-developed will of its own. Each major European power has its own interests and concerns; what Germany deems vital to its security and prosperity, England may regard as peripheral. To insist on joint intervention in such a case would only create friction where none previously existed...intervention in the complicated affairs of the Balkans and Eastern Europe, where the merits of the case are rarely obvious or entirely on one side and where many of the leading NATO states have had intense and emotion-laden involvement in the past, might prove seriously disruptive to alliance unity."[221]

That is why another option needs to be discussed: creating a collective defence structure, constituted by the former East European countries, located **between** and guaranteed **by** the two probable super-power alliances—NATO and the CIS (Commonwealth of Independent States)—and associated with NATO without any binding obligations to

---

[219]See Zbigniew Brzezinski, "Premature Partnership," Foreign Affairs, Vol.73, No.2, March/April 1994.

[220]James E. Goodby, "Collective Security in Europe After the Cold War," Journal of International Affairs, Vol.46, No.2, Winter 1993, pp.304-318.

[221]Owen Harries, "The Collapse of 'The West'," Foreign Affairs, Vol.72, No.4, September/October 1993, p.44.

an automatic military commitment. This collective defence structure, let us hypothetically call it the East European Union, might help to avoid the drawing of new demarcation lines in Europe. According to this option, "NATO would remain intact as a regional subgroup within the PfP; it would... support other regional groupings that would gradually evolve in Central and Eastern Europe and the former Soviet Union. The institutionalization of these regional groupings, not the expansion of NATO, would serve as the vehicle for erecting a pan-European security order."[222]

Such a regional security structure could provide security stability without any drastic change in the equilibrium, which is how Russia perceives the issue of NATO's extension eastwards. For that reason, Russian support for the idea is quite probable. At least it goes along with President Yeltsin's readiness to accept a joint Russian-NATO guarantee for the region's security, contained in his letter of September 1993 to the leaders of the United States, Great Britain, France, and Germany.

Other arguments in favour of such a structure on the part of the East European countries concern, first of all, these countries' similarities: similar problems and similar attitudes towards the big partners, i.e. the common quest for joining European integration structures and the common notion of a threat from renewed Russian domination. There also exist elements of common culture which may make the process of building common codes of understanding relatively easier. Levels of economic development are also more or less comparable or at least the gap between the East European countries seems to be less than that between the Visegrad Four and the European Union. And, last but not least, the existing incompatibility of military structures, weapons systems, and operational principles could be overcome through a gradual process of cooperation with NATO, extending the period during which the available equipment would be in use and thus postponing the necessarily heavy expenses on rearmament in accordance with NATO standards. The common floor for discussion between the three institutionalized alliances—NATO, the CIS, and the hypothetical East European Union—could be the framework of the PfP process.

---

[222]Charles A. Kupchan, "Strategic Visions," World Policy Journal, Vol.11, No.3, Fall 1994, p.120.

Paradoxically, the existing unstable equilibrium in Eastern Europe can only be maintained by preserving the security vacuum or, to put it another way, by preventing any super-power from entering the region and infringing the existing status quo. This status quo is the result of the establishment of a new—regional—edition of a balance-of-power system at the end of the Cold War, which can only be preserved at the regional level and with the consensus of the Great Powers. That is why such a security solution does not contradict the possibility of a new concert of powers appearing.[223]

Relations (and border lines) between the regional structure and the Great Powers are an important point of concern. These relations, especially between Russia and the Baltic states, Ukraine, and Belarus, determine the potential participants in the regional alliance. It is highly probable that the list would represent a residual value of Russia's interests and capabilities. According to James H. Brusstar, there are five general models of the limits to Russia's relations with the CIS and newly independent countries: "incorporation... into Russia (the USSR model); total political and economic domination by Russia but nominal independence (the old East European model); direct Russian control (formally or informally) over all security forces but political autonomy; Russian training and logistical support of indigenous forces, but political independence... and extensive Russian influence over security decisions, but political and economic independence."[224]

It is likely that only the countries of the former Eastern Europe would retain the possibility of conducting a completely independent security policy and that the fifth model would be applied to the Baltic states and the third to Ukraine and Belarus. Hence, the latter would not have the possibility of participating in any security alliances which excluded Russia. This is probably the reason why Ukraine is reluctant to adopt the regional approach and is opting for NATO membership or pan-European security solutions. According to a Ukrainian security analyst, "Kiev, however, fears that the establishment of a military and political alliance in the centre of Europe may once again lead to the

---

[223]In this respect Richard Rosecrance's vision of regionalism as an alternative to concert is extreme. Both options can but do not have to be exclusive. See Richard Rosecrance, "A New Concert of Powers," Foreign Affairs, Vol.71, No.2, Spring 1992, pp.75-79.

[224]Brusstar, "Russian," p.611.

division of the Continent. Without precluding its possible participation in such an alliance in the future, Ukraine will nevertheless attempt to avoid the creation of new military and political structures. Before taking such a step she must be convinced that hopes have fallen short for the integration of the new democracies into Western European structures and the transformation of the latter into all-European ones."[225]

Other possible and probable obstacles to the idea of a regional security alliance are posed by the East European countries themselves. Probably the Visegrad Four would be reluctant to join any common initiative that could delay their rapid integration into the EU and joining NATO.[226] The Four would resist any possible association with the other East European countries which are perceived as less developed and less advanced in their reforms (which is not far from the truth, especially in respect of economic reforms). Despite the achievements in their integration into all-European institutions, Central European policy makers and security specialists still fear "being caught in a 'no man's land' or 'security vacuum,' or being seen merely as 'buffer states'."[227]

However, limiting the possible regional structure solely to its military aspects may improve its chances, especially when it becomes evident that full NATO membership is unrealistic for practical reasons. At that point, a collective defence structure could turn into a reasonable compromise between the impossibility of satisfying expectations and the constant threat of a new division of Europe and its reseparation into

[225]Alexander Levchenko, "Ukranian Approaches to Regional Peacekeeping," in Peacekeeping Challenges to Euro-Atlantic Security, Ernest Gilman and Detlef E. Herold (eds.) (Rome: NATO Defense College, 1994), p.63. It seems however that among the emerging strategic community there is a much more favourable attitude towards regional solutions to the Ukraine's security concerns.

[226]From the very beginning of the Visegrad idea the possibility of a security aspect of integration was one of its significant elements. Shortly after the Visegrad summit a number of bilateral agreements were signed by the countries of the triangle but during the summit and after it "all three leaders emphasized that their cooperation efforts did not constitute a new bloc or alliance, perched between the Soviet Union and Western Europe." Milada Anna Vachudova, "The Visegrad Four: No Alternative to Cooperation?" RFE/RL Research Report, Vol.2, No.34, August 1993, p.40.

[227]Joshua Spero, "The Budapest-Prague-Warsaw Triangle: Central European Security after the Visegrad Summit," European Security, Vol.1, No.1, Spring 1992, p.70.

Great Powers' spheres of influence. It is also highly probable that such an alliance may even open the way to a normalized dialogue that is free of suspicion between Russia and her former Warsaw Pact allies.

That is why the crucial point in any discussion of the subject will be, first and foremost, clarifying attitudes. This means that a unanimous decision on the issue of NATO enlargement is necessary—be it support or rejection. The decision must not leave any possibility for different interpretations in terms of wishful thinking on the part of the countries concerned. Promises which cannot be fulfilled have been the worst source of conflict in the twentieth century.

Balkan security concerns are not only connected with the conflict in former Yugoslavia which could spill over into the whole region, but they are also part of a broader issue: East European security after the collapse of communism. In this respect the crisis in former Yugoslavia was symptomatic of the shape of the East European security environment after the collapse of the USSR and the dissolution of the WP. Lack of consensus on crucial issues, the internal instability of the newly established states, and the role of Russia as a source of concern—all these dimensions of the conflicts in the Balkans are also valid on the broader scale of Eastern Europe.

The currently existing security vacuum in Eastern Europe is perceived as a source of instability, linked mainly to a possible Russian threat. The events in Chechnya in December 1994-January 1995 have demonstrated Russia's determination to act in an imperial way inside Russia and most likely in the territories of the near abroad too, presumably with the exception of the Baltic states and Ukraine. Although less probable, an analogy can be made with the former Soviet republics and even with Eastern Europe. This gives grounds for concern about the possibility of maintaining the existing equilibrium in these regions.

But even more serious is the problem of the lack of a security concept. In fact the only new idea is the quest for NATO's extension eastwards. It seems however that this tempting idea is an unrealistic one, not only because of Russia's possible opposition but because any enlargement would influence the Alliance's effectiveness and involve additional expenditures, which the electorates in NATO countries would have to be persuaded to support. Since the collapse of communism, however, the dominant expectation is a reduction, not an increase, in defence budgets. But probably the main obstacle to Eastern Europe's membership in NATO is the inevitable new division of Europe along new demarcation lines as a result of any such extension. In fact, it would mean a renaissance of deterrence policy.

In this respect, one possible alternative might be the promotion of a regional security alliance guaranteed by the Great Powers. Such an alliance would not only offer a reasonable compromise between the security vacuum and the new division of Europe but it would also create optimum conditions for building common codes of understanding which are in fact a necessary condition for NATO membership. At the same time, it would not rule out the possibility of NATO's enlargement in the future and it could provide a more secure environment for the democratization process and market reforms over the next few decades.

CHAPTER 8
FINAL CONCLUSIONS

We have now witnessed a significant escalation in all the post-Yugoslav states involved in the conflict in the former Yugoslavia. At the end of 1994 and the beginning of 1995, the conflict entered a new phase in which open clashes occurred in Tetovo and Macedonian-Albanian tensions increased in Macedonia; a serious crisis broke out over the status of UN troops in Croatia; and the winter truce in Bosnia was effectively used by all parties to the conflict for substantially improving their fighting capabilities. After another round of heavy fighting in Bosnia, NATO launched air strikes against Serbian positions, to which the Bosnian Serbs retaliated by taking UNPROFOR troops as hostages. The next phase was marked, significantly, by the shooting down of a US plane over Bosnia on 2 June 1995 and reached its climax when the Croats launched their Operation "Storm" at the beginning of August.

Clearly, the pace of events had now considerably accelerated and, consequently, the situation on the ground underwent serious changes which were considered by some analysts as drastic. But are these changes really drastic, and have the events of the last few months actually changed the nature of the security and minorities' issue in the region?

What has changed?

First, the political map has changed and the republic of Serbian Kraina, which was not even recognized by Belgrade although it was an important regional political actor, ceased to exist. The political and military causes underlying its disappearance are still unclear, but this change has established an important precedent that may be applied to other self-proclaimed territories which have been unfortunate enough to exercise the right to self-determination, not within former republican borders but in territories which are predominantly populated by one nationality.

Second, the ethno-national map has changed too and at least one of the minorities analysed in this monograph—the Serbs in Croatia—has ceased to exist or, rather, has ceased to exist in its former shape and territory. As a result, we are now witnessing the biggest flow of refugees in Europe since World War II, with thousands of people in the Balkans being forced to leave their homes just as they were forced to do at the end of the nineteenth century. However, it is not only and not even mainly the Serbs in Croatia—or the former Serbs in Croatia—who are affected by the changes on the ethno-national map. Since most of the refugees will probably remain in Bosnia-Herzegovina, this will not only boost the percentage of the Serbian population there but will also change the different sides' justificatons for territorial claims.

Third, the moral context has changed because the Serbs have now become the victims, contrasting sharply with the commonly held conflict perceptions of the last few years. By leaving their homes the Serbian refugees have cast a peculiar vote of confidence in the Croatian regime's respect of human rights and ethnic co-existence. As a result, we now have another "bad guy" in the Balkan conflict—and perhaps a third one in the making too. More importantly, however, is the retroactive use to which the new moral context will be put as further justification for the crimes which have already been committed. The tragic situation of these new refugees will not only foster the Serbs' perception of their policy as the last resort of a just resistance in defence of Orthodox values but it will also deepen the different sides' perceptions of their respective policies as the only just and reasonable ones.

Fourth, the combination of a new ethno-national map and a new moral context has produced a change in the rationale for settling the Serbs in Bosnia-Herzegovina—although this was in fact enforced by the Croatian offensive—and increased the percentage of Serbs in Bosnia-Herzegovina. Consequently, the Serbs' previously unrealistic claims have now become more substantial.

Fifth, there has been a change in the approach to the very concept of the existence of a strategic Serbo-Croatian relationship. For some time, the Croats seemed to have only two alternatives: a tactical one—siding with the Serbs against the Bosnian Muslims—and a strategic one—siding with the Muslims against the Serbs. As a result of Operation "Storm" and in view of the fact that Belgrade may and probably will use the Serbian exodus from Kraina as a strong political argument, the Croats now have a third option: continuing as the Muslims' nominal ally and fighting the Serbs in Kraina but at the same time helping the Serbs in Bosnia-Herzegovina and Kosova. This third option provides one of the few pieces of indirect evidence pointing towards some sort of a deal between Zagreb and Belgrade.

Does all this indicate a drastic change in the minorities' and security issue? Unfortunately, it does not because the most important elements, i.e. the nature of the conflict and the rationales for the conflicting sides' policies, have not changed at all.

What has remained unchanged?

First, the approach to the conflicts in the region has not changed. Although these conflicts have been widely interpreted as ethnic ones, they have in fact always been economic and political conflicts. Indeed, they are conflicts of interests camouflaged as ethnic conflicts. The Croatian regime needed Operation "Storm," on the one hand, to demonstrate the power and viability of the Croatian state and, on the other, to ensure that Croatia's territorial integrity does not depend on any kind of negotiations with any minority, as in the case of other smaller-scale operations conducted earlier by the Serbs and the Muslims.

Second, minorities continue to play the role of flash points indicating potential broader conflicts. In fact, the minorities have not changed either so that the Kraina Serbs will remain Kraina Serbs no matter where they settle. This applies to all the other refugees, both Christian and Muslim, who will all be betrayed and will, therefore, continue to be prey to manipulation. One can already speculate about the creation of future organizations of displaced minorities, perhaps along the lines of the Sudeten Germans, with annual gatherings for their veterans to commemorate the exodus date. However, the real problem lies in the personal human drama and sentiments of these minorities, which may be, and most probably will be, used at the appropriate time for some questionable political purpose.

Third, there has been no change in the tradition of using people as cogs in some sort of sophisticated machinery or as stakes in political gambling. There are many strange aspects to the sudden disappearance of Serbian Kraina but the strangest part of it all is how it happened so easily. The Serbs demonstrated organized evacuation instead of organized defence and this is further indirect evidence of a possible deal between Zagreb and Belgrade. The problem is that it cost thousands of refugees.

Fourth, the approach to the existing problems remains unchanged. Politicians on all three sides are still searching for solutions to the minority issue in the creation of monoethnic nation-states. And if the political or ethno-national map does not match their rationales, they simply change the map. As a result of the inevitable territorial and population exchanges, dreams about an all-Croat or an all-Serb state flourish, and in this context Operation "Storm" is just the most recent but not the last example.

Fifth, the Americans' misunderstanding of Balkan problems has not changed. Their persistent quest for one guilty side, which must be condemned and punished, inevitably leads to biased policy. In some cases, it even looks as if US policy precedes and governs assumptions and not vice versa, as in the case of the assessment of the Sarajevo shelling on 29 August which provided the justifification for massive NATO air strikes.

What kind of a solution can be envisaged to the crisis in Bosnia-Herzegovina?

Probably only a temporary one because any solution that is militarily imposed on the Serbs will be perceived by them as unjust and encourage their claim to self-determination. The negative side of the Serbs' motivations, the attitudes based on the assumption of a "besieged fortress," will no doubt continue to prevail, thereby freezing democratic reform, the only guarantee of minority rights in Serbia, for some time to come.

The next flash point will probably be Kosovo where most of the refugees from Serbian Kraina will settle. This will not affect the Albanians' absolute majority, because even if all the Serbs from Kraina settle in Kosovo this will only increase the Serbian share in the population from 10% to 15%. Nevertheless, it will be another sign of political determination, the importance of which should not be underestimated in terms of a strong-handed Serbian policy to match the already dominating political discourse. Following the example of Serbian ethnic cleansing, the Croats have developed this "technology" further and even set a precedent in terms of scale. The territories of Serbian Kraina have been "cleansed" of the population which was predominantly of one nationality and had in many cases lived there for centuries. The case is similar in Kosovo and this makes the Croats' example extremely tempting.

In any case, it seems that the age of nation-states has just begun to dawn in the Balkans and, ironically enough, the so-called international community has become an active participant in this process.

In the meantime, the socialist (former communist) government in Bulgaria has taken its first concrete steps. And this cannot be termed recommunization because all communists are now capitalists. More important is the rapid growth of ethnic intolerance and the government's increased use of nationalistic appeals to gain support. However, it is still too early to say whether the Serbian approach of the late 1980s is now being applied in Bulgaria because many of the trends there are confusing and difficult to interpret.

At the same time, the debate over NATO's enlargement is slowly turning into two parallel monologues: one against its extension—Russia—and the other treating NATO membership as the one and only solution to security concerns—the rest of the former communist bloc. However, the NATO member countries seem to be becoming less and less enthusiastic about enlargement although one thing at least is now clear, and that is that there will be only one round of extension, if any.

Under these circumstances, minority issues can be approached in one of two ways. One of them, which is already being applied in the former Yugoslavia, can be described as getting rid of minorities, and the other one, which is still being applied in Bulgaria, although it is becoming increasingly difficult to do so, can be described as tolerating minorities as the lesser evil. While the former approach does not need any broader security framework, the latter constitutes an important prerequisite for such a framework.

Nevertheless, in both cases the outlook for security issues in the Balkans is not very bright, not least because so far no answer has been found to the question of who needs a broader security framework in the Balkans and who is willing to help to build it.

2 September 1995

Map 1: The Balkans (B. Jelavich, 1983)

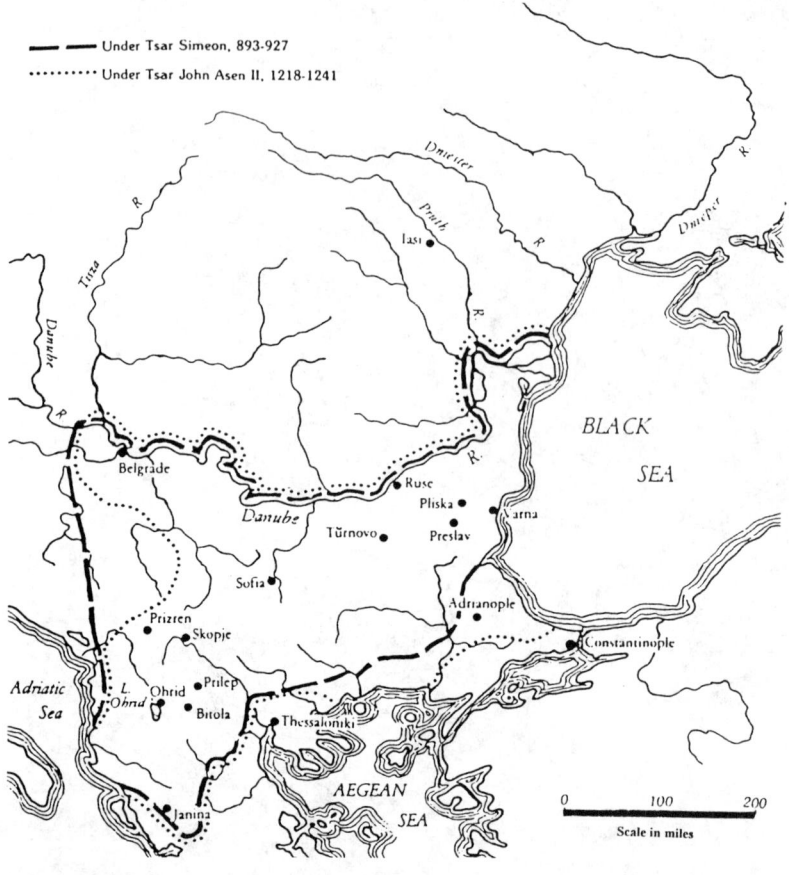

━━━━ Under Tsar Simeon, 893-927
⋯⋯⋯⋯ Under Tsar John Asen II, 1218-1241

Map 2: Bulgaria in the Middle Ages (B. Jelavich, 1983)

Map 3: Serbia under the Nemanja dynasty (B. Jelavich, 1983)

Map 4: The Macedonian Contested Zone, 1913 (R.R. King, 1973)

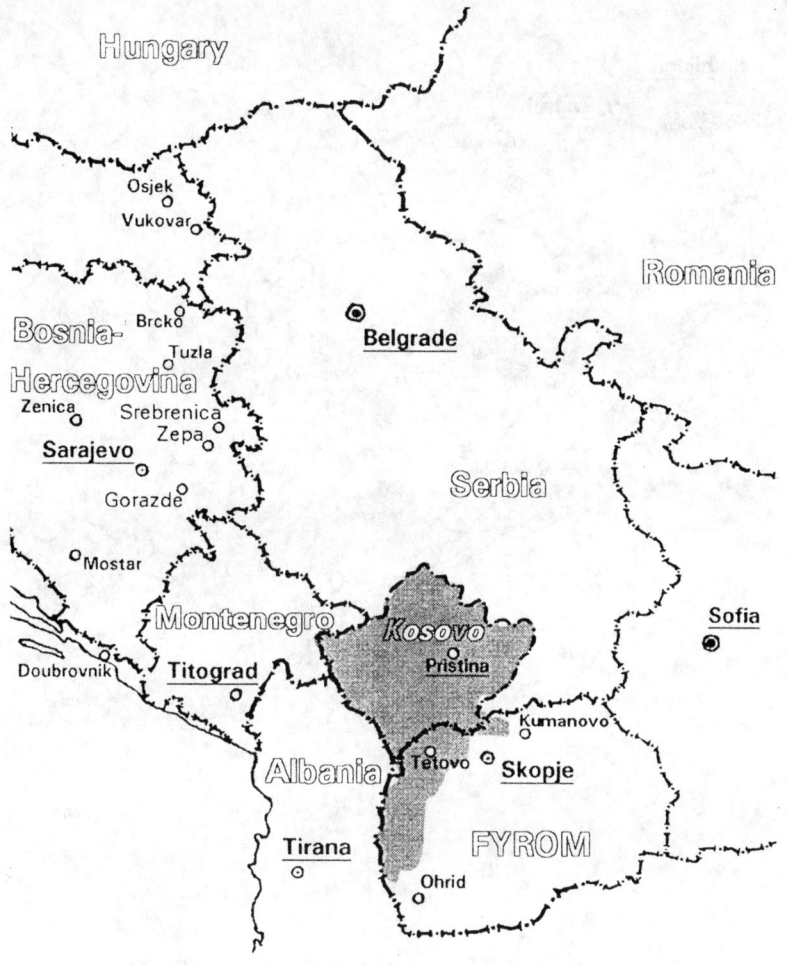

Areas with predominant Albanian populations

Map 5: FYROM and Serbia (A. Ivanov, Situation as at April 1995)

Areas with predominant Bosnian Muslim populations

Map 6: Bosnia-Herzegovina (A. Ivanov, Situation as at April 1995)

Areas with predominant Croat populations ▬▬

Map 7: Bosnia-Herzegovina (A. Ivanov, Situation as at April 1995)

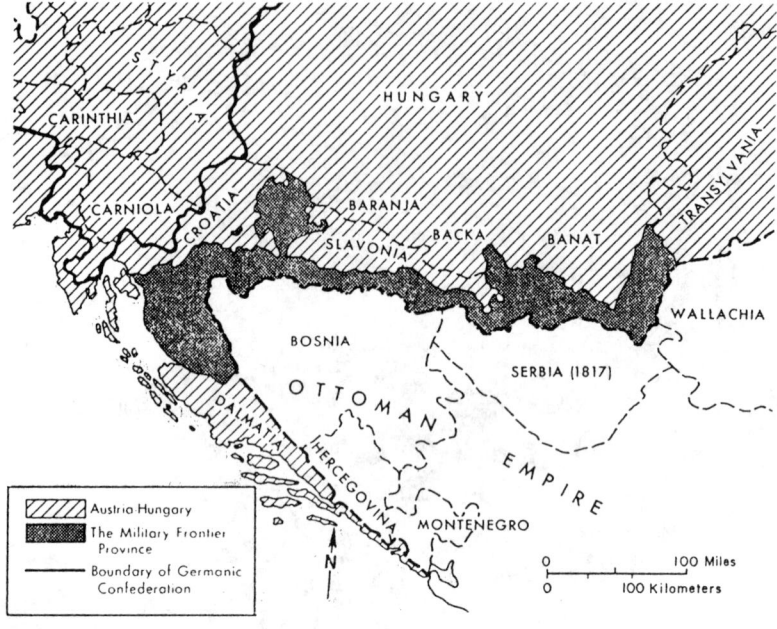

Map 8: Military Frontier Province between the Habsburg
and Ottoman Empires, ca. 1600-1800 (R.F. Nyrop, 1981)

Areas with predominant Serb populations ▨▨▨

Map 9: Bosnia-Herzegovina and Croatia (A. Ivanov, Situation as at April 1995)

Area with supposed Macedonian minority

Area with Pomak population

Area with concentrated Turkish populations

Map 10: Bulgaria (A. Ivanov, Situation as at April 1995)

Balkan Minorities according to Religion, Ethnicity, and Culture

Balkan Minorities	Religion					Ethnic roots		Cultural roots	
	Muslims		Christians						
	Shiits	Sunits	Orthodox	Catholic	Protestant	Slavs	Non-slavs	Roman	Byzantian
Albanians in Kosovo		■					■		■
Albanians in FYROM		■					■		■
Bosnian Muslims		■				■	■	■	■
Croats in Bosnia-Hercegovina				■		■		■	
Serbs in Bosnia-Hercegovina			■			■			■
Macedonians in Bulgaria and Greece			■			■			■
Pomaks in Bulgaria	■					■			■
Serbs in Croatia			■			■			■
Turks in Bulgaria	■						■		■

Table 1: Balkan Minorities according to Religion, Ethnicity, and Culture (A. Ivanov, 1995)

BIBLIOGRAPHY

Rabia Ali and Lawrence Lifschultz, "Why Bosnia?" Third World Quarterly, Vol.15, No.3, September 1994, pp.367-401

Anne Applebaum, "The Fall and Rise of the Communists," Foreign Affairs, November/December 1994, Vol.73, No.6, pp.7-13

Ronald D. Asmus, Richard L. Kugler and Stephen Larrabee, "Building a New NATO," Foreign Affairs, Vol.72, No.4, September/October 1993, pp.28-40

Aspekti na Etnokulturnata situazia v Balgaria (Sofia: CSD, FNST, 1992)

Robert Austin, "What Albania Adds to the Balkan Stew," Orbis, Vol.37, No.2, Spring 1993, pp.259-279

Robert Austin, "Albanian-Macedonian Relations," RFE/RL Research Report, Vol.2, No.42, 22 October 1993, pp.21-25

Etienne Balibar, Immanuel Wallerstein, Race, Nation, Class: Ambiguous Identities (London: Verso, 1992)

Ivo Banac, The National Question in Yugoslavia: Origins, History, Politics (Ithaca: Cornell University Press, 1984)

Ivo Banac, "The Fearful Asymmetry of War: The Causes and Consequences of Yugoslavia's Demise," Daedalus, Vol.121, No.2, Spring 1992, pp.141-174

Ivo Banac, "Nationalism in Serbia," in Balkans: A Mirror of the New International Order,Gunay Goksu Ozdogan, Kemali Saybasili (eds.) (Istanbul: Eren, 1995), pp.133-152

Zoltan Barany, "Mass-Elite Relations and the Resurgence of Nationalism in Eastern Europe," European Security, Vol.3, No.1, Spring 1994, pp.162-181

Boguslawa Bednarczyk, Nationalism, Ethnic Minorities and Human Rights in Post-Cold War Central and Eastern Europe (Rome: NATO Defense College, 1994)

Charles R. Beitz, Political Theory and International Relations (Princeton: Princeton University Press, 1979)

Andrew Bell-Fialkoff, "A Brief History of Ethnic Cleansing," Foreign Affairs, Vol.72, No.3, Summer 1993, pp.110-121

Hedva Ben-Israel, "Nationalism in Historical Perspective," Journal of International Affairs, Vol.45, No.2, Winter 1992, pp.367-397

184

Elez Biberaj, Kosova: The Balkan Powder Keg (London: Research Institute for the Study of Conflict and Terrorism, 1993)

Klaus Bitterman (ed.), Serbien Muss Sterben. Wahrheit und Lüge im jugoslawischen Bürgerkrieg (Berlin: Edition Tiamat, 1994)

Ljubo Boban, "Jasenovac and the Manipulation of History," East European Politics and Societies, Vol.4, No.3, 1990, pp.580-592

Juris Bojars, "Human and Minority Rights in Latvia," Research Paper, Riga, 1994

Milica Bookman, Economic Decline and Nationalism in the Balkans (New York: St. Martin's Press, 1994)

Stephen R. Bowers, Ethnic Politics in Eastern Europe (London: Research Institute for the Study of Conflict and Terrorism, 1992)

Paul Brass, Ethnicity and Nationalism: Theory and Comparison (Newbury Park, Ca: Sage, 1992)

Philippe Braud, François Burdeau, Histoire des Idées politiques depuis la Révolution (Paris: Editions Montchrestien, 1983)

Aurel Braun, Small-State Security in the Balkans (London: Macmillan Press, 1983)

Crane Brinton, The Anatomy of a Revolution (New York: Vintage Books, 1965)

Peter Brock, "Dateline Yugoslavia: The Partisan Press," Foreign Policy, No.93, Winter 1993-1994, pp.152-172

James F. Brown, Nationalism, Democracy and Security in the Balkans (Brookfield: Dartmouth Publishing Company, 1992)

Michael E. Brown (ed.), Ethnic Conflict and International Security (Princeton: Princeton University Press, 1993)

James H. Brusstar, "Russian Vital Interests and Western Security," Orbis, Vol.38, No.4, Fall 1994, pp.607-619

Zbigniew Brzezinski, "Premature Partnership," Foreign Affairs, Vol.73, No.2, March/April 1994, pp.67-82

Allen Buchanan, Secession: The Morality of Political Divorce from Fort Sumter to Lithuania and Quebec (Boulder: Westview Press, 1991)

Allen Buchanan, "Self-Determination and the Right to Secede," Journal of International Affairs, Vol.45, No.2, Winter 1992, pp.347-365

Lee C. Buchheit, Secession. The Legitimacy of Self-Determination (New Haven: Yale University Press, 1978)

Janusz Bugajski, Nations in Turmoil: Conflict and Cooperation in Eastern Europe (Boulder: Westview Press, 1993)

R.V. Burks, The National Problem and the Future of Yugoslavia (Santa Monica: Rand Corporation, 1971)

Barry Buzan, People, States and Fear: An Agenda for International Security Studies in the Post-Cold War Era (New York: Harvester Wheatsheaf, 1991)

Barry Buzan, "From International System to International Society: Structural Realism and Regime Theory Meet the English School," International Organization, Vol.47, No.3, Summer 1993, pp.327-352

Barry Buzan, Morten Kelstrup, Pierre Lemaitre, Elzbieta Tromer, Ole Waever, The European Security Order Recast. Scenarios for the Post-Cold War Era (London: Pinter Publishers, 1990)

Marie-Janine Calic, "The Serbian Question in International Politics," Aussenpolitik, No.2, 1994, pp.146-155

F.W. Carter, "Ethnicity as a Cause of Migration in Eastern Europe," GeoJournal, Vol.30, No.3, 1993, pp.241-248

Gérard Chaliand, Minority Peoples in the Age of Nation-States (London: Pluto Press, 1989)

Norman Cigar, "The Serbo-Croatian War, 1991: Political and Military Dimensions," The Journal of Strategic Studies, Vol.16, No.3, September 1993, pp.297-338

Jonathan Clarke, "Replacing NATO," Foreign Policy, No.93, Winter 1993-1994, pp.22-40

Oscar W. Clyatt, Jr., Bulgaria's Quest for Security After the Cold War (Washington: Institute for National Strategic Studies, 1993)

Lenard J. Cohen, Broken Bonds: The Disintegration of Yugoslavia (Boulder: Westview Press, 1993)

Constitution of the Federal Republic of Macedonia (Skopje: NIP, 1991)

W. Harriet Critchley, "The Failure of Federalism in Yugoslavia," International Journal, Vol.11, No.8, Summer 1993, pp.434-447

Suzanne Crow, "Russia Adopts a More Active Policy," RFE/RL Research Report, Vol.2, No.12, 19 March 1993, pp.1-6

Robert Cullen, "Human Rights Quandary," Foreign Affairs, Vol.71, No.5, Winter 1992-1993, pp.79-88

Ian M. Cuthbertson (ed.), Minorities: The New Europe's Old Issue (Boulder: Westview Press, 1993)

Christopher Cviic, Remaking the Balkans (London: The Royal Institute of International Affairs, 1992)

Robert A. Dahl, A Preface to Democratic Theory (Chicago: The University of Chicago Press, 1956)

Istvan Deak, "Uncovering Eastern Europe's Dark History," Orbis, Vol.34, No.1, Winter 1990, pp.51-65

Bogdan Denitch, Ethnic Nationalism: The Tragic Death of Yugoslavia (Minneapolis: University of Minnesota Press, 1994)

Anton W. DePorte, Europe Between the Superpowers. The Enduring Balance (New Haven: Yale University Press, 1979)

Karl Deutsch, Nationalism and its Alternatives (New York: Knopf, 1969)

Larry Diamond (ed.), Nationalism, Ethnic Conflict, and Democracy (Baltimore: Johns Hopkins University Press, 1994)

C.J. Dick, "Serbian Responses to Intervention in Bosnia-Herzegovina," British Army Review, No.102, December 1992, p.18

Dimitrije Djordjevic, "The Yugoslav Phenomenon," in The Columbia History of Eastern Europe in the Twentieth Century, Joseph Held (ed.) (New York: Columbia University Press, 1992), pp.306-344

Nina Djulgerova, "The Macedonian Bulgarians Through the Eyes of Austrian and Russian Diplomats in the 1890s and the Beginning of the 20th Century," Etudes Balkaniques, No.4, 1993, pp.12-17

John S. Duffield, "Explaining the Long Peace in Europe: the Contributions of Regional Security Regimes," Review of International Studies, Vol.20, No.4, October 1994, pp.369-388

Raymond Duncan (ed.), Ethnic Nationalism and Regional Conflict: The Former Soviet Union and Yugoslavia (Boulder: Westview Press, 1994)

Spyros Economides, "The Balkans and the Search for Security: From Inter-War to Post-Cold-War," Arms Control, Vol.13, No.1, April 1992, pp.121-139

Rupert Emerson, From Empire to Nation (Cambridge: Harvard University Press, 1960)

Milton J. Esman, "Political and Psychological Factors in Ethnic Conflict," in Conflict and Peacemaking in Multiethnic Societies, Joseph V. Montville (ed.) (Lexington: Lexington Books, 1990), pp.53-64

Milton J. Esman, Ethnic Politics (Ithaca: Cornell University Press, 1994)

Amitai Etzioni, "The Evils of Self-Determination," Foreign Policy, No.89, Winter 1992-1993, pp.21-35

"Europe. Another Destructive Year in the Balkans," Strategic Survey, 1993-1994, pp.98-106

"Europe. Fear and Loathing in the Balkans," Strategic Survey, 1992-1993, pp.83-94

Gareth Evans, "Cooperative Security and Intra-State Conflict," Foreign Policy, No.96, Fall 1994, pp.3-20

Graham Evans, Jeffrey Newman, The Dictionary of World Politics (New York: Harvester Wheatsheaf, 1990)

Stephen Van Evera, "Hypotheses on Nationalism and War," International Security, Vol.18, No.4, Spring 1994, pp.5-39

Timothy M. Frye, "Ethnicity, Sovereignty and Transitions from Non-Democratic Rule," Journal of International Affairs, Vol.45, No.2, Winter 1992, pp.599-623

Francis Fukuyama, "The End of History," The National Interest, No.16, Summer 1989, pp.3-18

Ernest Gellner, Nations and Nationalism (Oxford: Basil Blackwell, 1983)

Ernest Gellner and E.H. Carr, "Nationalism Reconsidered," Review of International Studies, Vol.18, No.4, October 1992, pp.285-293

Ernest Gellner, Encounters with Nationalism (Oxford: Basil Blackwell, 1994)

Tsvetana Georgieva, "Coexistence as a System in the Everyday Life between Christians and Muslims in Bulgaria (Ethnological Study)," in Relations of Compatibility and Incompatibility between Christians and Muslims in Bulgaria, Antonina Zheliazkova (ed.) (Sofia: International Centre for Minority Studies and Intercultural Relations Foundation, 1995), pp.151-178

Branko Geroski, "Macedonia: Post-Election Jockeying," War Report, No.30, December 1994/January 1995, p.11

Symeon A. Giannakos, "The Macedonian Question Reexamined: Implications for Balkan Security," Mediterranean Quarterly, Vol.3, Summer 1992, pp.26-47

Ernest Gilman, Detlef E. Herold (eds.), Peacekeeping Challenges to Euro-Atlantic Security (Rome: NATO Defense College, 1994)

Bojan Gjuzelev, "Die Minderheiten in Bulgarien unter Berücksichtigung der letzten Volkszählung vom Dezember 1992," SüdostEuropa, Vol.43, Nos.6-7, 1994, pp.361-373

Charles L. Glaser, "Why NATO is Still Best. Future Security Arrangements for Europe," International Security, Vol.18, No.1, Summer 1993, pp.5-50

Misha Glenny, The Fall of Yugoslavia: The Third Balkan War (London: Penguin, 1992)

Vladimir Gligorov, "Balkanization: A Theory of Constitution Failure," East European Politics and Societies, Vol.6, No.3, Fall 1992, pp.283-302

Davor Glovas, "The Roots of Croatian Extremism," Mediterranean Quarterly, Vol.5, No.2, Spring 1994, pp.37-50

James E. Goodby, "Collective Security in Europe After the Cold War," Journal of International Affairs, Vol.46, No.2, Winter 1993, pp.299-321

Gidon Gottlieb, Nation Against State: New Approaches to Ethnic Conflicts and the Decline of Sovereignty (New York: Council on Foreign Relations Press, 1993)

James Gow, Legitimacy and the Military: the Yugoslav Crisis (London: Pinter, 1991)

Liah Greenfield, Nationalism: Five Roads to Modernity (Cambridge: Harvard University Press, 1992)

Liah Greenfield, "Transcending the Nation's Worth," Daedalus, Vol.122, No.3, Summer 1993, pp.47-62

Ted Robert Gurr, Minorities at Risk: A Global View of Ethnopolitical Conflicts (Washington, D.C.: US Institute of Peace Press, 1993)

Ted Robert Gurr, "Peoples Against States: Ethnopolitical Conflict and the Changing World System," International Studies Quarterly, Vol.38, No.3, September 1994 pp.347-377

David G. Haglund, S. Neil MacFarlane, Joel J. Sokolsky (eds.), NATO's Eastern Dilemmas (Boulder: Westview Press, 1994)

John A. Hall (ed.), States in History (Oxford: Basil Blackwell, 1986)

John A. Hall, "Nationalisms: Classified and Explained," Daedalus, Vol.122, No.3, Summer 1993, pp.1-28

John A. Hall and Ian Jarvie (ed.), Transition to Modernity (Cambridge: Cambridge University Press, 1992)

Morton H. Halperin, David J. Scheffer, Patricia L. Small, Self-Determination in the New World Order (Washington: Carnegie Endowment for International Peace, 1992)

Owen Harries, "The Collapse of 'the West'," Foreign Affairs, Vol.72, No.4, September/October 1993, pp.41-53

Pierre Hassner, "Culture and Society," The International Spectator, Vol.26, No.1, January/March 1991, pp.136-153

Pierre Hassner, "Beyond Nationalism and Internationalism: Ethnicity and World Order," Survival, Vol.35, No.2, Summer 1993, pp.49-65

Robert M. Hayden, "Constitutional Nationalism in the Formerly Yugoslav Republics," Slavic Review, Vol.51, No.4, Winter 1992, pp.654-673

Derek Heater, National Self-Determination: Woodrow Wilson and his Legacy (Basingstoke: Macmillan Publishers, 1994)

Martin O. Heisler, "Ethnicity and Ethnic Relations in the Modern West," in Conflict and Peacemaking in Multiethnic Societies, Joseph V. Montville (ed.) (Lexington: Lexington Books, 1990), pp.21-52

Joseph Held (ed.), The Columbia History of Eastern Europe in the Twentieth Century (New York: Columbia University Press, 1992)

Gerald B. Helman and Steven R. Ratner, "Saving Failing States," Foreign Policy, No.89, Winter 1992-1993, pp.3-20

Alexis Heraclides, The Self-Determination of Minorities in International Politics (London: Frank Cass, 1991)

Alexis Heraclides, "Secession, Self-Determination and Nonintervention: In Quest of a Normative Symbiosis," Journal of International Affairs, Winter 1992, Vol.45, No.2, pp.399-420

Alexis Heraclides, "Secessionist Conflagration. What is to be Done?" Security Dialogue, Vol.25, No.3, 1994, pp.283-293

Rosalyn Higgins, "The New United Nations and Former Yugoslavia," International Affairs, Vol.69, No.3, 1993, pp.465-483

Eric J. Hobsbawm, The Age of Empire, 1875-1914 (New York: Pantheon Books, 1987)

Eric J. Hobsbawm, Nations and Nationalisms since 1870. Programme, Myth, Reality (Cambridge: Cambridge University Press, 1990)

Donald L. Horowitz, Ethnic Groups in Conflict (Berkeley: University of California Press, 1985)

Donald L. Horowitz, "Making Moderation Play: The Comparative Politics of Ethnic Conflict Management," in Conflict and Peacemaking in Multiethnic Societies, Joseph V. Montville (ed.) (Lexington: Lexington Books, 1990), pp.451-476

Henk Houweling, "Peacekeeping After State Collapse," in Peacekeeping Challenges to Euro-Atlantic Security, Ernest Gilman, Detlef E. Herold (eds.) (Rome: NATO Defense College, 1994), pp.85-102

Samuel P. Huntington, Political Order in Changing Societies (New Haven: Yale University Press, 1968)

Samuel P. Huntington, "How Countries Democratize," Political Science Quarterly, Vol.106, No.4, Winter 1991-1992, pp.579-616

Samuel P. Huntington, "The Clash of Civilizations?" Foreign Affairs, Vol.72, No.3, Summer 1993, pp.22-49

Dennis P. Hupchick, The Bulgarians in the Seventeenth Century: Slavic Orthodox Society under Ottoman Rule (Jefferson: McFarland and Co., 1993)

John Hutchinson, Anthony D. Smith (eds.), Nationalism (Oxford: Oxford University Press, 1994)

Adrian G.V. Hyde-Price, "After the Pact: East European Security in the 1990s," Arms Control, Vol.12, No.2, September 1991, pp.279-302

Ivan Ilchev, Duncan M. Perry, "Bulgarian Ethnic Groups: Politics and Perceptions," RFE/RL Research Report, Vol.2, No.12, 19 March 1993, pp.35-41

Andrei Ivanov, "Zweideutige Prioritäten. US-amerikanische Aussenpolitik und der Krieg auf dem Balkan (bis Sommer 1993)," SüdostEuropa, Vol.43, Nos.3-4, 1994, pp.126-150

Rita Jalali, Seymour Martin Lipset, "Racial and Ethnic Conflicts: A Global Perspective," Political Science Quarterly, Vol.107, No.4, Winter 1992-1993, pp.585-606

Branimir M. Jankovic, The Balkans in International Relations (London: Macmillan Press, 1988)

Barbara Jelavich, History of the Balkans. Twentieth Century, Vols.1 and 2 (Cambridge: Cambridge University Press, 1983)

Mark Juergensmeyer, The New Cold War? Religious Nationalism Confronts the Secular State (Berkeley: University of California Press, 1993)

Antoni Kaminski, "East-Central Europe Between the East and the West," European Security, Vol.3, No.2, Summer 1994, pp.301-317

Stefan Karastoyanov, "Macedonia (An Ethno-Geographical Profile)," Bulgarian Military Review, Vol.2, No.2, 1994, pp.55-84

Charles W. Kegley, Jr., Gregory A. Raymond, "Must We Fear a Post-Cold War Multipolar System?" Journal of Conflict Resolution, Vol.36, No.3, September 1992, pp.573-585

James G. Kellas, The Politics of Nationalism and Ethnicity (New York: St. Martin's Press, 1991)

Robert R. King, Minorities under Communism. Nationalities as a Source of Tension among Balkan Communist States (Cambridge: Harvard University Press, 1973)

Aleksander Kiossev (ed.), Post-Theory, Games and Discursive Resistance. The Bulgarian Case (Albany: State University of New York Press, 1995)

Stanley Kober, "Revolutions Gone Bad," Foreign Policy, No.91, Summer 1993, pp.63-82

Evangelos Kofos, National Heritage and National Identity in Nineteenth- and Twentieth-Century Macedonia (Athens: Hellenic Foundation for Defence and Foreign Policy, 1991)

Hans Kohn, The Age of Nationalism. The First Era of Global History (New York: Harper & Brothers Publishers, 1962)

Julia Kristeva, Nations without Nationalism (New York: Columbia University Press, 1993)

Krishan Kumar, "The 1989 Revolutions and the Idea of Europe," Political Studies, Vol.19, No.3, September 1992, pp.439-461

Milan Kundera, "The Tragedy of Central Europe," New York Review of Books, 26 April 1984

Charles A. Kupchan, "Strategic Visions," World Policy Journal, Vol.11, No.3, Fall 1994, pp.112-122

Charles A. Kupchan (ed.), Nationalism and Nationalities in the New Europe (Ithaca: Cornell University Press, 1995)

Charles A. Kupchan and Clifford A. Kupchan, "Concerts, Collective Security, and the Future of Europe," International Security, Vol.16, No.1, Summer 1991, pp.114-161

Ruth Lapidoth, "Sovereignty in Transition," Journal of International Affairs, Vol.45, No.2, Winter 1992, pp.325-346

Stephen Larrabee, "Instability and Change in the Balkans," Survival, Vol.34, No.2, Summer 1992, pp.31-49

Stephen Larrabee, East European Security after the Cold War (Santa Monica: RAND, 1993)

Paul Latawski, The Security Route to Europe: The Visegrad Four (London: Royal United Services Institute for Defence Studies, 1994)

Paul Latawski (ed.), Contemporary Nationalism in East Central Europe (London: The Macmillan Press, 1995)

Richard Ned Lebow, "The Long Peace, the End of the Cold War, and the Failure of Realism," International Organization, Vol.48, No.2, Spring 1994, pp.249-277

Alexander Levchenko, "Ukrainian Approaches to Regional Peacekeeping," in Peacekeeping Challenges to Euro-Atlantic Security, Ernest Gilman, Detlef E. Herold (eds.) (Rome: NATO Defense College, 1994), pp.57-66

Arend Lijphart, Democracy in Plural Societies. A Comparative Exploration (New Haven: Yale University Press, 1977)

Michael Lind, "In Defense of Liberal Nationalism," Foreign Affairs, Vol.73, No.3, pp.87-99

Paula Franklin Lytle, "U.S. Policy Toward the Demise of Yugoslavia: The Virus of Nationalism," East European Politics and Societies, Vol.6, No.3, Fall 1992, pp.303-318

Macedonia and the Macedonian Question (Thessaloniki: Society for Macedonian Studies, 1983)

Macedonia: Basic Economic Data (Skopje: Statistical Office of Macedonia, 1992)

Macedonia. Documents and Material (Sofia: Bulgarian Academy of Sciences, 1978)

Noel Malcolm, Bosnia: A Short History (London: Macmillan/ Papermac, 1994)

Michael Mann, "Nation-States in Europe and Other Continents: Diversifying, Developing, Not Dying," Daedalus, Vol.122, No.3, Summer 1993, pp.115-140

Stan Markotich, "Ethnic Serbs in Tudjman's Croatia," RFE/RL Research Report, Vol.2, No.38, 24 September 1993, pp.28-33

Charles William Maynes, "Containing Ethnic Conflict," Foreign Policy, No.90, Spring 1993, pp.3-21

Hans J. Michelmann, Panayotis Soldatis (eds.), Federalism and International Relations. The Role of Subnational Units (Oxford: Clarendon Press, 1990)

Benjamin Miller, "Explaining the Emergence of Great Power Concerts," Review of International Studies, Vol.20, No.4, October 1994, pp.327-348

Diana Mishkova, "Literacy and National-Building in Bulgaria 1878-1912," East European Quarterly, Vol.29, No.1, Spring 1994, pp.63-93

Petar Mitev, "Relations of Compatibility and Incompatibility in the Everyday Life of Christians and Muslims in Bulgaria (Sociological Study)" in Relations of Compatibility and Incompatibility between Christians and Muslims in Bulgaria, Antonina Zheliazkova (ed.) (Sofia:

193

International Centre for Minority Studies and Intercultural Relations Foundation, 1995), pp.179-230

Joseph V. Montville (ed.), Conflict and Peacemaking in Multiethnic Societies (Lexington: Lexington Books, 1990)

Patrick Moore, "Croatia and Bosnia: A Tale of Two Bridges," RFE/RL Research Report, Vol.3, No.1, 7 January 1994, pp.111-117

Edward Mortimer, "European Security After the Cold War," in Adelphi Paper 271, Summer 1992

Alexander J. Motyl, "The Modernity of Nationalism. Nations, States and Nation-States in the Contemporary World," Journal of International Affairs, Winter 1992, Vol.45, No.2, pp.307-321

Daniel Patrick Moynihan, Pandaemonium: Ethnicity in International Politics (New York: Oxford University Press, 1993)

Ivanka Nedeva, Bulgaria's Relations with Greece and Turkey and the Idea of Trilateral Cooperation (Sofia: Free Initiative Foundation, 1993)

Renée de Nevers, "Democratization and Ethnic Conflict," Survival, Vol.35, No.2, Summer 1993, pp.31-48

Rada Nikolaev, "Bulgaria's 1992 Census: Results, Problems, and Implications," RFE/RL Research Report, Vol.2, No.6, 5 February 1993, pp.58-62

Richard F. Nyrop (ed.), Yugoslavia. A Country Study (Washington, D.C.: US Government Printing Office, 1981)

Conor Cruise O'Brien, "The Wrath of Ages. Nationalism's Primordial Roots," Foreign Affairs, Vol.72, No.73, November/ December 1993, pp.142-149

The Other Balkan Wars: A 1913 Carnegie Endowment Inquiry in Retrospect with a new Introduction and Reflections on the Present Conflict by George F. Kennan (Washington, D.C.: Carnegie Endowment, 1993)

Gunay Goksu Ozdogan, Kemali Saybasili (eds.), Balkans: A Mirror of the New International Order (Istanbul: Eren, 1995)

M.R. Palairet, "How Long Can the Milosevic Regime Withstand Sanctions?" RFE/RL Research Report, Vol.2, No.34, 27 August 1993, pp.21-25

Raymond Pearson, National Minorities in Eastern Europe, 1848-1945 (London: Macmillan Press, 1983)

Raymond Pearson, "The Geopolitics of People Power: The Pursuit of the Nation-State in East Central Europe," Journal of International Affairs, Winter 1992, Vol.45, No.2, pp.499-518

Duncan M. Perry, Stefan Stambolov and the Emergence of Modern Bulgaria, 1870-1895 (Durham: Duke University Press, 1993)

Duncan M. Perry, "Politics in the Republic of Macedonia: Issues and Parties," RFE/RL Research Report, Vol.2, No.23, 4 June 1993, pp.31-37

Duncan M. Perry, "Macedonia," RFE/RL Research Report, Vol.3, No.16, 22 April 1994, pp.83-86

Michael B. Petrovich, A History of Modern Serbia, 1804-1918, Vol.1 (New York: Harcourt Brace Jovanovich, 1976)

William Pfaff, The Wrath of Nations: Civilization and the Fury of Nationalism (New York: Simon & Schuster, 1993)

Athanassios G. Platias, R.J. Rydell, "International Security Regimes: the Case of a Balkan Nuclear-Free Zone," in South-Eastern Europe After Tito. A Powder-Keg for the 1980s?, David Carlton, Carlo Schaerf (eds.) (London: Macmillan Press, 1983), pp.105-130

Barry R. Posen, "The Security Dilemma and Ethnic Conflict," Survival, Vol.35, No.1, Spring 1993, pp.27-47

Barry R. Posen, "Nationalism, the Mass Army, and Military Power," International Security, Vol.18, No.2, Fall 1993, pp.80-124

Hugh Poulton, The Balkans. Minorities and States in Conflict (London: Minority Rights Publications, 1991)

Uri Ra'anan, Maria Mesner, Keith Armes, Kate Martin, State and Nation in Multi-Ethnic Societies: The Breakup of Multinational States (Manchester: Manchester University Press, 1991)

Pedro Ramet, Nationalism and Federalism in Yugoslavia, 1963-1983 (Bloomington: Indiana University Press, 1984)

Pedro Ramet (ed.), Yugoslavia in the 1980s (Boulder: Westview Press, 1985)

Sabrina P. Ramet, Nationalism and Federalism in Yugoslavia, 1962-1991 (Bloomington: Indiana University Press, 1991)

Sabrina P. Ramet, "The Breakup of Yugoslavia," Global Affairs, Vol.6, No.2, Spring 1991, pp.93-110

Sabrina P. Ramet, Nationalism and Federalism in Yugoslavia: 1962-1991 (Bloomington: Indiana University Press, 1992)

Sabrina P. Ramet, "How Democracy Fares: Balkan Pluralism and Its Enemies," Orbis, Vol.36, No.4, Fall 1992, pp.547-564

Sabrina P. Ramet, "The Yugoslav Crisis and the West: Avoiding 'Vietnam' and Blundering into 'Abyssinia'," East European Politics and Societies, Vol.8, No.1, Winter 1994, pp.189-219

Robert B. Reich, "What is a Nation?" Political Science Quarterly, Vol.106, No.2, Summer 1991, pp.193-209

Robin Alison Remington, "Bosnia: The Tangled Web," Current History, Vol.92, No.577, November 1993, pp.364-369

M.A. Riff (ed.), Dictionary of Modern Political Ideologies (Manchester: Manchester University Press, 1990)

Richard Rosecrance, "A New Concert of Powers," Foreign Affairs, Vol.71, No.2, Spring 1992, pp.64-82

Jakob Rösel, "Ethnic Nationalism and Ethnic Conflict," Internationale Politik und Gesellschaft, No.2, 1995, pp.117-130

Michael G. Roskin, "The Bosnian-Serb Problem: What We Should and Should Not Do," Parameters, Vol.22, No.4, Winter 1992-1993, pp.21-32

Donald Rothchild, Alexander J. Groth, "Pathological Dimensions of Domestic and International Ethnicity," Political Science Quarterly, Vol.110, No.1, Spring 1995, pp.69-82

Jay Rothman, From Confrontation to Cooperation: Resolving Ethnic and Regional Conflict (Newbury Park: Sage, 1992)

Joseph Rothschild, Ethnopolitics: A Conceptual Framework (New York: Columbia University Press, 1981)

Joseph Rothschild, Return to Diversity: A Political History of East Central Europe since World War II (New York: Oxford University Press, 1981)

Jean-Jacques Rousseau, "The Social Contract or Principles of Political Right," in Great Books of the Western World, Vol.38. Montesquieu, Rousseau (Chicago: Encyclopedia Britannica Inc., 1952), pp.387-439

Richard E. Rubenstein, Jarle Crocker, "Challenging Huntington," Foreign Policy, No.96, Fall 1994, pp.113-128

Lothar Ruehl, "European Security and NATO's Eastward Expansion," Aussenpolitik, Vol.45, No.2, 1994, pp.115-122

Jacques Rupnik, "Europe's New Frontiers: Remapping Europe," Daedalus, Vol.123, No.3, Summer 1994, pp.91-114

Trevor C. Salmon, "Testing Times for European Political Cooperation: The Gulf and Yugoslavia, 1990-1992," International Affairs, Vol.68, No.2, 1992, pp.233-253

Bruno Schoch, To Strasbourg or to Sarajevo? On Nationalism in the Postcommunist Transitional Societies, PRIF Reports No. 28 (Frankfurt: Peace Research Institute, 1992)

George Schopflin, "Nationalism and National Minorities in Eastern and Central Europe," Journal of International Affairs, Vol.45, No.1, 1991, pp.51-65

George Schopflin, Politics in Eastern Europe, (Oxford: Basil Blackwell, 1993)

George Schopflin, "Postcommunism: The Problems of Democratic Construction," Daedalus, Vol.123, No.3, Summer 1994, pp.127-141

Gertrude E. Schroeder, "On the Economic Viability of New Nation-States," Journal of International Affairs, Vol.45, No.2, Winter 1992, pp.549-574

Hugh Seton-Watson, Nations and States. An Enquiry into the Origins of Nations and Politics of Nationalism (London: Methuen, 1977)

Kemal S. Shehadi, Ethnic Self-Determination and the Break-Up of States (Adelphi Paper 283, December 1993)

Paul S. Shop (ed.), Problems of Balkan Security (Washington D.C.: Wilson Center Press, 1990)

Harvey Sicherman, "Winning the Peace," Orbis, Vol.38, No.4, Fall 1994, pp.523-544

Thomas W. Simons, Jr., Eastern Europe in the Postwar World (London: The Macmillan Press, 1993)

Anthony D. Smith, The Ethnic Revival (Cambridge: Cambridge University Press, 1981)

Anthony D. Smith, Ethnic Origins of Nations (Oxford: Basil Blackwell, 1986)

Anthony D. Smith, "National Identity and the Idea of European Unity," International Affairs, Vol.68, No.1, 1992, pp.55-76

Anthony D. Smith, "The Ethnic Sources of Nationalism," Survival, Vol.35, No.1, Spring 1993, pp.48-62

John E. Smith, Quasi-Religions: Humanism, Marxism and Nationalism (London: Macmillan Publishers, 1994)

Jack Snyder, "Nationalism and Instability in the Former Soviet Empire," Arms Control (Contemporary Security Policy), Vol.12, No.3, December 1991, pp.6-16

Jack Snyder, "Nationalism and the Crisis of the Post-Soviet State," Survival, Vol.35, No.1, Spring 1993, pp.5-26

Louis L. Snyder, Encyclopedia of Nationalism (New York: Paragon House, 1990)

Joshua Spero, "The Budapest-Prague-Warsaw Triangle: Central European Security after the Visegrad Summit," European Security, Vol.1, No.1, Spring 1992, pp.58-83

Krassen Stanchev, "Can Economic Reforms Overcome Ethnic Tensions?" Paper, Institute for Market Economics, Sofia, 1994

"Strategic Policy Issues. The Challenge of Self-Determination," Strategic Survey, 1992-1993, pp.16-23

Peter F. Sugar, Ivo J. Lederer, Nationalism in Eastern Europe (Seattle: University of Washington Press, 1969)

Bogdan Szajkowski (ed.), Encyclopedia of Conflicts, Disputes and Flashpoints in Eastern Europe, Russia and the Successor States (London: Longman Group, 1993)

Yael Tamir, Liberal Nationalism (Princeton: Princeton University Press, 1993)

Mikulas Teich, Roy Porter (eds.), The National Question in Europe in Historical Context (Cambridge: Cambridge University Press, 1993)

Timothy L. Thomas, "Ethnic Conflict: Scourge of the 1990s?" Military Review, December 1992, pp.15-26

Mark Thompson, A Paper House (New York: Pantheon Books, 1992)

Charles Tilly, Coercion, Capital and European States (Oxford: Basil Blackwell, 1990)

Charles Tilly, European Revolutions, 1492-1992 (Oxford: Basil Blackwell, 1993

Maria Todorova, "Ethnicity, Nationalism and the Communist Legacy in Eastern Europe," East European Politics and Societies, Vol.7, No.1, Winter 1993, pp.135-154

Maria Todorova, "The Balkans: From Discovery to Invention," Slavic Review, Vol.53, No.2, Summer 1994, pp.453-482

Maria Todorova, "The Ottoman Legacy in the Balkans," in Balkans: A Mirror of the New International Order, Gunay Goksu Ozdogan, Kemali Saybasili (eds.) (Istanbul: Eren, 1995), pp.55-74

US Department of State Dispatch, Vol.2, No.32, 1991, p.596

Ustav na Republika Makedonija (Skopje: NIP Magazin 21, 1991)

Krasimir Uzunov, Evelina Csaneva, Hristos na Balkanite (Sofia: 1993)

Milada Anna Vachudova, "The Visegrad Four: No Alternative to Cooperation?" RFE/RL Research Report, Vol.2, No.34, 27 August 1993, pp.38-47

Tibor Varady, "Collective Minority Rights and Problems in Their Legal Protection: The Example of Yugoslavia," East European Politics and Societies, Vol.6, No.3, Fall 1992, pp.260-282

Katherine Verdery, "Whither 'Nation' and 'Nationalism'?" Daedalus, Vol.122, No.3, Summer 1993, pp.37-46

Katherine Verdery, "Nationalism and National Sentiment in Post-Socialist Romania," Slavic Review, Vol.52, No.2, Summer 1993, pp.179-203

Garrison Walters, The Other Europe. Eastern Europe to 1945 (Syracuse: Syracuse University Press, 1988)

Michael Walzer, Edward T. Kantorowicz, John Higham, Mona Harrington, Politics of Ethnicity (Cambridge: The Belknap Press of Harvard University Press, 1982)

David Welsh, "Domestic Politics and Ethnic Conflict," Survival, Vol.35, No.1, Spring 1993, pp.63-80

Gerhard Wettig, "Shifts Concerning the National Problems in Europe," Aussenpolitik, Vol.44, January 1993, pp.67-76

Gerhard Wettig, "Moscow's Perception of NATO's Role," Aussenpolitik, Vol.45, February 1994, pp.123-133

Stephen White, John Gardner, George Schopflin, Tony Saich, Communist and Postcommunist Political Systems (New York: St. Martin's Press, 1990)

H. Williams (ed.), National Separatism (Cardiff: University of Wales Press, 1982)

Robert Lee Wolff, The Balkans in our Time (Cambridge: Harvard University Press, 1956)

Pia Christina Wood, "France and the Post Cold War Order: The Case of Yugoslavia," European Security, Vol.3, No.1, Spring 1994, pp.129-152

Christopher M. Woodhouse, Modern Greece, (London: Faber and Faber, 1984)

World Directory of Minorities. Longman International Reference (London: Longman, 1990)

Victor Zaslavsky, "Nationalism and Democratic Transition in Postcommunist Societies," Daedalus, Vol.121, No.2, Spring 1992, pp.97-121

Philip Zelikow, "The New Concept of Europe," Survival, Vol.34, No.2, Summer 1992, pp.12-30

Antonina Zheliazkova, "The Problem of Authenticity of Some Domestic Sources on the Islamization of the Rhodopes, Deeply

Rooted in Bulgarian Historiography," Etudes Balkaniques, No.4, 1990, pp.105-111

Antonina Zheliazkova, "The Penetration and Adaptation of Islam in Bosnia from the Fifteenth to the Nineteenth Century," Journal of Islamic Studies, Vol.5, No.2, 1994, pp.187-208

George B. Zotiades, The Macedonian Controversy (Salonica: Institute for Macedonian Studies, 1961)

EURO-ATLANTIC SECURITY STUDIES

Edited by the Nato Defense College